Malcolm Andrews is a respected Australian author and journalist. In a career spanning almost fifty years, he has worked for such media institutions as *The Australian*, the *Daily Telegraph* (Sydney), the *Daily Express* (London) and the Nine Network's current affairs program *Today*. In the early 1970s, he spent five years in Munich working for the US State Department at *Radio Free Europe*, which broadcast news behind the Iron Curtain.

Malcolm has written twenty-seven books on subjects ranging from history and trivia to travel and sport. They include *Quest for Gold*, chronicling the efforts of a group of Aussie medal hopefuls at the 2000 Olympics; *The Fabulous Fairstar*, a nostalgic history of the famous cruise liner that sailed into the sunset after thirty-five years of plying the world's sea lanes; and *Kostya — From Russia with Gloves*, the ghosted pictorial autobiography of world boxing champion Kostya Tszyu, which made the non-fiction bestselling lists.

These days he operates as a freelance writer and broadcaster based on the New South Wales north coast.

# HUBERT WHO?

War hero. Polar explorer. Spy.
The incredible life of unsung adventurer Hubert Wilkins.

## MALCOLM ANDREWS

ABC
Books

The ABC 'Wave' device is a trademark of the
Australian Broadcasting Corporation and is used
under licence by HarperCollins*Publishers* Australia.

First published in Australia in 2011
by HarperCollins*Publishers* Australia Pty Limited
ABN 36 009 913 517
harpercollins.com.au

**HarperCollins*Publishers***
Level 13, 201 Elizabeth Street, Sydney NSW 2000, Australia
31 View Road, Glenfield, Auckland 0627, New Zealand
A 53, Sector 57, Noida, UP, India
77–85 Fulham Palace Road, London W6 8JB, United Kingdom
2 Bloor Street East, 20th floor, Toronto, Ontario M4W 1A8, Canada
10 East 53rd Street, New York NY 10022, USA

National Library of Australia Cataloguing-in-Publication entry:

Andrews, Malcolm, 1944–
    Hubert who? War hero. Polar explorer. Spy. The incredible life of
    unsung adventurer Hubert Wilkins / Malcolm Andrews.
    ISBN: 978 0 7333 2300 3 (pbk.)
    Wilkins, G. H. (George Hubert), Sir, 1888–1958.
    Nautilus (Submarine)
    Air pilots – Australia – Biography.
    Explorers – Australia – Biography.
    Photographers – Australia – Biography.
    Arctic regions – Aerial exploration – History.
910.92

Cover design by Christa Moffitt, Christabella Designs
Cover images: H. Wilkins, *Nautilus* crew member, in cold weather gear © The American
    Philosophical Society; Wilkins on an abandoned tank, recording the breaking of the Hindenburg
    Line, France, in late 1918 (E03915) by Australian War Memorial; Wilkins submarine *Nautilus* ©
    Schenectady Museum, Hall of Electrical History Foundation/CORBIS; Iceberg and ice by
    iStockphoto.com
Typeset in 11.5/17pt Bembo by Kirby Jones
Printed and bound in Australia by Griffin Press
70gsm Classic used by HarperCollins*Publishers* is a natural, recyclable product made from
wood grown in sustainable forests. The manufacturing processes conform to the
environmental regulations in the country of origin, Finland.

5 4 3 2 1        11 12 13 14

TO MY DAD AND MY HERO
KEN ANDREWS
(1911–1998)

A pioneer in aircraft design, your great regret was that you were too old to have had the chance to travel to the moon.

I know, if you had met him, you would have enjoyed the company of Hubert Wilkins.

# CONTENTS

# PREFACE

WE WERE ALL taught in school about Australia's great heroes and adventurers.

We know that Charles Kingsford Smith was the pilot of the first aircraft to fly across the Pacific. Douglas Mawson explored Antarctica. Charles Sturt befriended the local Aboriginal people as he traced the waterways of inland Australia. Frank Hurley made a name for himself photographing the Antarctic and the bloody battlefields of France in World War I. James Cook made voyages no one else would have considered attempting, even in their wildest dreams. And Nancy Wake worked as a journalist for the newspaper magnate William Randolph Hearst before living on her wits as a member of the French Resistance — a spy behind enemy lines.

Wrap all these great Australian heroes into one, add a few more adventures — such as pioneering movie coverage of news events that grabbed the world's attention and trying to be the first to manoeuvre a submarine under the Arctic icecap — and you have Sir Hubert Wilkins. Yet few Australians have even heard of the man, let alone his exploits.

'Hubert *who*?' they wonder.

Australia's commanding officer in World War I, General Sir John Monash, called Wilkins 'the bravest man I have ever seen — Australia's answer to Lawrence of Arabia'. That's some compliment indeed considering that among Monash's forces were no less than sixty-four servicemen who were awarded the Victoria Cross.

Away from the battlefield, legendary Hollywood director Cecil B. deMille reckoned Wilkins was an inspiration to all the world's filmmakers that followed him. And Wilkins is the hero of modern-day Australian adventurer Dick Smith.

But still: Hubert … *who*?

I first became aware of this incredible Aussie hero in 2000 while writing *The Ultimate True Blue Trivia Book* — wherein I compiled thousands of facts about Australia and Australians. Scattered throughout the book were what I called 'True Blue Icons' — identities, real or otherwise, from the likes of cricketer Don Bradman, our most famous nude, Chloe, and rock 'n' roll star Johnny O'Keefe, to Harry's Café de Wheels pie stall, the Chiko Roll and Chesty Bond. It was then that I discovered a brief biography of a South Australian named George Hubert Wilkins and listed him under a logo that read *He deserves to be a True Blue Icon*, adding: 'Here are some facts that ninety-nine out of one hundred Australians don't know (but should).'

Then I started my search, the results of which left me shaking my head in amazement. Where most people would say, 'Why doesn't someone do such-and-such?', Wilkins didn't ask — he went out and did it. He stowed away on a ship that took him halfway around the world, took the first movie footage from an aircraft while strapped to its primitive fuselage, trekked more than 100 kilometres across frozen Arctic wastelands, undertook pioneering aircraft flights over the icy roof and base of the globe, became the only member of the media to win medals for gallantry in conflicts he was covering as a war correspondent, spied for the British in Russia and for the Americans in the Far East, lived with the local Aboriginal people in outback Australia … The list just went on and on.

Suitably astounded by the combination of this man's courage and achievements and his status as perhaps the world's greatest unsung hero, this book, *Hubert Who?*, gradually took shape. It seemed inconceivable to me that Hubert Wilkins was not a household name like Kingsford Smith, Sturt, Cook and the others — and it was important to right that wrong.

In most instances the amazing facts speak for themselves, but in telling Wilkins' story, I have occasionally taken a touch of poetic licence by turning what was a mere description of events into dialogue between those involved. In every case, however, there has been absolutely no deviation from the facts unearthed by my investigations and the research of others.

While Wilkins has been honoured by both Britain and the United States, he has basically been ignored in the land of his birth. Thankfully, though, historians are gradually recognising the great contribution to science and exploration that was made by Sir Hubert Wilkins. Maybe soon our educators will begin explaining his great legacy to young Australians, who are so in need of true blue role models.

And what a great role model he was!

*Malcolm Andrews*
*Port Macquarie*
*July 2011*

# PROLOGUE

THURSDAY, 31 OCTOBER 1912. The First Balkan War is in full cry. A battle is joined between the invading troops of Bulgaria and those of Turkey near the tiny town of Lule Burgas, west of the Bosphorus. Young Australian adventurer Hubert Wilkins rides out from nearby Chorlu on a magnificent Arab stallion. It is his twenty-fourth birthday.

He is a little under 6 foot tall, with a prominent chin and eyebrows, and an expression that reminded friends back in London of Lord Kitchener, of Boer War fame. Wilkins is dressed like a Turk: a short jacket, sleeveless, over a loose woven shirt; ballooning Moorish trousers tucked into his riding boots; a fez on his head, holding down a rough, overlarge cravat that's wound around his chin and neck, Arab style. Well tanned from his years growing up in the Australian bush, Wilkins has the swarthy looks of the Turkish soldiers he passes on the road. The dust and grime of a week living rough since he left the luxury of Constantinople's Pera Palas Hotel adds to the authenticity. A halter, one end wound around his left wrist, is attached to a bulky movie camera. Spare film is stuffed under his shirt. Wilkins is here to record history as it happens for London's Gaumont Graphic newsreel company, looking for an eyewitness scoop as the Bulgarians sweep eastwards through the countryside towards the Turkish capital.

The Turks are in disarray. The panorama that stretches out before him is a maelstrom of confused retreat. Angry Turkish cavalry officers, overcome with rage, are charging at their own men, trying to turn the terrified rabble back against the advancing Bulgarians.

Camera balanced delicately on his lap, Wilkins cranks away, catching — for the first time in history — action from a major world battle. The glint from the waving swords of the cavalry officers … The puffs of smoke as Bulgarian guns discharge their complement of shells … Maimed men crawling in no particular direction to their inevitable death, pain contorting their faces into grotesque masks of fear … Wilkins' film and despatches from the front, the latter typed out on his battered Blickensderfer portable typewriter, will make a name for the young antipodean back in the English capital.

Wilkins rides on towards the action, with his mount, as if by second nature, avoiding the dead and dying that litter the battlefield. A couple of other reporters are following in his wake as he crosses the lone bridge that spans a river outside Lule Burgas. There is Bernard Grant from the London *Daily Mail* and Francis McCullagh, the veteran war correspondent for London's *Daily News* and the New York *World*, whose reputation was sealed five years earlier thanks to his dramatic coverage of the Russo–Japanese War in Manchuria.

The conflict is hotting up. Shells begin exploding around them. One lands directly in front of Wilkins, but by some miracle it fails to blow up. Suddenly, a detachment of Bulgarian cavalry officers gallop past the advancing foot soldiers and head straight for the trio.

'Oh, damn!' shouts Wilkins. 'They think we're bloody Turks! They didn't tell me about *this* back in London. Strewth, I'm outta here …'

He digs his spurs hard into the flanks of his trusty Arab mount and charges away from the Bulgarians. Across the battlefield. Through the panicking Turks. Around a low hill and back to the river. No time to find the bridge now — it's a case of straight into the water and a desperate swim across the fast-flowing stream. Bullets pepper the river bank as he and his horse clamber out the other side.

'Thank Christ they're dud shots,' Wilkins calls out as he turns and notes the successful escape of his companions. 'They wouldn't last long in the outback,' he adds with a chuckle, before galloping on to safety.

The other two men nod in agreement, even though they have no idea of the so-called outback to which Wilkins refers.

Later on, back in Chorlu, the full impact of what has happened finally strikes home and Wilkins visibly shivers in spite of the warmth of the evening. To be a successful war correspondent, one has to take risks, as Wilkins has done this day — and he will gamble with his life time and time again in the years to come, with almost monotonous regularity. On the killing fields of Flanders. In the untamed Australian bush. On, under and over the icefloes of the Arctic. In the skies above Antarctica. With the *R-34*, *Hindenburg* and *Graf Zeppelin* airships. And as a spy in Russia and South-East Asia.

He will shrug off any thought of the perils that confront him. To Hubert Wilkins, taking risks will just be part of everyday living.

# Chapter 1

# Enquiring Minds

IT HAS BECOME a popular pastime in Australia to chase one's family history, to chart out a family tree. Naturally enough, the majority of the forebears of Australian families stretch back to Britain. So it was with George Hubert Wilkins. According to those who have checked out the family tree, he could trace his lineage back to one of the most influential thinkers of the seventeenth century, Bishop John Wilkins.

At the very least, John Wilkins (1614–1672) showed many of the traits that drove the adventurous Hubert Wilkins three centuries later. The good bishop was well connected, having married Robina, the youngest sister of Oliver Cromwell, in 1656. She was said to have been the most eligible widow in England. Yet it was not for his personal life but his enquiring mind that Bishop Wilkins is best remembered. He chaired the first meeting of that august scientific body, the Royal Society, and became its first secretary. He developed a glass beehive from which honey could be removed without disturbing the bees, and a machine that could throw up an artificial water spray in gardens. He worked on an instrument that helped people with hearing problems. And he argued the theory of possible life on the moon and the ideas of submarines and heavier-than-air flying machines. All this was some 200 years before Jules Verne wrote about such things as mere fiction. The good bishop also tried to perfect a world language in which scientists could converse. He would have been proud had he known that a descendant would be part of the reality of many of his dreams.

Hubert Wilkins' immediate ancestors played a major role in the settling of Australia, even if they never experienced the privilege and position that the bishop enjoyed. Hubert Wilkins' grandparents, William and Mary Ann, were among the scores of Britons living close to the poverty line in the mid 1830s and looking for a new life. They were entranced by stories of success in the colonies and thus lured to an office in John Street, London, not too far from Gray's Inn. The

The enlightened seventeenth-century British scientist Bishop John Wilkins, an ancestor of the Australian adventurer.

South Australian Company owned the building and had already set in place its plans for a large township to be laid out for the would-be settlers quite remote from other settlements in the Great South Land.

One of the first emigrant ships to head for the new colony was the twelve-year-old, two-masted brig *Emma* of 167 tonnes, which sailed from London on 21 April 1836. On board were twenty-three passengers, including the Wilkinses and their two eldest sons, Frank and Albert. Mary fell pregnant on the voyage, which went via Madeira, the island of Martin Vaz in the South Atlantic, the Cape of Good Hope and St Paul, halfway across the Indian Ocean. The *Emma* finally arrived at Nepean Bay on Kangaroo Island on 5 October, after a journey of 166 days. There the South Australian Company had hoped to establish a whaling station. Later the planned township about which the Wilkinses had been told back in London would be set up on the mainland at Holdfast Bay. History would see it spread inland and eventually grow into the city of Adelaide, while the original site is today referred to as the suburb of Glenelg.

British Government officials arrived from Port Jackson (now Sydney) on 30 December and proclaimed the new colony of South Australia. Two days later, on 1 January 1837, Mary gave birth to another son, Henry — to be known in the family as Harry. Officially he was the first white child born in the colony, although there had been others before it was gazetted.

Despite the fact that the Wilkinses were later quite strict Methodists, the family's early life in the colony revolved around pubs. William was publican at several taverns around the fledgling city. But his life in South Australia was not a long one. He passed away on 23 January 1845, a little over eight years after he arrived. Mary remarried; her new husband was also a publican and mine host at the New Market Hotel in Adelaide.

It seems that young Harry and his stepfather may not have got along too well. Or was it just the lust for adventure manifesting itself in the Wilkins psyche that caused him to forsake the family fold? For when, in late 1851, news of the discovery of gold at Ballarat in Victoria reached Adelaide, Harry Wilkins was off like a shot to try his luck at the diggings. He was not yet fifteen years old — still wet behind the ears. More than £12 million worth of gold was uncovered in the first fifteen months of the Ballarat boom, but little if any of it seemed to find its way into young Wilkins' pockets. Within a couple of years, with a degree in learning from the school of hard knocks, he was back in South Australia, working as a drover.

Harry met his wife-to-be, Louisa Smith, at the Gallia Tassia Hotel in the town of Port Augusta, on the northernmost reaches of Spencer Gulf. Maybe he had dropped into the pub for a thirst-quencher while moving cattle. Or maybe it was a meeting arranged by the family, for Louisa, too, had a father who was a publican. Whatever the reason, they were married at the hotel in Port Augusta on 24 March 1863. The publican gave away the bride. A couple of years later, Harry and Louisa moved to Victor Harbor, on Encounter Bay, south of Adelaide, where her father ran a popular pub, the Port Victor Hotel.

Harry took over the pub's licence from his father-in-law and the couple's first four children were born there in Victor Harbor. Eventually they would have thirteen children. The eldest was stillborn; the second, Henry, and another son, Albert, died as infants, but eight of the others all lived to over seventy years of age.

It was at this stage that the government passed the *Waste Lands Amendment Act* of 1869, better known as the Strangways Act, after the South Australian premier Henry Strangways. He had been upset about the continual grab for land by the big pastoralists and believed that small farmers should be encouraged to become part of the expanding rural scene. The Strangways Act allowed would-be farmers to buy pastoral land from the Crown on time payment at £1 an acre. They would be required to make a 20 per cent deposit, with the remainder paid off over a period of four years. To prevent a new breed of pastoralists from getting a slice of the action, a farmer could only buy a maximum of 64 acres (260 hectares).

Much of it was poor-quality land, and Harry Wilkins got more than his fair share on his 'selection' at Mount Bryan East, around 200 kilometres north of Adelaide, near Burra, when he decided to change his life's direction. Most of the property, Netfield, was on dry barren land, where Harry tried to grow sheep, cattle and various grain crops. Several times he was almost sent bankrupt by drought. The memory of these harsh times would leave an indelible mark on the memory of his youngest son, George Hubert, leading him as an adult to search for ways of accurately forecasting the weather.

Harry Wilkins learned from his setbacks and when South Australia suffered one of the worst droughts in history, in 1902, he was prepared. He had put aside a large quantity of dry feed and was able not only to save all his animals, but also to buy even more from desperate neighbours. As a result, when the drought eventually broke, he was in a position to retire to Adelaide with a modest income.

George Hubert Wilkins — later to be known by his second name — was born at Netfield on 31 October 1888. He attended the one-teacher Mount Bryan East Public School, about 5 kilometres away from the Wilkinses' property. He had an advantage over the other pupils, in that the teacher lived with the Wilkins family and was able to give him extra tuition. But George Hubert was also a very bright child, with a thirst for learning. He was able to read and write by the age of four and at nine had passed the state exam, which qualified him to go to high school. He was hardly a nerd, however. He led an active outdoor life on the farm. He learned to ride at about the same time as he learned to walk. Before he was in his teens he had his own couple of horses, his own area of the farm to look after, and 200 head of sheep. In his early teens he was good enough to shear seventy-five head of sheep in a day — and that was at a time when there were no electric clippers. Almost every evening he and his brothers would ride out to hunt kangaroos.

As a boy he also came into contact with nomad Aboriginal tribes, forging a respect and admiration for Australia's indigenous people. In his teenage years he would often go hunting with them and stay overnight in their camps. He was struck by their system of laws, passed on by word of mouth and covering everything from principles of conduct to marriage and property ownership. Years later he explained: 'I always found them chaste, law-abiding and kind. I still think their behaviour was superior to much of ours in our supposedly high state of civilisation.'

When Harry and Louisa retired in 1905 and moved to a house in the Adelaide suburb of Parkside, George Hubert went with them. Simultaneously, he studied at the University of Adelaide (mechanical engineering), the South Australian School of Mines and Industry (electrical engineering) and the Elder Conservatorium of Music (singing, violin, cello, flute and organ).

One day during that first year at Parkside, a course of events changed his life. Wilkins was helping put the electric wiring into a new theatre in Adelaide when one of his colleagues mentioned that there was a travelling motion-picture tent show nearby and the entrepreneurs were having trouble with the diesel-powered generator. 'You might be able to lend a bit of your expertise to help them out,' the man suggested.

Wilkins wandered over to the tent and watched as two men tried to get the generator going. But every time they tried, it just spluttered and stopped.

'What's the trouble?' he asked.

'We've got to get this generator working. It's okay here in Adelaide — we can hook into the local power grid to run our movie projectors. But we're off on a country tour in a few weeks' time, and there's no power out in the bush. So we need this bloody generator to work.'

'Let me take a look at it.'

Within an hour, Wilkins had the generator running as smoothly as it did when it was new.

'What do we owe you?' the grateful entrepreneurs asked.

'I don't want any money,' the teenager replied. 'Just show me how your movie projector works.'

When he saw the movies for the first time, Wilkins was instantly hooked. From then on he was back at the tent at every opportunity, learning how to operate and repair the projector. The entrepreneurs even taught him how to make movies himself. And soon enough his musical talent also came into play. As there weren't enough movies to keep the punters entertained, the owners of the tent show included an hour or so of vaudeville acts, during which Wilkins, drawing on his expertise as a trained singer, was one of the stars. His signature tune was 'In the Valley Where the Bluebirds Sing', a popular song on Edison cylinder phonographs of that period.

As part of his apprenticeship, Wilkins was required to either work at Adelaide's main power station or take charge of a small power plant for six months. Showbiz was now in his blood, so he signed up with a travelling carnival of singers, dancers and acrobats as the foreman of its electricity workers. For the next eighteen months he toured South Australia and Victoria.

He would never return to his studies. Instead, sometime in 1907, he headed for Sydney and a job as a tent-cinema operator.

ONE OF THE pioneers of the film industry was Frenchman Léon Gaumont. His name remains part of movie history to this day as that of a chain of cinemas in Britain. The Gaumont company can be traced back to the late nineteenth century when a London surgeon, John Le Couteur, began importing the primitive Gaumont cameras and projectors into Britain. Eventually, under the enthusiastic control of brothers Alfred Claude and Reg Broomhead, the British company became bigger than the parent in France. The elder brother, known to everyone as 'AC', was the better known of the pair and was instrumental in setting up Gaumont Graphic, one of the world's first newsreel companies, in 1910. It immediately began a fierce competition with the established Pathé organisation for film coverage of the major events of each week for showing in theatres around Britain. In those early months, they captured the pomp and ceremony of the visit of US president Theodore Roosevelt to London, the funeral of King Edward VII, floods in Europe that killed thousands, protests by suffragettes, the launch of the SS *Olympic* (at that time the largest ship ever built), and the knighting of Antarctic explorer Ernest Shackleton.

The following year, 1911, AC toured the world, setting up branches in the far-flung outposts of the British Empire. And he was always on the lookout for eager young men willing to become Gaumont cameramen. In Sydney he met Wilkins and set in train the journey that was to take the Australian into a lifetime of adventure.

AC was impressed with the short features that Wilkins had filmed. They were a mixture of shots of real life, woven into a brief storyline acted out by friends and colleagues. Often that storyline was no more than the 'actors' adlibbing their gestures as the camera rolled. The fact that Wilkins operated out of a small office-cum-studio in North Sydney also meant that many of these mini-movies used the nearby Sydney Harbour as a spectacular backdrop.

Broomhead asked Wilkins to come and work for him in London. But he would have to make his own way to Britain; AC was not about to hand over an expensive ticket on a ship to an Australian who might go his own way once he reached his destination. The absence of a ticket wasn't going to deter Wilkins — but it would have dire consequences.

Wilkins immediately returned to Adelaide to bid farewell to his parents, not realising that it was to be the last time he would see his father, then aged seventy-four. The youngest Wilkins then planned to stow away on a coastal steamer back to Sydney and write about the adventure in an effort to help raise the fare for his trip to England. But he picked the wrong ship at Port Adelaide. It was only when the vessel was well out to sea and he was discovered that the truth dawned.

The captain was furious to find a stowaway aboard his ship. 'Wasn't the ship searched before we sailed, bosun?' he thundered.

'Yes, sir. I don't know how he managed to avoid us,' the hapless officer replied. 'It's never happened before, and I assure you it won't happen again.'

'Well, it's too late to put him ashore. Clean him up, bosun, and send him to my cabin.' He then stared straight at Wilkins: 'You had better think about what you plan to do when we throw you off the ship in Africa.'

Africa? Wilkins shivered. Where in Africa? Would it be Cape Town in South Africa, where at least they spoke English? Maybe Kenya, on the east coast, or Port Said, Tunis or Algiers ...

He had around a month at sea before he found out. During that time he helped the ship's engineer rewind the dynamo needed to run the ship's motor and learned a lot about the practical aspects of running a ship. It would come in handy in many of his future ventures. As they sailed through the Suez Canal, he at last discovered where he was to be dumped: the teeming North African city of Algiers.

THROUGHOUT HISTORY, ALGIERS has been a nest for intrigue. It was almost destroyed with the fall of the Roman Empire, but it had a renaissance during the sixteenth century. Under the control of the Ottoman beys (or rulers), it thrived as a port where, especially in the 1700s, pirates of all nationalities who plundered the Mediterranean and Atlantic could sell their ill-gotten gains. And historically, it was arguably the most significant city in North Africa for the sale of slaves. The navies of the European powers — notably France, Italy, Germany and Britain — would regularly attack Algiers, but without lasting success, until the city was annexed by France in 1830.

In the early years of the twentieth century, intrigue was the order of the day. The labyrinth of narrow streets and blind alleys that made up the city's old quarter, the kasbah, were home to spies and gun-runners from various nations. They had little regard for the laws of the French. Policemen may have roamed the new city, but in the kasbah, guns and money ran everyday life.

This was the hothouse of ferment into which the young Wilkins was suddenly thrust, in what by now must have been late 1911. A job may have awaited him in London but, virtually penniless in Algiers, he might as well have been back in Australia for all the hope he had of making it there.

Although Wilkins had mixed with the local Aboriginal people, the Nunga, as a youth, by and large in Australia there had been just white people, mostly of Anglo-Saxon stock. He was wide-eyed at this North African melting pot of humanity. Europeans, Arabs and Africans speaking a multitude of languages: the Babel of the twentieth century.

Language was most certainly a problem. So Wilkins was somewhat relieved when he fell into conversation with an intriguing character who spoke broken English. 'Intriguing' was the operative word. He claimed to be a member of the Italian secret service, trying to halt the ferrying of guns through Algiers to Arabs in what is now Libya. The weapons were to be used against Italian merchants and diplomats in the port of Tripoli, over which Italy claimed jurisdiction. Was he in fact an Italian spy? He could very well have been, for there were many going about their business in Algiers.

The stranger offered Wilkins a job patrolling the waterfront, checking out ships that arrived to see if they were discharging weapons of any sort. With the brashness of youth, Wilkins accepted, ignoring the obvious danger that would have persuaded a more worldly-wise man to send the Italian on his way. 'I was [around] twenty years old, with little experience of life,' he would later reflect. 'If I had been older and wiser, I would have handled the situation much differently. I would most certainly have been much more careful and suspicious of this fascinating, if suspect, Italian.'

One night the pair were doing a crawl of the bars in the kasbah. 'This is how you find out all the gossip,' the Italian told Wilkins. 'People let things slip when they've had too many drinks.'

A shady Arab approached the Italian and started whispering in his ear. Wilkins' mate nodded and slipped the Arab some money. 'He knows a fellow who's got some useful information for us,' he explained to Wilkins. 'I think we can trust him.'

The Arab led them out of the kasbah and off to an expensive house in the new city. There another man, a European, explained how they could be put onto a caravan route that was being used to ferry guns across the border into Tunisia and then on to the Arabs who were harassing the Italians in Tripoli.

The 'spy' was duly impressed and handed their host a note to be passed on to an Italian Government official in Algiers, who would provide the reward for this information. And he asked Wilkins to accompany him on his trip to find the gun-runners' route. Again, Wilkins should have known better — but his youthful exuberance blinded him to the obvious dangers. It was like something out of an adventure novel. And he was determined to be one of the central characters.

The pair travelled 300 kilometres west to Philippeville (today known as Skikda and a major port for the export of Algerian oil), and then another 250 kilometres south to Biskra, at the foot of the Saharan Atlas Mountains. In Roman times, Biskra was a military base, but by the twentieth century it had become a commercial centre for the nomad Arabs who wandered the Sahara Desert and beyond. At Biskra, agents told Wilkins and his companion that they must travel on further south, to Chott Melrihr, a huge salt lake lying some 40 metres below sea level. But before they were to leave, they dined with the agents. At the end of the evening, everyone raised their glasses to toast the success of the partnership.

That was all that Wilkins and the Italian remembered when they woke the next morning, each tied to the back of a donkey. They had been drugged and abducted. The only account of what happened then was in Hubert Wilkins' so-called autobiography, ghost-written in the late 1950s by a mate of his, US media personality Lowell Thomas.

The pair had been duped by the gun-runners themselves. The 'spy' was to be ransomed off to his family back in Italy and a couple of days later disappeared as the Arabs executed their plan. Wilkins' fate was unknown, but he believed he would eventually be killed. He tried to curry favour with his captors by following their rituals, even offering morning and evening prayers to Allah.

As it turned out, he befriended a young Arab woman travelling with the caravan. Sexual attraction is a marvellous thing — although Wilkins never admitted to any consummation of the partnership and claimed only to have seen her eyes, twinkling, as she stared at him over her yasmak. The girl arranged for his escape, wrapping him as a pack of goods and smuggling him onto a camel that was heading back to Biskra.

During the first night out, the pack in which he was hiding was unloaded from the camel and dumped before the entourage fell asleep. When they were dead to the world, he extricated himself and for the rest of the journey he mixed with those in the camel train. Wilkins never explained just how the others accepted him without question. He claimed to have scrounged scraps of food and drank at each oasis with the camels and donkeys.

Wilkins was always very vague about this time in his life, in fact. No dates, even for his eventual arrival in London, and the minimum of details. It's not inconceivable that in the youthful spirit of adventure he had been acting as a gun-runner himself — a fact that he no doubt soon regretted and would certainly never have wanted to share with anyone who met him through the highly respectable Gaumont organisation.

Once in Biskra, Wilkins managed to get a message to a British Government representative, who arranged money, clean clothes and a ticket on the first steamer out of Algiers to London, the cost of which the expat would have to repay from his first wage packets. Wilkins often claimed that the abduction was a watershed in his life. 'It showed me how to live on my wits,' he explained. 'How to survive on small amounts of water and types of food that Anglo-Saxons would never have considered eating. Most importantly, it proved to me that the human spirit is more than a match for any adversity that can be encountered. No desert … no Arctic wasteland … would ever threaten to conquer my mental determination to survive.'

# Chapter 2

# Those Magnificent Men in Their Flying Machines

CLAUDE GRAHAME-WHITE, the man regarded by many historians as the greatest of Britain's pioneer aviators, was never short of a quid. To use a familiar cliché, he was born with a silver spoon in his mouth. And when, as a young man, he joined the small band of enthusiasts enthralled by the innovation of flight, he never had to worry about how to pay for his outrageously expensive hobby.

Grahame-White attended the right schools and ended up with an engineering degree that looked good on the letterhead of the family business, a company that sold expensive motor cars to London's upper class. The young super-salesman operated from premises in the socially elite suburb of Mayfair, and his gift of the gab ensured many a sale of these early twentieth-century status symbols.

Despite his foppish 'Hooray Henry' mannerisms, Claude Grahame-White had the courage of a latter-day Dr Livingstone or Admiral Nelson and the vision of a Christopher Columbus or Guglielmo Marconi.

In 1909, he had been a spectator at the very first international aviation meeting, at Rheims in northern France. The aircraft on display were primitive machines. But Grahame-White believed they were the way of the future and bought himself a Blériot XII — one of the planes made by French pioneer Louis Blériot, the first man to fly across the English Channel. Grahame-White worked in Blériot's factory for six weeks helping to build it. Such was the bravado of the Englishman that he even attempted a few hops along the runway at Rheims before he'd been taught how to fly this new heavier-than-air machine that would eventually make him a household name back in Britain.

He had the plane shipped over to London by road and sea before engaging on a campaign of self-publicity. He set up his own airfield, flying school and factory at Hendon, to the north of London, with which he hoped to start an English aviation industry.

In 1910, Grahame-White narrowly missed out on a £10,000 prize offered to the first person to fly from London to Manchester in twenty-four hours, having made just two stops on the way. But in October that year, in the United States, he earned for himself a universal reputation at the International Aviation Tournament held at Belmont Park Race Track, near New York. It was billed as 'the Greatest Show Above Earth', and with good reason. The Wright brothers were there to lend it authenticity; so too was the French pioneer Roland Garros, posing for photographs alongside the scores of fragile wood-and-fabric biplanes from all over the world.

Grahame-White won the $5000 Gordon Bennett Trophy for the fastest flight of twenty laps of the racetrack (a total of 10 kilometres). He then posted the fastest time in a race from the track, around the Statue of Liberty and back again, but was disqualified and prevented from claiming the $10,000 prize money because he had allegedly fouled a pylon at the start. Frenchman Count Jacques de Lesseps pocketed the cash instead.

The pretentious Grahame-White was to later fly around Britain in a Farman Boxkite aircraft that had been equipped with light bulbs

British aviator Claude Grahame-White, who taught Wilkins how to fly, mixed in exalted company. Here he is about to land in a street adjacent to the White House in Washington in 1910 for a meeting with President William Taft.

spelling out the message 'Wake up, England'. He wanted the British to wake up to the possibilities presented by aviation.

WILKINS QUICKLY MADE his mark in London as a photo-journalist with Gaumont, shooting the major stories of the day. Although no records exist of exactly which events he covered, there are a number of stories that his bosses would surely have passed his way when allocating jobs to their team of cameramen. The Australian cricketers were over during the northern summer of 1912, for instance, for the triangular tournament with England and South Africa, and it's hard to imagine the young cameraman not being there at Old Trafford when a fellow South Australian, Tom Matthews, bowled his way into the history books with two hat-tricks on the one day. And Wilkins had a lifelong friendship with the celebrated playwright George Bernard Shaw — perhaps it began while he was filming Shaw's appearance at an opening night in London's West End. Then there were the suffragettes' demonstrations, the launch of the *King George V*, Britain's biggest battleship, and the departure of the ocean liner *Titanic*, on her doomed maiden voyage. One can only speculate that Hubert Wilkins filmed at least some of these historic events.

At the same time, Broomhead agreed to let him write stories and take still photographs for Fleet Street's *Daily Chronicle*. AC knew that a byline in the newspaper would have a positive effect at the cinema box office, but the Gaumont boss demanded that his newsreel camera work be a priority.

By now, surrounded by a world that five years before in Adelaide he could only have imagined existed, Wilkins had become captivated by the thought of flying and the possibilities of taking photographs from the air. It would give everyone a whole new perspective on life, he realised. He was well aware of the ostentatious aerial displays of Claude Grahame-White — quite frankly, he felt Grahame-White

Wilkins covering the news in London on horseback.

was, in the words of the old Aussie idiom, up himself. Yet Wilkins had a healthy respect, a fascination even, for the dangers involved in what the Englishman was doing. It was this fascination that drew Wilkins to Hendon Aerodrome one day in early 1912.

While scouting around for potential photographs he fell into a conversation with a stranger. The pair discussed the future of flying and the exploits of some of the pioneers.

'While he's achieved some great things, I'm told that Grahame-White is a conceited ass,' Wilkins told the stranger. 'Despite all that, I admire what he has done, because aircraft and those that fly them will one day prove to be of immense benefit to the world.'

'Oh, really?' came the reply.

'Oh yes, planes are the future of the world,' said the cocky young

Wilkins. 'Have you, by any chance, ever met Grahame-White?' he added.

'Met him? I am Claude Grahame-White. I *am* the pompous ass!' With that, the British aviator dissolved in a fit of laughter as Wilkins squirmed with embarrassment.

That same afternoon, Grahame-White took an enthralled Wilkins up for his first flight. And the foundation was laid for the Australian's flight into the history books. He was thrilled by the experience of the wind blowing in his face, the noise of the propellers that drowned out any hope of conversation, and the view of houses and people below, the latter resembling tiny ants scurrying from their nests.

Wilkins was determined to learn how to fly and soon began lessons under Grahame-White. Ironically, for a man whose name was to be writ large in the history of aviation, he never completed the pilot's course with the British ace; he didn't have sufficient money. It was, after all, a rich man's pastime.

WILKINS BEGAN MIXING with some of the great pioneer aviators. One of them was Lieutenant (John) Cyril Porte, of the Royal Navy, who was to later become involved in several attempts by contemporaries to fly across the Atlantic.

One day in the spring of 1912, Wilkins was photographing Porte testing a new Deperdussin monoplane that boasted a 100-horsepower engine — something considered quite daring and revolutionary. Like Grahame-White, Porte knew the advantages of publicity for the fledgling industry. He suggested that Wilkins should fly with him and shoot some film from the air. It had never before been attempted. Why not? thought Wilkins. A world first!

The Aussie tied his movie camera to wires stretching from just behind the propeller on the Deperdussin's fuselage to the starboard wing, and pointed it at a downward angle. He then had himself strapped to the fuselage, behind the camera, with his right arm able to reach forward and across to crank the film past the lens. Porte was in the cockpit, about a metre behind Wilkins.

The two men were quite nervous, but for different reasons. Porte was tense because he was unsure if the Deperdussin would handle what was at the time the most powerful engine tried in such an aircraft, and Wilkins because he was about to take the most unusual flight of his life, with no way to save himself if the plane crashed.

Wilkins recalled the flight as being like riding a giant bucking bronco at some outback rodeo in Australia. He had trouble catching his breath as the plane zoomed into the air, vibrating violently. Porte did just one circuit of the airfield before landing while Wilkins cranked away in desperation. As he alighted, the Australian cameraman was shaking like a leaf, petrified with the fear of what could have happened to him.

It was a hairy flight with Lieutenant Cyril Porte when Wilkins shot the world's first moving pictures from a plane.

That first historic film was almost useless. But Wilkins was able to modify the way he and the camera were mounted for future flights on various aircraft. And he was able to capture some memorable aerial shots that brought him justified kudos from his peers.

Indeed, a couple of months later, he accepted a commission from Gaumont to film a hare hunt in France. He sat on a bicycle seat that had been affixed to the front of a Farman biplane (constructed by the famous French aircraft designer Henri Farman III). The pilot then proceeded to skim along the course of the hunt just a couple of metres above the ground. It's not certain what frightened the hare in Wilkins' sights the most — the baying hounds or the roar of the aircraft. Wilkins admitted that this was one of his most worrying early flying experiences. 'But I was never as frightened as I was the first time I went up with Porte,' he added.

# Chapter 3

# Like Carbine in the Cup

OVER THE CENTURIES, Europe had become quite used to wars. Every century there would be two or three major conflicts as countries cast envious eyes at their neighbours. But there had been a lull since the Franco–Prussian War of the early 1870s — four decades of peace. Not that there had been an absence of sabre-rattling; it was simply that the tensions had never quite boiled over into open warfare.

In the northern autumn of 1912, all that changed. A loose alliance of Bulgaria, Greece, Serbia and Montenegro decided on a pre-emptive strike against the Ottoman Empire of Turkey, on the pretext of the latter's alleged repressive policies against their ethnic citizens living under Ottoman control. In early October, more than 1 million troops invaded the Turkish-held territories in Europe. The leaders of the European superpowers such as Britain, France, Germany and Italy eyed the conflict with more than a passing interest: they knew it would be the first confrontation that would be won and lost by a new warfare involving the latest technological advances.

Wilkins' bosses at Gaumont and the *Daily Chronicle* were eager to send him into the fray. And Wilkins was keen to go, hoping to become the first man in the world to shoot moving pictures of a battle. He would cover the war from the Turkish side, but he was not alone. When he arrived in the city of Constantinople, he found twenty-six like-minded journalists, all hungry to get to the front.

The conflict was not going well for the Turks, who really didn't want correspondents snooping around and reporting on the chaos, which had even engulfed the capital, far away from the action on the front line. There in Constantinople, every able-bodied young man was being conscripted and every half-decent horse compulsorily purchased from reluctant owners. Indeed, a couple of the journalists found themselves stranded halfway between the wharf where they'd disembarked and the inner-city hotels into which they had been booked, after military officers stopped their hansom cabs and appropriated the horses.

Most of the correspondents, including Wilkins, had booked into the famous Pera Palas Hotel. Almost a century after Wilkins arrived in the Turkish city, the Pera Palas Hotel still evokes the mood of those exhilarating times in which spies and smugglers rubbed

The Pera Palas Hotel in Constantinople, Wilkins' base before covering the First Balkan War battles.

shoulders with Europe's royalty, politicians and diplomats. It was no coincidence that the United States Embassy was next door to the hotel and the British Embassy only a couple of blocks away. That was why most news organisations wanted their employees to stay in the Pera Palas. It had been officially opened in 1892 to cater for travellers on the Orient Express. The railway firm that owned the celebrated train, Compagnie des Wagons-Lits et des Grands Express Européens, also owned the hotel. Porters would meet the train at the railway station in the old city and carry the passengers in special cushioned chairs to a wharf on the Golden Horn estuary, from where they were rowed north across a small stretch of water to near the hotel. There an underground funicular railway would transport them during the minute-and-a-half journey to the hotel's foyer.

WILKINS HAD PLANNED down to the finest detail how he intended covering the war. In London he bought a motorcycle and sidecar, which he would transport to Constantinople by train. He mounted his movie camera onto a special shelf bolted underneath the handlebars of the bike. There was a second shelf mounted above the bars, on which his still camera could rest. That way he could click off photographs at the same time as cranking the movie camera. The sidecar, normally used to carry a passenger, would be packed with spare parts for both the motorcycle and the cameras, a supply of film, his Blickensderfer typewriter, food, and a small one-man tent and sleeping bag. A motorised, travelling photographic unit.

But when he rode his bike from the railway station to the Pera Palas Hotel, he was greeted with general derision by the locals. They knew he had wasted his time converting this newfangled motorcycle, because their own General Abdullah Pasha had already taken steps to thwart the foreign correspondents. The Turkish general decreed that for each journalist to be given accreditation, he must employ a servant, and each group had to have a dragoman (professional interpreter). In addition, each person had to have a horse — and it was a near impossibility for most people to buy one themselves in chaotic Constantinople.

Soon Wilkins had made a pact to share resources with two other journalists. One was Bernard Grant, who was taking still photographs for the London *Daily Mail* newspaper; the other was John Banister, a freelance reporter, also from London. As Wilkins was the only one who knew anything about horses, he was sent out to try to buy mounts for the trio. And with plenty of ingenuity he managed it, paying around £50 worth of gold for each horse, although the acquisition of the third one proved quite elusive for a while.

An elderly Greek cab driver, who had persuaded Wilkins to employ him to look after the horses, provided the answer. He took the Australian to a slum on the outskirts of the city, where the owner of a house in advanced stages of disrepair led him inside and up the stairs to a first-floor bedroom. There in the corner was a wonderful black Arab stallion. The owner had been keeping it hidden inside so the military wouldn't requisition it. He promised to lend the horse to Wilkins for the length of his stay in Turkey, for a 'present' of gold worth around £100.

Wilkins was over the moon. Here was a mount that would be the envy of every one of the opposition newsmen. He was grateful to the Greek cabbie. In relating the story later in life, Wilkins would explain how he and his two London companions never managed to work out the Greek's unpronounceable name, instead dubbing him 'Marcus Aurelius'. The nickname was Roman — but who was quibbling?

The other support crew consisted of a Maltese fellow called Godfrey, whom Wilkins had met in the Pera Palas. Godfrey spoke no less than seven languages fluently and could converse in a couple more. A reformed alcoholic Englishman named Henry was also signed up to be part of the team. Somehow the Turkish officials did not realise that the party of correspondents was one short of the designated number for their entourage.

In the wee hours one morning, those correspondents who had managed to fulfil the Turkish criteria by somehow finding horses, servants and provisions were loaded onto a military train that headed out of Constantinople. They had hoped to make it to the city of Adrianople, about 220 kilometres to the north-west, where the fighting was reported to be at its fiercest. But the Turks unloaded the correspondents at the small town of Chorlu, less than 100 kilometres west of the capital, where the army kept them under tight control. Any photos or stories they wanted to send to their employers were highly censored. Wilkins was frustrated. It was okay for the writers:

A rare photograph of the chaos on the bridge over the Sakarya River during the Battle of Lule Burgas.

they could type up a story using hearsay. But there were only so many photos or so much film of military camps that could be sent back to London.

One day the army officer assigned to shadow the journalists ordered them out of camp and back towards Constantinople. The war was going worse for the Turks than they ever could have imagined — and they didn't want the outside world to know. Wilkins and Bernard Grant by this time had teamed up with veteran American war correspondent Francis McCullagh and the new trio decided to make a dash for 'freedom'. Wilkins staged a mishap during the journey, whereby all his provisions on the trailing packhorse spilled over the ground; the other two came back, supposedly to see what had happened, closely followed by a couple of soldiers. The three media men then bribed the guards and galloped off to the front with their interpreter in tow.

After half an hour or so riding north-west, they reached the top of a hill where, finally, they were able to watch first-hand as a battle unfolded. The date was 31 October and this action was to go into the history books as the Battle of Lule Burgas, named after a nearby town. Indeed, historians regarded it as one of the most significant of the short war.

'The Turks are goners,' said Grant. 'Just look at the panic.'

It certainly was panic. Local peasants, fearing terrible retribution from the Bulgars, had loaded their farm carts with what few possessions they had and were trying to flee to the south. But it was a futile exercise. There was just one bridge across the Sakarya River, a magnificent stone structure with many arches and a wide roadway. But not wide enough. Frightened soldiers elbowed the peasants to one side as they not so much retreated as took flight in absolute terror across the bridge. In addition to this mayhem, angry Turkish cavalry officers were trying to prevent the rout, hacking at the deserting infantrymen with their swords.

Grant was to describe the scene vividly:

*Never before had I seen men so mad with fear. I hope that never again shall I see a great mass of humanity so lost to all reason, so impelled by the one terrible instinct of flight. I saw the final but fruitless struggle of many of them as they tried to keep their feet and then fall. I saw the pain which twisted the faces of those who were grievously wounded. I saw the last rigors of men as death came upon them.*

The three correspondents left Godfrey, the Maltese dragoman, with their provisions and rode down towards the bridge to get the necessary movie footage and photos that would win them fame back in the capitals of Europe and America. As they did so, they were swept up in the wake of the Turkish cavalry, who had suddenly decided on a last-ditch counterattack against the invaders.

Words could hardly describe the emotion of the moment. Hundreds of soldiers, resplendent in their crisp uniforms, urging on their steeds with shouts of encouragement. Sabres waving above them, the riders with their testosterone levels skyrocketing, hoping to find victims to either behead or run through as they galloped into the midst of the enemy. The horses smelt the excitement, pricked their ears and, with nostrils flared, swept into this incredible charge.

Wilkins' Arab stallion needed no urging. He was bred for such excitement and took off like a latter-day Carbine in his charge around Flemington on Melbourne Cup Day. The Aussie could not have reined him in even if he'd wanted to do so.

Wilkins understood that he was about to play a major role in breaking history. In front of him were thousands of Bulgarian infantry troops; behind them, waiting for the right moment to pounce, were thousands of cavalry. And all of them supported by cannon.

As he rode along, he cranked the movie camera that was soon to be his passport to fame. Here he was, capturing the moment on film. It was the first movie coverage in history of a battle — although he didn't think of this at the time. It was all instinct. Like cameramen in later years, in world wars and other international conflicts, he thought not of history but of the need to show people who were not 'lucky enough' to be present what was happening on the world stage.

But, when an artillery shell landed between Wilkins and McCullagh, the Australian realised that discretion might well have been the better part of valour after all. It was time to make a quick exit.

He stopped filming, shouted to his companions and, wheeling his stallion around, began to gallop back towards where they had left Godfrey. There was no time to negotiate the bridge, as a cluster of Bulgarian cavalry wheeled around the wings of the infantry and set off in hot pursuit of what they thought were three young Turks on the run. It was like a Melbourne Cup, with the strongest stayers triumphing. Around a couple of hills before a mad dash for the river. Wilkins thought of the words of Banjo Paterson in *The Man from Snowy River* — how the Man's pony was given its head and he raced down the mountain 'like a torrent down its bed'. But the Man from Snowy River certainly didn't have cavalrymen on his tail, bent on killing him, like Wilkins and his mates did.

Wilkins urged his horse on and they jumped into the river at full gallop. The stallion and the other two mounts were sturdy creatures and swam strongly across the fast-flowing stream. Bullets fired by the pursuing cavalrymen ricocheted off the opposite bank as the horses struggled out of the water. They had escaped. It was a hell of a way for the young Australian to celebrate his birthday.

The historic moment had an unusual postscript. When Wilkins' bosses at Gaumont received his film they were less than pleased. They fired back a cable pointing out that 'the opposition', their great rival Pathé, had been showing movie footage of the conflict in London cinemas for the previous two days, and that it was much more dramatic than Wilkins' shots of the chaos at the Battle of Lule Burgas. Wilkins was bemused. He knew his was the first and only movie of the battle. There was another movie camera in the area, but it had broken down before the French photographer who owned it had had a chance to use it.

A few days later Wilkins received another cable — this time an abject apology. It transpired that the other film was a fake. It had been shot using actors at a location near Paris. Only when the genuine movie taken by Wilkins was aired in British cinemas did the penny drop: the actors in the Pathé newsreel had been wearing the wrong uniforms. The opposition did not try the con trick again.

IT WAS PERHAPS lucky for Wilkins, Grant and McCullagh that they'd left Godfrey back well away from that first skirmish. As it turned out, the interpreter did not have the stomach for a battle, even though in the social circles back at the Pera Palas he had always boasted of his bravery when confronted by thieves and vagabonds.

A week or so later, in early November, Wilkins decided it was time to return to the front and again seek out stories and film first-hand. By this time, the foreign correspondents had been permitted to return to Chorlu after their forced withdrawal in late October. He had heard the sound of the heavy artillery booming out from the west of the camp, where, as before, the Turkish authorities were trying to keep the war correspondents on a leash. Wilkins was having none of that and talked to Grant and another London-based journalist, (George) Ward Price of the *Daily Mail*, later to make a name for himself in World War I, about again defying the Turks and heading for the front to see for themselves what was really happening.

After filming some graphic scenes — one where Turks are seen being blown up by Bulgarian shelling — Wilkins readied himself to gallop closer to the scenes of carnage. His man Godfrey, who was there to hand him replacement film for his camera, then panicked and started screaming at the Australian.

'We're all going to die!' he cried. 'We are finished. We are history.'

Wilkins was desperate to get better shots of the battle — but Godfrey was holding on to his arm, threatening to drag him off his horse. Angrily, Wilkins pulled out the revolver he was carrying and was about to shoot his servant when Ward Price rode up and slapped Wilkins with his riding whip.

'He's not worth it, dear boy!' the Englishman shouted. 'Let's leave the stupid man to his fate.' Which is what they did.

It was now clear that Hubert Wilkins no longer worked according to the Turkish rules. He and his colleagues did their own thing, sneaking film and stories back to Constantinople using locals. It was wonderful what the greasing of a palm with some gold would do. Back in London, the Gaumont chiefs were delighted as they sold movie clips and single frames from Wilkins' efforts to cinemas and newspapers not only in Britain but on the Continent and in Canada and the United States as well. What a goldmine they'd found in this daring young Australian.

The longer he stayed in Turkey, the easier it became. Wearing local clothes, the suntanned Wilkins looked like a Turk and could casually stroll past army checkpoints whenever he walked into a town to organise the transportation of his film back to Gaumont. He learned to conceal the rolls of film in his Arab clothes. At the checkpoints, the soldiers would only search his baggage, thrown over the back of the Arab stallion. Wilkins also perfected the simple peasant's blank look and shrug of the shoulders for the times when the soldiers did decide to question him; frustrated at their inability to make him understand the simplest of questions, the guards would wave him on.

After a week or more, Price parted company with the other two correspondents. Wilkins and Grant found an accommodating retired priest in a tiny nondescript village away from the prying eyes of the Turks. There the two men continued their first-hand coverage of the conflict. One day, however, they were surprised to encounter a dapper Englishman in the village. He had suddenly appeared in a chauffeur-driven automobile — a rare sight in Constantinople, let alone in this remote area. When he introduced himself as Ellis Ashmead-Bartlett, the penny dropped. The two correspondents had read his despatches from war zones around the world for the news agency Reuters. He was a friend of the Turkish sultan, Mehmed V, and, as such, was allowed to roam freely around the country, unlike other journalists. This time he was reporting for the London *Daily Telegraph*.

Wilkins and Grant suggested he stay with them in the priest's house. After all, what better way to keep a close watch on what the opposition was doing? That first night they dined on food brought in the car by Ashmead-Bartlett, including some of the finest Russian caviar and a couple of bottles of Veuve Clicquot champagne. They toasted Veuve's Grande Dame over and over again while discussing the war.

At one point during the evening, their new companion made a lame excuse to go outside and talk to his chauffeur. 'I'm sending him back to Constantinople to get me some soda water for tomorrow's foray into the battle,' said Ashmead-Bartlett. 'Would there be anything you'd like him to bring back for you?'

There wasn't. But when the visitor was gone an unusually long time, Wilkins realised that the *Telegraph* man had almost certainly written a story from the events they had just related to him, and that was the real reason for the chauffeur's sudden return to the Turkish capital. Before the driver left, though, the Australian managed to pull him aside — and, with a hefty bribe of gold, persuaded the man to also take their stories and photos to their representatives in Constantinople.

Late in the night, when the champagne had taken its toll, Ashmead-Bartlett confessed to his ruse. 'Really, chaps, you're not in my class as a war correspondent,' he said with a condescending toss of the head. 'That's why it is so easy to scoop you fellows. Tomorrow the readers of the *Daily Telegraph* in Britain will be reading my exclusive reports from the front. Never mind, you will have learned a fine lesson tonight: never trust an opposition journalist.'

'We don't,' Wilkins replied with a smile. 'That's why we sent our reports and photos back with your chauffeur. Your story is only hearsay. Ours are dramatic, first-person accounts of the fighting. And the pictures ... spectacular stuff, if I may say so myself.'

British war correspondent Ellis Ashmead-Bartlett was scooped by Wilkins during the First Balkan War but later made a name for himself by helping expose the disastrous World War I campaign at Gallipoli.

The blood drained from Ashmead-Bartlett's face. It was he who had been scooped. He left at dawn in high dudgeon.

Before long, the Bulgarians were bearing down on the village. And, as they did, the locals decided to abandon their homes and head for the capital. The news team dined that night on some turkeys left behind by the villagers, after which Wilkins and Grant fell violently ill. According to Wilkins, the symptoms were those of cholera. The disease was rampant and he wondered if the turkeys had been infected. As Bulgarian shells began raining down on the village, their man-servants, Marcus Aurelius and Henry, loaded the by-now unconscious pair onto their horses, tied them securely with rope and led them to safety well behind the Turkish lines.

Over a period of a week or two, the correspondents slowly regained their health, with the help of local peasants who provided herbal remedies handed down through the generations. By now the Turkish Army was being thoroughly routed, and Wilkins and Grant knew their graphic photos of the starving deserters and the hotchpotch of grimy homeless peasants would most certainly be censored at the telegraph offices in Constantinople. But they also knew there was a wireless link to the rest of the world about 240 kilometres to the north, in the Black Sea port of Constanta, the so-called 'Lung of Romania' at the mouth of the River Danube.

It was too far and too dangerous to make the journey on horseback, so the team headed for the coast to the north with a plan to commandeer a boat and travel across the Black Sea. At the ancient town of Midye (now Kiyikoy), they hijacked a tugboat at gunpoint after the chief engineer, the only man on board, had refused to accept a bribe. The voyage to Constanta would take them about thirty-six hours — but by the time they passed the Bulgarian–Romanian border the chief engineer had decided that perhaps, if a little gold came his way, he would be happy to co-operate and get them back to Turkey.

# Best of British

Ellis Ashmead-Bartlett was one of the most famous of all British war correspondents. Hubert Wilkins may have believed that his ego was far too inflated, but the Australian did admit he was good company — especially when relating his experiences at the front in several wars.

In 1897, at the age of sixteen, the Englishman had accompanied his father, the American-born but English-educated Sir Ellis Ashmead-Bartlett, to Turkey as guests of Sultan Abd-ul-Hamid II, who was engaged at the time in a war with Greece. It fuelled the younger Ashmead-Bartlett's enthusiasm for analysing the conflicts of the ever-changing world.

He fought in the Boer War of 1899–1902, but was repatriated because of illness. His career as a war correspondent began in 1904 when he covered the siege of the Russian port of Port Arthur by the Japanese. As a globetrotting correspondent for the British news agency Reuters, he reported on the French Army's campaigns in Morocco in 1907 and 1908, the Spanish efforts in the same country the following year, and the Italian Army's battles in Libya in 1911. A year later the *Daily Telegraph* commissioned him to cover the first of the two Balkan Wars.

The suave English journalist is best remembered for his reporting of the Anzac landing at Gallipoli in April 1915. Historians have attributed his reports, and those of Australian war correspondent Keith Murdoch, of the debacle at Gallipoli and the ineptitude of the British command as the major reasons behind the eventual withdrawal of the troops from the Dardenelles and the resignation of Winston Churchill as Britain's First Lord of the Admiralty.

Ashmead-Bartlett later covered conflicts in China (1927), the Soviet Union (1928), Palestine (1929) and India (1930). He took ill and died in Lisbon on 4 May 1931.

Wilkins and Grant concocted a wonderful story about being captured by a drug-runner for the engineer to explain his absence to the captain of the tugboat. They were wordsmiths, after all.

At Constanta the two men took it in turns to telegraph their stories and pictures. The stories caused a sensation in London, as Wilkins and Grant were thought to have died while under Bulgarian shell-fire, and all enquiries to the Bulgarians — who'd been offered a sizeable ransom for their return, unharmed, if they had taken them prisoner — had drawn a blank. When the pair eventually returned to London at the end of the year, they were able to read their own obituaries. What was it that Mark Twain noted? Something along the lines of 'Reports of my death have been greatly exaggerated'.

BACK IN CONSTANTINOPLE, Wilkins and Grant heard a story that set their blood racing. Philip Gibbs, a senior war correspondent on Wilkins' paper, the *Daily Chronicle*, had been stationed with the Bulgarians who had been laying siege to Adrianople from the Bulgarian side. This was a fortress city west of Lule Burgas and had remained a Turkish enclave despite the rest of the area being overrun by the Bulgarian troops. The 35-year-old Gibbs, who was to become one of Britain's best-known war correspondents in World War I and later a successful novelist and a knight of the realm, had witnessed the first use of an aircraft in battle. A monoplane flown by a Bulgarian pilot had circled above the city to check out the extent of the Turkish defences. After a while, as shells exploded around it, the plane flew off to report to the Bulgarian commanders. An hour or so later it was back for a second reconnaissance. Again it was greeted by a fusillade of fire. Its task complete, it flew off once more.

Gibbs thought the pilot must have flown off to safety 'from his chase of death'. 'But later that day,' he explained, 'I heard that the unfortunate aviator and his plane had fallen from the sky when he was within sight of his home aerodrome. This hero's body ended up lifeless in the tangled wreckage.'

'A hero, indeed!' Wilkins told Grant when he heard the story. 'But, you mark my words, there will be many more like him in years to come. I predict they'll also mount guns on these aircraft and fight the enemy in the air, just as they do now on land and sea.' Wilkins also saw the possibilities of filming battles from an aircraft, just as he had filmed the hare hunt in France. What an adrenalin rush that would be.

By this time the Turks had retreated to the so-called Chatalja Line. The town of Chatalja was near the Bosphorus, just 40 kilometres from Constantinople. Here they had dug trenches — in what was the first use of trench warfare in history — to hold off the Bulgarians. Wilkins and Grant returned to the front, this time armed with a letter of introduction for Prince Abd-ul-Aziz, a member of the reigning Ottoman royal family. The prince directed his army officers to offer help and hospitality to the two correspondents.

The order was promptly ignored, however, and when Wilkins started filming the conflict, he and Grant were arrested and held for a week without food. Then there was a sudden change of heart, with the two men being taken to the tent of Turkey's minister for war, Nazim Pasha. Nazim, a genial and popular politician, apologised and assigned the man who had detained them, one Captain Haji Ali, to be their personal aide-de-camp. Haji looked after the pair before returning them to Constantinople in early December. Nazim Pasha and the country's grand vizier (prime minister), Kiamil Pasha, had sued for peace.

The war was over and Wilkins and Grant headed home ... Actually, the war would soon restart and then drag on for another four months. Nazim was assassinated on 23 January by Enver Bey, one of the youthful politicans whose names have gone into the English language as 'the Young Turks', and later the country's minister for war during World War I. Kiamil was then forced to resign and the new

Turkish leadership decided to continue the war — a decision that soon proved to be disastrous as even more concessions of territory resulted from the resumption of hostilities.

By then, Wilkins was back in London, basking in the success of his Balkan mission. Gibbs, Wilkins and Grant decided to write a book on the conflict, titled *Adventures of War with Cross and Crescent*. According to Wilkins, he and Grant decided to toss a coin to see whose name would accompany that of Gibbs on the front cover. Wilkins lost the toss. But, truth be known, Wilkins was never one to indulge in self-promotion; he was happy to stay out of the limelight.

HE MAY HAVE come out of the First Balkan War alive, but Hubert Wilkins had no sooner returned to Britain than he was risking his life again — this time in a hot-air balloon. Wilkins arrived home from the front in the third week of December. He had hoped for a short break and a relaxing yuletide but his bosses at Gaumont had other ideas. They ordered Wilkins to film what promised to be a spectacular publicity stunt, planned by Sandow's Cocoa Company, for two days before Christmas.

Eugene Sandow was the world's first recognised body builder. The vaudeville strongman is credited with turning body building from physical culture for a tiny minority of men, regarded by society as cranks, into a major sport with a massive marketing potential. The son of a Prussian father and Russian mother, he was born Friedrich Mueller in 1867, but changed his name as a teenager when he ran away from home to join a circus as an acrobat. He became famous under the tutelage of renowned American showbiz entrepreneur Florenz Ziegfeld, of *Broadway Follies* fame. In 1901, Sandow organised the world's first body-building contest, at London's Royal Albert Hall, with Sir Arthur Conan Doyle, creator of the fictional detective Sherlock Holmes, as one of the judges. Sandow then branched out into the cocoa business, adopting the slogan 'A Perfect Sweetmeat — A Perfect Food' for his Health & Strength Cocoa. And now, having built a factory at Hounslow on the western outskirts of London, he was intending a foray into the chocolate market.

The company had signed up the famed Spencer brothers for the high-profile launch. Back in 1902 Stanley Spencer had been the first Englishman to fly a powered airship (as distinct from a balloon) and his brother Frank was an expert balloon pilot, too. Frank would be joined in the stunt by a Sydney daredevil dubbed 'Captain Penfold' (real name Vincent Patrick Taylor), famous for scaling the outside walls of tall buildings, parachuting from balloons over Sydney Harbour, and jumping with a parachute from cliffs and bridges. He was arguably the world's first exponent of what today is known as BASE-jumping.

On this particular day, 23 December, Captain Penfold was dressed as Santa Claus, white beard and all. He was due to jump from the

CAPTAIN TAYLOR PENFOLD, THE AUSTRALIAN AERONAUT.

Vincent Patrick Taylor aka Captain Penfold. A balloon ride with the eccentric Australian adventurer almost cost Wilkins his life.

balloon and parachute into London's Hyde Park, where he would hand out Sandow's new chocolates to children.

It was a miserable winter's day when Wilkins filmed the preparations for the ascent of the balloon, 4 kilometres south of Hyde Park, near the River Thames. Frank Spencer was worried there was not enough ballast on board to prevent the balloon from ascending too high, so Wilkins suggested he tag along for the ride, thus adding a bit of weight, as well as giving him the chance to get some great aerial shots of the city.

Once aloft, he realised there wouldn't be too much chance for photography, as the balloon was suddenly engulfed by thick cloud. What's more, they were heading in the wrong direction for Hyde Park. Then, about thirty minutes into the flight, there was a break in the cloud.

'I'm off,' shouted Captain Penfold. And, with his bag of chocolates, he jumped out of the basket hanging below the balloon.

Wilkins managed to film him — but only for a few seconds, as the balloon was suddenly back in the cloud. The parachutist would land in a field at Chelmsford, about 55 kilometres north-east from where he was supposed to touch down. But he handed out the chocolates anyway, to the children of local farmers.

Meanwhile, all the activity had unbalanced the balloon and the gas release cord became entangled in the ropes — meaning there was no way the duo could descend. Frank did some calculations and pointed out that even as the gas cooled, it would be at least twenty-four hours before the balloon managed to drop back down to earth. Then the realisation hit. At the speed they were being carried by the wind, they would be well off the coast of Britain, over the North Sea, by the time they came down.

Fortunately, the winds changed overnight, and when dawn broke they found themselves over the English Channel, slowly, ever slowly, descending and drifting back towards the coast. Several times the gondola hit the water with a thud. As the pair hung on for grim death, Wilkins' movie and still cameras were jolted overboard. Several hours later, he and Spencer eventually came ashore and crashed into a ploughed field, lucky to be alive.

Wilkins' bosses at Gaumont were furious. There was no insurance on the cameras and there was not one piece of film to justify the risks he had taken.

The publicity hardly worked for Sandow's either. Within a couple of years the company was in liquidation, forced out of business by the likes of Cadbury and Rowntree, both of which had lowered their prices to scuttle the interloper. But the executives at Cadbury were impressed by the enterprise of Wilkins, and signed him up to do a film and brochure on the production of cocoa in the West Indies. Film pioneer Léon Gaumont hand-painted every single frame of the movie. It was released as *Food of the Gods* in 1914 and is recognised as one of the first colour movies in history.

But it was to be several years before Wilkins saw the final product of his efforts in the West Indies. As he was boarding the ship from Barbados for his return to England, in April 1913, he received a cable from his bosses in London, asking whether he would like to join an expedition to the Arctic. Would he ever … He immediately replied in the affirmative.

It was only when his ship was at sea that Wilkins realised he had misread the cable. He'd thought the expedition was going to the Antarctic. He had been entranced by the stories of Sir Ernest Shackleton's first expedition there, on the *Nimrod* in 1907–09, during which the famed explorer reached the South Magnetic Pole, and had asked the intrepid Englishman if he could come along on his next mission to the South Pole.

Instead he would go north with a Canadian named Vilhjalmur Stefansson. And, once again, Wilkins would push his luck to the limit.

# Chapter 4

# North from Alaska

VILHJALMUR STEFANSSON WAS born in 1879 in Ames, north of the
Canadian city of Winnipeg, the son of Icelandic immigrants. Indeed,
the area in which their log cabin was built was known locally as New
Iceland because of the number of residents from that country. His
parents wanted him to be accepted by Canadian children so they
baptised him William, but as an adult, his pride in his ancestry saw him
change it back to the Icelandic equivalent. Sadly, their stay in Canada
was short. The family farm was wiped out by floods and when two of
Vilhjalmur's siblings died in a smallpox epidemic that swept through
the Canadian province, they moved south to the US state of North
Dakota. He graduated from Harvard, where he studied anthropology,
and immediately turned his attention to the life of the Inuit (Eskimos)
of North America.

With his first two ventures into the Arctic, Stefansson became
something of an authority on the Inuit. During the first, the Anglo–
American Polar Expedition of 1906–07, he spent eighteen months
living with the indigenous people of the Mackenzie Delta, in the far
north-western corner of Canada, learning their language and recording
the society's history as passed down verbally from generation to
generation.

Canadian explorer Vilhjalmur Stefansson who took Wilkins on the Australian's first venture into the Arctic.

On his second expedition, in 1908–12, Stefansson discovered a group of Inuit with distinct European features. American newspapers went over the top when reporting the existence of these so-called 'Blond Eskimos' (now described as the Copper Inuit). There was speculation that they were perhaps descendants of the Vikings. Although critics among the scientific community ridiculed his findings, the saga ensured that the 33-year-old had no trouble gaining finance for his next journey into the Arctic, especially after he'd published a bestselling book, *My Life with the Eskimo*.

Most of his considerable backing came from the Canadian Government. Among the aims of his expedition, which was to take five years, was to prove the existence or otherwise of a massive continent alleged to be concealed under the polar icecap. And because of his celebrity status, he found it relatively easy to attract other young scientists to accompany him. The top-notch scientific crew comprised the following:

- Diamond Jenness, a Rhodes Scholar from New Zealand, as one of two anthropologists on the expedition. At age twenty-six, Jenness was already well respected in his field, thanks largely to his efforts of the previous two years in studying the natives of the d'Entrecasteaux Islands, off north-eastern New Guinea.

- Professor Henri Beuchat, a renowned French anthropologist and colleague of the famous Marcel Mauss. Together, the two Frenchmen had published a book and several academic papers. Beuchat was regarded as an expert on North American anthropology.

- Dr Alistair Forbes Mackay, the expedition's surgeon and one of only two members with experience of the conditions they would face in the Arctic. Mackay had been assistant surgeon with Ernest Shackleton's British Antarctic Expedition and was among the first people to ever reach the South Magnetic Pole.

- George Malloch, a respected Canadian geologist. There is a mountain in the Canadian Rockies named after Malloch, in recognition of the fact that he was the first to climb the 3068-metre peak and map its features.

- Bjarne Mamen, a Norwegian forester, as the group's topographer, assisting Malloch.

- William McKinlay, a 24-year-old Glasgow teacher known to his mates as 'Wee Mac' (he was just 1.62 metres tall), as the team's meteorologist.

- James Murray, the oceanographer, and another Glaswegian. Murray had also been a member of Shackleton's 1907–09 foray to Antarctica, having earlier conducted extensive biological research on Scotland's freshwater lochs.

The secretary for what would come to be known as the Canadian Arctic Expedition (or CAE) was a local man, Burt McConnell. These were the key personnel whom Wilkins would be joining as the

CAE's official cameraman and cinematographer. It was hoped that he would have the opportunity to send photos and news reports to the *Daily Chronicle*, but Stefansson would be venturing into largely undiscovered territory, so the chances of this happening before the end of the expedition were slim.

The mother ship taking the team north from Victoria in British Columbia on 17 June was the *Karluk*, a wooden former whaler that was almost thirty years old. There were other ships involved — the *Alaska*, *North Star*, *Polar Bear* and *Mary Sachs* — making up what was christened 'the Expedition Navy'.

Master of the *Karluk* was Robert A. 'Bob' Bartlett, who had a wealth of experience, having sailed more than forty voyages and a total of around 200,000 nautical miles in Arctic waters. He was best known as the skipper of *Roosevelt*, which in 1909 had taken Robert Peary to within 215 kilometres of the pole, from where the American

Bob Bartlett, captain of the ill-fated *Karluk*.

naval lieutenant and explorer became the first man to reach the North Geographic Pole.

THE STORY OF the *Karluk* has become one of the great epics of history. And depending on whom you believe, Stefansson was the villain and Bartlett the hero ... or vice versa. Indeed, there are two conflicting stories on how the tragic demise of the *Karluk* occurred.

What is undisputed is the fact that the *Karluk* was not a suitable ship to use in the expedition. The 255-tonne, square-rigged barquentine was basically a tub. She was in need of a good coat of paint, reeked of whale oil and was infested with cockroaches. Her construction meant there was no possibility of breaking free if the ship became trapped by ice. And that proved to be her downfall.

Stefansson's Expedition Navy sailed out of Nome, Alaska, in July 1913 and headed north into the Arctic Ocean. Once past Point Barrow, on the northernmost tip of Alaska, Captain Bartlett decided to head into the icefloes instead of sticking to the open water closer to land.

On the first night, the *Karluk* became stuck in the ice about 15 nautical miles away from the Alaskan landmass. Meanwhile the other ships had passed by near the shore and headed east towards the Beaufort Sea. As the ice pushed in around his vessel, Bartlett predicted they might be stuck there until the following spring. This threw the whole expedition into chaos. The ships had planned to rendezvous at Herschel Island, about 650 kilometres east of Point Barrow; from there, various teams would head out on different scientific research projects. As it turned out, the other ships got only halfway when, in mid September, ice off Point Collinson trapped them for the winter.

It is at this point that the stories of what happened differ.

Captain Bartlett claimed that Stefansson, McConnell, Wilkins and Jenness left the barquentine to hunt caribou, to provide sufficient food for those on board. And that Stefansson's party then failed to return, abandoning everyone on the *Karluk* to a horror fifteen months. The version as told by the expedition leader, and corroborated by Wilkins and others in his team, was very, very different.

Stefansson claimed he had planned to go ashore and recruit a group of Eskimos to join them on board and help the expedition members survive the winter by teaching them the ways of the local indigenous people. On the first night out from the ship, the four men were engulfed by an Arctic storm that raged for almost four days. Once it had cleared and they emerged from the tent in which they'd taken refuge, the group found themselves trapped on a small island of ice floating in the ocean — with the *Karluk* nowhere in sight. Nor were they ever to see her again.

Stefansson said he had ordered Bartlett, in the event of the ice breaking up, to burn beacons so that the ship could be located on

The *Karluk* trapped in the Arctic ice, before it was finally crushed in January 1914.

their return journey. He never saw a beacon during the several weeks in which he, McConnell, Wilkins and Jenness struggled along the northern coast of Alaska in a horrendous 250-kilometre trek west to Point Barrow. Along the way, the four met a family of Eskimos who reported seeing the *Karluk* drifting west; they'd wondered why the crew hadn't tried to reach land in their lifeboats, as the way the ice was moving, the ship would eventually be taken deep into the Arctic Sea.

For five months the *Karluk* drifted, a prisoner trapped in the ice. Eventually, in January 1914, the ice crushed the barquentine, which sank without trace near Wrangel Island (now known as Ostrov Vrangelya), off the north coast of Siberia. Bartlett had seen this coming and had unloaded most of the sled dogs and provisions for the twenty-five survivors.

Two groups of four then set out across the ice to the east in an attempt to reach Herald Island, often a stopover for whalers and other ships. The first group — Mackay, Beuchat, Murray and a seaman named Stanley Morris — were never seen again. The other four — all members of the *Karluk*'s crew, led by First Officer Sandy Anderson — managed to reach Herald Island but died there soon after, asphyxiated by the fumes from a faulty stove. Their bodies were not discovered until eleven years later.

Eventually, Bartlett decided to make his own attempt to save those who were left. With an Eskimo hunter, Claude Kataktovik, he set off on foot across the icefloes on a 250-kilometre journey to the Russian mainland. Reaching what was then known as Emma Harbor (today's Komsomolskaya Bay), the pair were taken aboard a passing trading ship, the *Herman*, skippered by a renowned Arctic maritime veteran named Captain Christian Pedersen, who took them back to Nome. There Bartlett arranged for a rescue mission by an American coastguard ship, the USS *Bear*.

By the time the *Bear* reached the makeshift camp at Wrangel Island in the autumn of 1914, another three members of the expedition had perished. The geologists Malloch and Mamen died of nephritis (kidney infection), and Seaman George Breddy from gunshot wounds. There was a suggestion of murder since Breddy had been accused of stealing food from his crew-mates.

Until the day he died, Wilkins blamed Robert Bartlett and his crew for the disastrous end to the *Karluk* and so many of those on board. Wilkins claimed that the advice of the people with experience of Arctic conditions had been ignored. He scoffed at the decision to head for Herald Island and questioned the amount of supplies taken on the sleds and clothing worn by the two ill-fated parties of four.

AFTER RECOVERING AT Point Barrow in August 1913, under the care of the American trader Charlie Bower and his Eskimo wife, Stefansson's party were ready to resume the expedition. Wilkins and Jenness were first to set off, heading east. They were to rendezvous with Stefansson and McConnell at a lake near Point Collinson, some 500 kilometres away, near the US–Canadian border. They arrived just before Christmas 1913. Wilkins put on a movie show to celebrate the yuletide.

For the next two years, the group conducted exploration and scientific experiments around the area. Many times the men were separated and often believed lost. Wilkins suffered frostbite and snow blindness, but invariably he was helped by the survival techniques taught to him by the local Eskimos.

On one occasion during 1914 when Stefansson had disappeared, Wilkins took the *Mary Sachs* and four crew-members to search for him on Banks Island, off Canada's Northwest Territories. They reached the island after four months' sailing, during which time the ship almost sank off the mouth of the Mackenzie River. It was touch and go, as for fifty-six hours the crew battled huge seas whipped up by a raging storm. They sought refuge in the lee of a grounded iceberg, only to have the ship drift onto land after the sailor on watch had fallen asleep. The bow was staved in, her two rudders loosened and a propeller smashed. Yet, thanks to temporary repairs and Wilkins' extraordinary seamanship, the stricken vessel managed to make it to Cape Kellett on Banks Island, where the arrival of autumn ice trapped them for the 1914–15 winter.

Still, Wilkins was determined to check for any signs of Stefansson and, accompanied by two Eskimos, decided to make a 700-kilometre trek around the perimeter of the island. Just four days into the journey, he found evidence of Stefansson having recently made a camp. Returning to the *Mary Sachs*, he decided to prepare for a blanket search of the area. But the next day, while the crew were out hunting for caribou and polar bears to provide food, Stefansson suddenly appeared, none the worse for wear.

During the wait through winter the following year, Wilkins learned from Stefansson and the Eskimos in the party the art of making igloos, and Wilkins and the expedition leader spent long hours discussing ways of exploring the Arctic. While the Australian was keen on the use of aircraft, Stefansson suggested that a submarine might be better suited. Submarines had been used during the American Revolution and, as the twentieth century had dawned, the British Admiralty had purchased five as possible weapons of war. Stefansson believed that submarines would provide a safe environment for the explorers of the future and would be able to force their way up through the icefloes of the Arctic Ocean just as giant whales were able to do. History was to prove him right.

The seeds of ideas for a couple of new forms of exploration were sewn in Hubert Wilkins' mind that winter of 1915–16. And he was to eventually try both.

EARLY IN 1916, as the winter ice began to melt, Wilkins received his first mail from England in almost two years. There were letters from his family in Australia, giving him the sad news that his father, Harry Wilkins, had passed away on 10 December 1914, and asking him to come home for a visit. And there were letters from both Gaumont and the *Daily Chronicle* in London, asking him to return to cover a new war that had broken out in Europe, just as he had the First Balkan War.

The Canadian Government reckoned the CAE had done its job, even though Stefansson intended to stay for another couple of years. The government was also uncomfortable about the *Karluk*'s fate and the death of so many of the ship's crew. The politicians back in Ottawa were keen to sweep as much adverse publicity under the carpet as possible, and demands by some of the survivors for a royal commission into the disaster were summarily rejected. The government preferred to emphasise the positives of the CAE's efforts.

Stefansson's team had discovered four new islands that were claimed for Canada. They had mapped new parts of the wilderness and corrected mistakes in many of the existing maps, especially those of Banks Island. For his part, Wilkins had taken hundreds of photos that are regarded almost a century later as classics. Other members of the expedition party had commemorated his efforts by naming prominent geographic features in the Arctic after him: Wilkins Bay, on the north-west coast of Banks Island; Wilkins Strait, off the small Jenness Island (north-east of Banks); and Wilkins Point, on the Canadian mainland.

Wilkins estimated that while on the expedition he had traversed some 8000 kilometres on foot — much of it from going back and forth over ground already covered. By June 1916, with his task finished, Wilkins was packing up and heading back to civilisation.

# Chapter 5

# The Western Front

As STEFANSSON'S EXPEDITION was making its way north in July 1913, the nations of Europe had begun the sabre-rattling that would culminate in the outbreak of the Great War — or World War I, as it would come to be known later in the century. At the time of the Balkan Wars, few people had fully realised what a threat to world peace the conflicts posed. But the European nations were grouped in various alliances, all struggling for influence in the region, and now the great powers mobilised for what was to be an inevitable war.

It is said that the bullet that killed Archduke Franz Ferdinand of Austria on 28 June 1914 was the shot that started the war. It was fired by a Serbian nationalist, in Sarajevo, but the assassin could have come from any of the states ruled against their will by the Austro-Hungarian Empire. A month later, the Austro-Hungarian Government declared war on Serbia. Within another week, Germany had declared war on Russia and France and invaded Belgium, thus forcing Britain into the conflict, on 4 August. The following day, half a world away in Canberra, Prime Minister Joseph Cook announced that Australia was now at war also: 'Our duty is quite clear — to gird up our loins and remember we are Britons.' Cook immediately offered Great Britain an expeditionary force of some 20,000 troops.

In September, the forces allied to Britain and Germany, respectively, dug themselves into trenches opposite each other on battlefields across northern France and Belgium. At sea, the two greatest navies of the world prepared to fight for control of the sea lanes. The conflict was on in earnest.

Wilkins had fully expected the war to have been over long before the end of his time with the CAE. After all, the British pundits had predicted that the Tommies would clean up the Huns in just a few weeks. But this 'war to end all wars' surprised everyone, as the two sides dug in for years of horrific trench warfare. Wilkins had enthusiastically embraced the Balkan conflict in 1912 as a war correspondent. He would do likewise in the Great War, although at first he had no intention of photographing the action. Rather, he wanted to fight.

In the northern summer of 1916, he set off from Alaska to return to Australia, but as at almost every point in Wilkins' life, he had a brush with death on the journey home. A train journey across Canada and then down to New York passed without incident, after which followed the most dangerous leg: a voyage across the Atlantic to Britain. The steamer on which he had managed to procure a berth would have to run the gauntlet of German U-boats eager to sink any ship sailing under the flag of Great Britain or its empire, whether it be a Royal Navy vessel or a passenger or merchant one.

It is difficult to piece together exactly what happened on this voyage. The only hint came in a later British radio series on Wilkins' exploits, *True Adventure Thrills*, in which it seems there was more than a little journalistic licence — something commonplace in today's media, but quite unusual in that era. According to the depiction on radio, Wilkins' ship (the name is never mentioned) was part of a small convoy of vessels. Within a day of leaving New York, two of the ships had been sunk, with much loss of life. Many of the survivors, most of them the families of Canadian officers who were heading for England to be with their husbands and fathers, were picked up by his ship. On the third day, the steamer was attacked by a German U-boat and had its hull ripped apart by torpedoes. As it began to sink, Wilkins and another man managed to climb down a swaying rope into a lifeboat. It was a difficult task for the women and impossible for the children on board, so men up on the deck would throw the kids bodily down into the boat, where Wilkins and his companion caught them and thrust them into the arms of whichever woman happened to be the nearest. Wilkins' description continued: 'Finally the boat was jammed full. Many on deck were pleading to be helped in, but we could take no more ... [and] the young officer in charge ordered us to move out free from the ship.'

After twenty-four hours of drifting aimlessly in the Atlantic, so the radio adaptation maintained, a Royal Navy corvette appeared on the horizon. It had heard the SOS radioed by the captain of the doomed vessel and had sailed through the ring of U-boats to rescue the survivors.

The *True Adventure Thrills* episode implied that many passengers didn't make it. But the facts tell a different story. There were no lives lost at all in U-boat attacks around this time. It would seem that the vessel *U-53*, skippered by Kapitänleutnant Hans Rose, could have been the sub involved. One of the German Navy's most decorated officers, Rose sank eighty-one ships during the war, including five off Nantucket Lightship on 8 October 1916 — but even then, as during this earlier encounter, without inflicting any casualties. (Ironically, Rose found out about the departure of those five ships while reading a newspaper on a 'courtesy visit' to nearby Newport Harbor, in the then-neutral United States.)

From London, there was another worrying two months of sailing dangerous sea lanes for Wilkins, down the African coast and finally across the Indian Ocean to Australia. In Adelaide, in early April 1917, he was reunited for the first time in six years with his widowed mother and seven siblings. However poignant the reunion must have been — his brother Peter had also died during his absence — it was destined to be a brief one, with a war raging on the far side of the globe. Four of Wilkins' five surviving brothers were well into middle age by now and it is unlikely that they would have been accepted for military service. Not so 28-year-old Hubert, the baby of the family, who quickly headed off to Melbourne to enlist.

Wilkins thought his experience with ships on the Stefansson explorations could be utilised in Australia's fledgling navy. But when he heard the powers-that-be wanted him to run a training school for young men who would pilot motorboats, he baulked at the idea. It was then that an old acquaintance from his time as a cameraman in Sydney came to the rescue.

When Wilkins had first met Brigadier General Hubert John Foster, the Englishman had been a colonel and the head of the University of Sydney's school of military science. These were the days long before Australia had a dedicated college to train its army and navy officers, so it was the job of Foster, who had been a British military attaché in Washington, and previously quartermaster-general of the Canadian forces during the Boer War, to train the country's future military leaders in the finer points of warfare. Some of the textbooks written by Foster were essential reading for the military hopefuls, especially *War and the Empire: The Principles of Imperial Defence* and, later on, *The War in Europe: A Sketch of the Main Operations up to August 1915*.

At the time Wilkins renewed their acquaintance, Foster had recently become chief of the Australian General Staff — the supreme head of the nation's army. Foster suggested a spot for him in the Australian Flying Corps, formed just eighteen months earlier;

Wilkins' experiences with the likes of Claude Grahame-White and Cyril Porte would be invaluable to this new arm of the military, based at Point Cook, west of Melbourne. Foster brushed aside the South Australian's protests that it had been some years since he'd been aloft in any kind of aircraft. 'Why don't you see what you can do in a plane?' the general said while his batman was driving them down to Point Cook.

And Wilkins did, going up in a training aircraft with an instructor and realising that he knew more about flying than his companion.

'I suppose it's a bit like the old saying, "You never forget how to ride a bicycle",' Wilkins joked to Foster after he had landed.

General Foster used his influence, putting in a special request to Prime Minister Billy Hughes. Within forty-eight hours, Wilkins had been granted a commission in the Australian Flying Corps, at the rank of lieutenant. A week later, in early May 1917, he was back at sea en route to Europe.

But he still hadn't passed an official medical examination, such was the speed at which Foster's hand had guided events. That would come in England, in July, before the trip across the Channel to the front.

And Wilkins failed it, on two counts. First, there were his feet and legs: they had been irreparably damaged during his long treks across the Arctic ice.

'You cannot walk properly,' said an officious doctor at the headquarters of the Australian Imperial Force, located at 130 Horseferry Road, Westminster.

'So what?' Wilkins responded.

'Well, you have to be able to walk to be in the armed forces,' came the frosty reply.

'Fair enough. And since the original damage was done, I've regularly averaged slogs of more than 16 miles a day over ice and snow.' Over 25 kilometres a day — that was impressive.

'Absolute rubbish. No man could manage that on your legs and feet.'

Wilkins recalled an adage he had once heard — 'You can't put brains in statues' — and just smiled.

The new AFC lieutenant then failed the eye test, because he was allegedly colour blind. This truly surprised Wilkins, as he dabbled in art and had produced some wonderful watercolour paintings that now hung on friends' walls. They would hardly have displayed paintings with the wrong colours just to humour a friend.

The doctor, knowing he was fighting a losing battle against this determined man, caved in. The fact that Billy Hughes and General Foster had recommended Wilkins would no doubt have helped in the decision. In his report the doctor suggested that Lieutenant Wilkins was not colour blind; it was just that his knowledge of the names of basic colours was poor.

Throughout his life, Wilkins would tell the story of the medico's findings and wonder aloud how many fit Australian men were denied from serving in the war because their feet weren't right or they were supposedly colour blind, or whatever. 'Just because your toes point the wrong way doesn't mean you can't fight for your country!' he would fume.

Regardless of his influential friends, Wilkins never did get to fly with the AFC, in fact. Instead he was to join arguably Australia's greatest war correspondent and military historian, C.E.W. Bean, in the newly created War Records Section.

CHARLES EDWIN WOODROW Bean was born in Bathurst, New South Wales, in November 1879 but moved with his family to England, where he received his formal education. After returning to Australia in 1904, he practised law for four years until switching careers to become a reporter for the *Sydney Morning Herald*, a position he still held at the outbreak of war. When the British defence chiefs asked each of the countries from the British Empire to provide an official war correspondent, Bean won the Australian ballot.

Bean went ashore at Anzac Cove on Gallipoli at about 10 am on 25 April 1915, some five and a half hours after the first landing. A fortnight later he was with two Australian brigades that made an unsuccessful attack at Cape Helles. Throughout the bitter fighting on that night of 8 May, he ignored the Turkish gunfire to help tend dozens of wounded Diggers. For his efforts he was recommended for the Military Cross, but it couldn't be awarded as he was not in the armed forces. Instead, Bean was Mentioned in Despatches.

The first news of the Anzac landings to be published in Australia was a story by Wilkins' old Balkan War acquaintance Ellis Ashmead-Bartlett. Bean had been scooped because the British authorities in Alexandria wanted their man to get the kudos and held up Bean's first story until Ashmead-Bartlett's had been published.

Bean was the only correspondent to stay on at Gallipoli until the withdrawal in December. On 6 August, he was hit by a bullet in his right leg. He was offered a place on one of the hospital ships, but turned it down; instead, he had medicos dress the wound each day as he lay in great pain in his dugout. After almost three weeks, he was able to hobble out and continue his coverage of the action.

The reporting by Bean and the stories of his bravery brought him to the attention of the Australian Government, which was keen for the Diggers' part in the war to be recorded. Hence the establishment of the War Records Section in 1917, with Bean at its head.

He chose as his two official photographers men who, coincidentally, had both been involved in polar explorations, Hubert Wilkins and Frank Hurley, the latter having served as photographer on Sir Ernest Shackleton's failed Antarctic expedition of 1914–17. The two men's approach to their job was as different as chalk and cheese. And Bean used them accordingly — Hurley for the 'propaganda' photos, sometimes faked, that were sent to newspapers and magazines in Australia, and Wilkins for the historically accurate shots that would be the visual backbone of the official history of the war. Bean also had official war artists at his disposal. Among them were the acclaimed Arthur Streeton, Will Dyson and Fred Leist, on the Western Front, and George Lambert in Palestine.

Wilkins was told of his new job by Colonel Thomas Griffith, commandant of the AIF headquarters in London. 'This job is more important than flying,' the colonel declared. 'You will keep your rank in the Flying Corps and you can fly whenever you think it necessary to get photographs from the air. But your main task will be to link with every section of the AIF and get pictures of the soldiers in action. You'll be off to the front in a couple of days.'

Bean met Wilkins and Hurley when they disembarked at the French port of Boulogne. Basically, he had just one instruction for

Fellow World War I photographer Frank Hurley.

them: 'I want an honest pictorial coverage of Australian soldiers both in battle and at times of relaxation away from the hostilities.' To history's great loss, Wilkins made few notes, left almost no details of his experience on the Western Front and rarely spoke about it after the war.

The photographers arrived at the front towards the end of July 1917, just before the Third Battle of Ypres. Ypres was a small town in Belgian Flanders, just across the border with France, and was razed during the hell of the first three years of the war. The Third Battle is these days remembered as Passchendaele, after the village east of Ypres that was also wiped out. The slaughter on the yellow mud-fields of Passchendaele inspired British war hero and renowned poet Siegfried Sassoon to write 'Memorial Tablet', a poem that has become perhaps the most quoted verse of the Great War, with its immortal lines: 'I died in Hell — / (They called it Passchendaele) ...'

Bean decided that Wilkins and Hurley needed to be shocked into the horrors of the war immediately and so took them on a tour of the Australian front line, just a few metres from the German trenches. He showed them what remained of Hill 60, an artificial incline once 60 metres high, made from the spoil of a railway cutting, that had given its name to one of the more recent battles. But it was no longer a hill; Australian engineers had tunnelled under it and simultaneously exploded around twenty mines, levelling it to the ground. For the two new arrivals, the noise from massive guns discharging their shells behind the front line, and of the shells screaming overhead, was deafening. They winced at the sight of pieces of dead German soldiers and their broken weapons littering the area between the opposing trenches. And the cacophony did not halt at sunset, but continued twenty-four hours a day. That first night, they came under attack from above — a German squadron flying over the trenches, pilots dropping bombs from their open cockpits.

Years later Wilkins was to tell his good friend Lowell Thomas of his first impressions: 'When the Germans attacked, it seemed like a trip into Hell. The black night lighted by flames of guns and by signal flares, the air shaking with noise, and the earth shaking underfoot. Human beings seemed insignificant in the midst of all this. It didn't seem possible that men could go through it and live.'

He would also tell Thomas of a bizarre incident that occurred as he was walking with some other Australians along the duckboards in the front-line trenches, when one of the Diggers was hit by a shell. The man's head was blown off and landed on a post, at the sight of which those who had survived the explosion broke up into hysterical laughter, such was the surreal nature of the poor bloke's fate. Each man knew it could have been his head sitting on the pole, his shattered body on the other side of the trench.

An iconic photo shot by Wilkins shows fellow cameraman Frank Hurley among wounded and dead Australian soldiers at Broodseinde Ridge on 12 October 1917 (National Library of Australia).

WILKINS AND HURLEY soon fell into a regular routine. They rose at 5 am, snatched a bite to eat and were at the front when the sun rose. They took photos of the front-line infantry, machine guns and heavy artillery in action, and twice a week Wilkins would go up in an Australian Flying Corps plane to shoot the action from the air. On one of these occasions he watched as seven Zeppelins were destroyed, the hydrogen gas inside them turning the airships into burning infernos as they crashed down to the earth.

At sunset each day, the two Australians returned to their headquarters at the French village of Steenvoorde, some 10 kilometres behind the lines. There they had dinner before developing their films for despatch to the censors in Warlencourt, close to the town of Pozières, which was the site of a battle in 1916 that had seen some 23,000 Australians perish in just seven weeks. It was rare for them to get to bed before midnight. Bean realised the toll this took on the photographers and ordered them to take a day's leave in London once a month.

They came to understand the enemy's tactics, soon learning that the safest time to take photos on the battlefield was immediately after it had been strafed by the German artillery. There was usually a two- or three-minute window of opportunity at this point, allowing them a pretty good chance of safety while they got to work with the cameras. The ice-cool Wilkins was also known to crawl out of the Allied trenches before the Aussies launched an attack, so that he could get dramatic photos as they came over the top on their rush through no-man's-land towards the German trenches.

There were countless acts of heroism by Australian soldiers during the various battles and skirmishes that made up the Third Battle of Ypres, and Hubert Wilkins was on the scene during or just after many of them. Five members of the AIF won the Victoria Cross, three of them being awarded posthumously. Private Reg Inwood, a miner from Broken Hill before his enlistment, was honoured at Polygon Wood for his capture of two separate machine-gun emplacements on the opening couple of days of the hostilities there, in late September. Second Lieutenant Fred Birks, a Welshman who emigrated to Australia to join relatives, died at Glencourse Wood on 20 September after overcoming twenty-five Germans to capture a machine-gun position. He was killed while trying to dig out his mates after they'd been buried under mud by a shell explosion. Lance Corporal Wally Feeler, from the Victorian town of Castlemaine, performed three acts of valour at Broodseinde Ridge on 4 October, killing thirty enemy troops in all. He was later to work as the custodian of Melbourne's Shrine of Remembrance. On the same day at Broodseinde, former Tasmanian train driver Sergeant Lewis McGee rushed and captured a pillbox while armed only with a revolver. He was killed in battle eight days later. And finally there was Captain Clarence Jeffries, from the Hunter Valley in New South Wales, who died while leading a bombing party on the second of two pillboxes they attacked on 12 October, at Augustus Wood.

Wilkins' bravery over these weeks did not go unnoticed either, and he was awarded a Military Cross (second only to the Victoria Cross) for his efforts. The citation hardly tells the full story:

*During the five battles before Ypres, from September 20th and October 12th, and in the fighting in between those dates and since, Lieutenant G.H. Wilkins acted as the Australian Records photographer. On September 20th, early in the fight forward of our old trenches a shell bursting beneath a tank from which he was operating broke some of the gear which he was carrying. In spite of this he continued to obtain records of every subject of value for Australian history, procuring invaluable pictures of the front line during a period of fighting in Polygon Wood. In the subsequent fighting he again had the gear which he was carrying broken by a shell, but he persisted with his work passing daily through the barrages, without relief, during a period when almost all other officers engaged in work of equal danger were relieved. He was round the front line during the Battle of Broodseinde Ridge on October 4th, obtaining records beyond our furthest objective, the valuable pictures of consolidation. Late in the month he was blown from the Zonnebeke duckboards and picked up by a passing party of Canadians, but he has continued his work during the winter without relaxation. This work has been imposed on Lieutenant Wilkins by his own sense of duty, the results being invaluable as records while he rarely obtains the credit of publication. His demeanour has been markedly gallant and his noticeability [that is, his presence in the thick of the action] brought credit upon his office amongst the 'troops'.*

That incident on the Zonnebeke duckboards happened while he was returning from the front with some graphic shots of the action. A shell exploded near Wilkins and blasted him into a nearby water-filled bomb crater. He landed with his camera equipment underneath him — and it was this equipment that saved his life. He was unconscious, but the camera and bulky film plates kept his head out of water, saving him from almost certain drowning. When the shelling briefly stopped, a party of Canadian gunners (who had tried to warn him of his imminent danger) arrived and took him to the nearest field hospital. During the night, Wilkins defied doctors' orders, left his hospital bed and made his way back to his headquarters, ready for the next day's work.

A year later, on 27 September 1918, Wilkins was with the AIF's 3rd and 5th divisions, supported by troops from the American 27th and 29th divisions (the United States having officially entered the war in April 1917), as they attacked the Hindenburg Line. Named after German commander Paul von Hindenburg, this was a 160-kilometre-long defensive trench with a second trench a few hundred metres behind it; in front of the Hindenburg Line was several hundred metres of open land that would make attackers sitting ducks for the German machine-gunners. The Australians were by this time controlled, not by British generals, but by their own leader, General Sir John Monash. And, with the October Revolution having taken Bolshevik-controlled Russia out of the war and freed up whole divisions of German troops from the Eastern Front, the Allies' eventual victory in this battle would be the turning point in the so-called One Hundred Day Offensive that ultimately led to the end of the Great War.

Now promoted to captain, Wilkins had taken so many photographs in the area in which this battle was being waged, he knew it like the back of his hand. And he made a special effort to help the Americans, who, while fighting courageously, seemed confused when trying to work out just where the enemy was located. And their inexperience meant that often they allowed the Germans to regroup after being overrun.

It was just such a situation that Wilkins saw on the morning of 29 September. He noticed a group of confused soldiers arguing among themselves in a front-line trench. Dodging German bullets, he raced across some open land and leaped into the trench.

'G'day. Are you Yanks okay?' Wilkins asked as he and his assistant tumbled in with their camera equipment.

'No. We don't know what to do,' an agitated American private replied. 'We've lost all our officers, and the Germans are up the other end of the duckboards with a group of our men that they've captured.'

'Just stay calm,' Wilkins told him. 'I'll organise everything.'

'How can I stay calm? You'll be a lot of help — you don't even have a gun!'

# Who killed the Red Baron?

Without doubt the greatest name in the skies over the battlefields of World War I was Baron Manfred von Richthofen. It could even be said that in the history of aviation, there has never been a fighter pilot the equal of him. During the Great War, with the primitive aircraft made of wood and fabric, a pilot who managed twenty kills in dogfights with the enemy was regarded as a legend. So what does that make von Richthofen, whose final tally was eighty?

He was known in his native Germany as '*der Rote Kampfflieger*' (the Red Battle-flyer). The French described him as '*le Petit Rouge*' (Little Red). But he is probably best known by his Anglo-Saxon nickname: the Red Baron. It was von Richthofen who made famous the German award for gallantry, the Orden Pour Le Mérite — nicknamed 'the Blue Max', after the first German airman to win it, Max Immelmann, when it was awarded for eight kills. The medal achieved iconic status once the qualification was raised to sixteen enemy aircraft shot down, and the Red Baron was the first to win the Blue Max under these conditions.

Von Richthofen was born at Breslau, in what was then Germany (now Wroclaw in Poland), on 2 May 1892. He began training in military schools at the age of eleven and before he was twenty had reached the rank of lieutenant in the cavalry. But cavalry charges were soon to become a thing of the past, and at the start of the Great War he joined the German air service. After one day's instruction he became a pilot, making his first solo flight on 10 October 1915. In his first dogfight — on just his second solo effort — he shot down a French plane. And his reputation soon gathered strength.

In 1917, Jagdgeschwader (Fighter Wing) 1 was formed, with von Richthofen in command. In July that year he was shot down. But while he landed safely, he suffered a serious bullet wound to the head and was plagued by headaches for the rest of his life.

On 21 April 1918, von Richthofen was following the Sopwith Camel flown by an inexperienced young Canadian RAF pilot, Wilfred 'Wop' May, as it veered away from a dogfight involving around forty aircraft. While the Red Baron chased May, the Canadian's squadron leader, Captain Roy Brown, was chasing the German.

Wilkins was on his way to the front to take photos of the action when he saw the battle overhead and stopped his car to watch. He recalled looking on as May, trying to shake off the German air ace, put his plane into an almost vertical dive. Miraculously, as he neared the ground, May pulled out of the dive and disappeared from Wilkins' view, over a hill. The Red Baron, in hot pursuit, also pulled out of his dive. Then suddenly, there was the crackle of a single machine gun, at which point von Richthofen's Fokker triplane seemed to go out of control and sideslip. It, too, disappeared from view.

Wilkins found a telephone, checked with headquarters and found that the Red Baron had crashed and died. The cameraman quickly drove to the scene to photograph the wreckage. By the time he arrived, the German hero's body had already been taken to RAF headquarters, located on the front between the townships of Albert and Harbonnières. Wilkins never saw von Richthofen's body but took a series of shots of the mangled wreck of his famous red aircraft.

There has always been some dispute over who actually shot down the Red Baron. The Canadians were convinced it was Brown, but Diggers in an Australian machine-gun emplacement claimed they hit the Red Baron's aircraft with ground fire as it pulled out of the dive. Wilkins later recalled how, because of ill-feeling at the time between the Australians and the Canadians, he was asked not to take sides. Still, he would always insist that the Red Baron was in perfect control of the Fokker until moments after he (Wilkins) heard the machine-gun fire. And as an experienced aviator himself, Wilkins would surely have known.

Von Richthofen was buried with full military honours by the Allies, with the propeller of his downed aircraft fashioned into a memorial cross on his grave. There was even a truce to enable German pilots to fly across the area and drop wreaths of flowers onto the grave. Wars were different back then.

'But I've got you blokes, right? You look likely lads, and I reckon you're good soldiers. Come on, we'll stop any of the Hun who dare to show their faces — don't you reckon?'

The private nodded in agreement. And so did those behind him. The cool, calm Australian had given them all hope.

'There'll be others with us soon, mark my words,' Wilkins said with a reassuring nod of the head. He wasn't really sure about that, but all those crises in the Arctic had instilled an incredible optimism in him. 'In the meantime, let's go get the Huns.'

They moved forward and, in some bitter close fighting, overwhelmed the enemy and released the captured Americans. By this time Wilkins and his assistant had been joined by an Australian liaison officer. The three of them climbed to the rim of a crater so that Wilkins could explain to the officer what had been happening. Suddenly there was a burst of machine-gun fire — lead raining down mercilessly on their mud-splattered khaki uniforms, and the trio of bodies fell limply back into the crater …

When Hubert Wilkins recovered consciousness, he was bleeding from multiple bullet wounds: seven bullets had grazed his chest, there was a scalp wound and another on his right foot. The other two men were dead. A group of Australians, seeing what had happened, had charged and captured the German machine-gun nest.

Covered in blood from head to foot, Wilkins was evacuated to safety and treated by the AIF medicos. Next morning, still swathed in bandages, he left his hospital bed — and headed back to the front line. 'I've got work to do,' was his only comment.

That day he was shot three more times, but dismissed his wounds as being no more than superficial: 'Lots of blood, but not too much damage. All part of a day at the office!'

The efforts by Wilkins during this period saw a bar added to his Military Cross. The citation explained:

*Captain G.H. Wilkins, Australian Official Photographer, during the whole period of the German offensive, and the British offensive that followed it, carried out his duties in a manner which brought a most marked credit to his unit amongst all the troops engaged. During the period in which the Australian Corps was attacking, from August 8th to October 3rd, he was in the front line at some period during the day of every battle, and on six occasions during that period went over with the attacking infantry. During the attack on Mont St Quentin [captured by the Allies on 1 September] the coolness displayed by him was a marked encouragement to those around him. In the Battle of the Hindenburg Line of September 29th, Captain Wilkins went over shortly after the attacking Americans and found the Germans bombing the Americans back up the trenches on the left flank. Under machine gun fire at close range he worked forward to the trenches held by the Americans, together with his sergeant, and on reaching the position, organised the Americans, who had lost their officers, and directed operations until the German attack was checked and the supporting troops were arriving. He then left them and continued his duties, frequently under heavy fire, during the rest of the day.*

'A couple of colonels had witnessed what had happened,' Wilkins later explained, characteristically downplaying his heroics. 'They singled me out because they saw I was carrying a camera and, while there were plenty of rifles, there weren't many cameras on the Western Front.'

WILKINS WOULD DISMISS the prestige that resulted from both the Military Cross and Bar, as well as the time in November 1918 when he was Mentioned in Despatches. He was embarrassed when General Monash described him to colleagues as 'the bravest man I have ever seen' and claimed Wilkins was Australia's counterpart to T.E.

Lawrence — Lawrence of Arabia. 'His war record was unique,' the general noted. Indeed, Monash singled him out for special mention in the first edition of his war memoirs. (When it was pointed out that tradition dictated a commander should never make individual mention of anyone below the rank of general, however, he removed the reference to Wilkins from later editions.)

Records show that Captain Hubert Wilkins was wounded on at least nine different occasions while at the front. To Wilkins, that was inconsequential. All he cared about was recording the events of the war. Decades later, he would tell Lowell Thomas that when he first saw the completed *Official History of Australia in the War of 1914–1918*, he was consumed with pride. 'I derived great satisfaction from the way Charlie Bean had used so many hundreds of my pictures,' he said.

Yet just as the man appeared modest almost to a fault, there can be no denying his incredible bravery, although some critics may suggest there was an element of foolhardiness in his efforts to capture many of his exceptional photographs. It was as if he was born for the job of Australia's official war photographer.

There was, for example, the occasion when Wilkins went up in an observation balloon with a reconnaissance expert to take photographs of the German lines. The balloon was one of six grouped together along this part of the front line. It was dangerous work, because whenever a balloon was hit by shell or machine-gun fire, it usually exploded; plus, being such visible targets, they were a magnet for enemy aircraft. And sure enough, once Wilkins and the other reconnaissance teams were aloft, there was a German fighter plane heading right their way. As the crews on the ground frantically tried to winch them all back to the ground, the two balloons nearest to his exploded. The observers tried to parachute to safety, but as they descended, the men were sitting ducks. They were strafed by the German pilot and killed instantly.

Wilkins' companion shouted at him: 'Climb out of the basket and hang on with your hands! Let go if the balloon explodes, and just hope you're close enough to the ground to survive.'

Three times the pilot raked their balloon with machine-gun bullets, before turning his attention to the remaining three. The balloon from which Wilkins was dangling was the only one to survive the onslaught without exploding. But this was a fact not lost on the German airman, who soon returned and began strafing Wilkins during his descent, one bullet nicking the Australian's right cheek.

*Don't look down and don't look at the plane …* Wilkins kept willing himself. *Just concentrate on survival.*

Eventually he hit the ground and heard the comforting words of a soldier. 'Hey, at least there's one of them still alive …'

Wilkins would also make regular trips by aircraft over the German lines to get aerial shots of the enemy. A second plane would accompany his as protection from the inevitable German flyer that would soon arrive, hoping to shoot the interlopers out of the air. But Wilkins was under orders never to engage in a dogfight, and would instead turn tail and head back to the Australian Flying Corps air base. Many times Wilkins' plane would return riddled with bullet holes.

But even this sort of derring-do was tame stuff for the irrepressible adventurer from South Australia. In October 1918, around the time of his thirtieth birthday and just a month away from Germany's eventual capitulation, Wilkins approached Charles Bean to explain what he saw as a serious flaw in the unit's photographic coverage of the fighting on the Western Front.

'All our photographs show only the Allies in action,' he began. 'We haven't taken any suitable photos of the *German* infantry fighting. Now, I'm trying to find a pilot to fly me over the German trenches so low that we'll be almost at ground level. If we're low enough, we could get some sensational photos of the German Army in action. I just want to get your permission for the exercise.'

Bean looked at him in amazement. 'Hubert, you can't be serious.'

But he most certainly was. Bean would comment later on how glad he was that the war came to an end a few weeks after this conversation — before Wilkins could find a pilot with a similar disregard for the dangers that such a venture would involve. Wilkins had always approached his exploration adventures with the utmost care, and he had never taken any stupid risks. 'But no amount of care and planning could have prevented them being shot down by the German machine-gunners,' Bean said.

THE WAR WAS over, but not so Wilkins' work for the Australian Government. Charles Bean had an important task ahead of him.

Right from the start, Bean had been commissioned to write the official history of the war as seen through the eyes of the Australians who had fought on the many battlefields, from Mesopotamia (now Iraq), the Sinai and Palestine in the Middle East, Gallipoli and the Western Front. Bean had been diligent, writing up his diaries every night and making sure that Wilkins and Hurley had taken every possible photograph on the battlegrounds of Europe. He had also collected trunkfuls of relics from the Western Front — personal items discarded by Australian soldiers that, to Bean, provided a human side to the conflict. He had been at Gallipoli, of course, where the Anzac legend was born, and he had written stirring reports of the fierce encounters for the Australian media. But because of the hurried nature of the eventual retreat in December 1915, he had been unable to gather any trinkets or personal effects from that particular campaign. Now, with the world leaders gathering at Versailles outside Paris to hatch out a binding peace treaty, he wanted to return to the peninsula and collect the relics before they were 'souvenired' by visitors or destroyed by the elements. He also wanted to view the battlefields from the Turkish side, in order to give his history a proper perspective.

'I had become certain that the accepted story of the Anzac landing was far from the truth,' was the way Bean put it. 'The riddles might be solved by visiting Gallipoli while the ground was almost unchanged.'

He asked the politicians in Canberra to let him return to Australia via Gallipoli, something to which they agreed wholeheartedly. And thus the Australian Historical Mission of 1919 was established.

By January, Bean had gathered together five other officers and two sergeants to help him in his endeavours. One of these men was Wilkins. Bean chose him to take the official photographs of all the spots made famous by the Anzacs — Lone Pine, The Nek, Quinn's Post, Hell Spit, Shrapnel Valley et al. — rather than Hurley, because he was unhappy with the way the latter would regularly 'fake' photographs by superimposing two or three different images to achieve a more dramatic picture. 'Wilkins sought to provide our future historians with a record of places and events so accurate that they could be, and often were, relied on as historical evidence,' Bean explained.

Among the others in the team was war artist George Lambert, whose paintings of the Australian Light Horsemen in Palestine have since achieved iconic status.

Bean knew he had chosen well as the team scrambled over the rough terrain of Gallipoli in search of answers. Indeed, he publicly attributed much of the success of the venture to the enthusiasm and spirit of Hubert Wilkins. 'He was a born leader,' Bean said of his official photographer. 'As we strode and climbed about the hills, the rest of the party unconsciously followed Wilkins' lead. If he used a certain path, climbed a cliff in a particular way, jumped a trench or even went round left or right of a bush, the rest of us usually did the same.'

Still, Australia's great war historian was to muse after the mission how the trip to Gallipoli was probably the most unadventurous expedition of Wilkins' life.

BEFORE REACHING GALLIPOLI, Bean and Wilkins had spent some time in Constantinople, talking to the right people and shaking the right hands. It was a necessary task, but something that did not sit easily with either man. Bean had wanted Wilkins at his side because of the important contacts he'd made while reporting on the First Balkan War.

One day while Wilkins was walking near the Pera Palas Hotel, there was a shout as a cab screeched to a halt next to him. He looked around as jumping down from the vehicle came the man he knew as Marcus Aurelius — the Greek old-timer who had tended his and Bernard Grant's horses six years before. He demanded to drive the pair around without payment for the entire time they were in the city.

Their only free night in Constantinople was spent at a cabaret in the renowned Tokatlion Hotel. Bean was unimpressed, describing it as a 'tawdry place'. When a waiter appeared with a couple of bottles of the finest French bubbly and some hors d'oeuvres, they were baffled. 'Compliments of the manager,' said the waiter. 'He will be along shortly.'

And who was this manager so keen to offer largesse? None other than Godfrey, the untrustworthy Maltese dragoman from the earlier conflict.

Wilkins bit his tongue and suppressed his anger so as not to cause a scene. But his opinion of Godfrey was confirmed when the manager boasted how he had spied for both sides during the Great War. 'The

British thought I was a double agent working for them, and the Turks believed I was on their side!' he laughed. 'I was too clever for both of them. All the time I was just working for myself!'

As they trudged back to their hotel that night, Wilkins turned to Bean and, with a shake of the head, muttered: 'I knew I should have killed him.'

Bean was unsure whether he was joking or not.

# Chapter 6

# The Race to Australia

WHAT WAS IT that drove so many Australian adventurers of the Wilkins era? Of all the countries in the world, Australia seemed to produce more than its fair share of young men determined to fly the newfangled, heavier-than-air machines across vast stretches of largely uncharted ocean, relying on the most basic navigational techniques. These early aviators didn't regard life as being cheap; they weren't fatalists. They had no perception that maybe, just maybe, they would disappear over the vast tracts of water, never to be seen again. Yet they challenged the elements, and many of them won.

There had been a huge influx of intrepid adventurers into Britain before the recent war, keen to learn how to fly. More came to serve the empire during the Great War, and when it was all over, so many were left deflated; to keep the adrenalin pumping, they too began to challenge the skies.

Harry Hawker was one such adventurer. Born in the Melbourne suburb of South Brighton (now Moorabbin) in 1889, the future co-founder of aircraft giant Hawker Aviation had arrived in Britain in 1911 with a single aim: to learn to fly. He got a job as a mechanic with the Sopwith Aviation Company and was soon being feted as the firm's top test pilot. His ice-cool flying made him so valuable that when war broke out, the British Government put pressure on the Australian authorities to refuse him a spot in the newly formed Australian Flying Corps. Instead, Hawker tested the planes that the likes of Hubert Wilkins flew over the enemy lines in Flanders.

Not long after the Germans surrendered, the *Daily Mail*, one of London's (or, indeed, the world's) most famous newspapers, launched a high-profile competition to find the first aircrew to successfully fly across the Atlantic Ocean. The prize was £10,000 — a tidy sum now but a king's ransom back then. It didn't matter whether the winners were British, although no doubt it would have been nice for the national daily. Next best would have been a crew of flyers from the British Empire.

As it was, the *Mail* got it both ways. The thirty-year-old Hawker seconded a British naval commander, Ken Mackenzie Grieve, to be his navigator as they tried for the prize. They took off in a Sopwith aircraft from St John's in Newfoundland, Canada, on Sunday, 18 May 1919, and headed off across the ocean. On the other side, the British waited with bated breath.

A day later there was a report that the plane had ditched in the sea near the mouth of the Shannon River in western Ireland, and the pair were alive. The relief of Hawker's wife, Muriel, who was nursing their two-month-old baby daughter, was overwhelming. Then came the letdown: the message was exposed as a hoax.

For almost a week there was no news. It was at that time that Muriel Hawker received a telegram from Buckingham Palace: 'The King, fearing the worst must now be realised regarding the fate of your husband, wished to express his deep sympathy and that of the Queen in your sudden and tragic sorrow.' Muriel was not convinced, however. The next day she went to church to pray that everyone else (including King George V) was wrong. They were. Some may say her prayers were answered; others would suggest that the general public, fed by the media, was premature in dismissing the survival chances of Hawker and Mackenzie Grieve.

On 25 May, the *Mary*, a Danish steamer that had been plying the Atlantic — but without a radio with which to keep in contact with the rest of the world — approached the Butt of Lewis in the Outer Hebrides, north-west of the Scottish mainland. From her mast the ship flew semaphore flags spelling out a simple but most important message: 'Saved hands Sopwith.' Coastguards quickly shot off a query: 'Is it Hawker?' The reply signalled from the *Mary* was quickly relayed around the world by telegraph. It said simply: 'Yes.'

It had been a terrifying journey for Hawker and Mackenzie Grieve, with the engine of the aircraft at one stage cutting out, only to roar to life again when the aviators were a couple of metres above the ocean waves. They'd made it just halfway across the Atlantic and thought all was lost, until they saw the *Mary*. They manoeuvred the Sopwith and ditched it in the swirling sea in front of the ship. It took the vessel's crew two hours to rescue them.

When Hawker finally set foot on British soil, he was able to read his own obituary in the Fleet Street newspapers. He and Mackenzie Grieve were then ferried across to the mainland before making the long train journey south to London. They may not have taken out the *Daily Mail* prize (the RAF's Captain John Alcock and Lieutenant Arthur Brown would do so less than a month later), but by the reception the pair received at each and every railway station along the way, you would never have believed it.

The enthusiasm with which the airmen were greeted in the British capital was especially incredible. Australian soldiers and airmen were among the thousands who flocked to pay tribute to their courage. Captain Hubert Wilkins would no doubt have felt the infectious excitement that prompted the outpouring of public passion. Certainly Hawker's efforts set in train the plans to meet the next great aviation challenge: an air race from London to Australia. And all the fledgling flyers, including Wilkins, quickly lined up to take part.

AFTER AUSTRALIA'S PRIME minister, Billy Hughes, had announced a prize to equal that of the trans-Atlantic challenge for the crew of the first aircraft to fly to Australia, one contemporary report noted that Australia House in London was 'thick with aviators anxious to fly home'. It was not an anxiety to get back to Australia per se; nor, in fact, was it the £10,000 prize money that lured them into the race. It was the innate derring-do of the scores of Australian airmen who had been involved in the world's first military battles of the air.

The rules of the race as defined by Hughes, the man they dubbed 'the Little Digger', demanded that the crew be Australian and the aircraft constructed of parts manufactured in the British Empire, that entrants should not take off before 8 September 1919, and that the journey be completed within a period of thirty days and finish before the end of the year. The aviators would fly easterly rather than west via North America, due to the scarcity of charted islands in the Pacific on which an aircraft could be landed. Without detours because of bad weather, the journey from London to Australia would involve flying a minimum of 25,000 kilometres. The rules also stipulated that at least one of the crew had to be an expert navigator, and each crew would include at least one skilled mechanic. As a result, most planes would be carrying a crew of three or four experienced aviators.

Back in Australia, the community was divided. Many thought Hughes' idea was foolhardy; others believed it was a great boost for Australian nationalism. The press took sides. *The Argus* reckoned it was a massive waste of taxpayers' money because the task ahead for the flyers was far too easy. Another Melbourne newspaper, *The Age*, was equally dismissive of what it described as 'a circus flight'.

But Hughes was a canny fellow. He recognised the international exposure that awaited the infant nation in the southern hemisphere. The Little Digger basked in the headlines, from London and Paris to New York and a host of other cities around the world — however doom-laden those headlines may have been. The *New York Times*, for one, was wary of possible disaster and suggested that the aircrews would be 'throwing dice with Death'.

Hughes took precautions against any adverse publicity that would follow should Death manage to throw the winning roll. Britain's Royal Aero Club was responsible for vetting all contestants, and insufficient flying experience or navigational skills would automatically rule out any novices. One such kid was 22-year-old Sydney flyer Charles Kingsford Smith. He had flown in aerial battles in France but his sparse knowledge of navigation went against him. Little did the boffins at the Aero Club know just what a great aviator Charles Kingsford Smith would one day become.

He had planned to fly with a crew led by a fine Queensland airman named Valdemar (Val) Rendle. The 23-year-old son of a Brisbane doctor, Rendle had taken up gliding as a teenager, in 1915, and had helped set up the Queensland Volunteer Gliding Civilians. When he'd tried to enlist with the Australian Flying Corps, the authorities in Sydney had turned him down because of his alleged defective eyesight. So Rendle took himself to England, learned to fly and was accepted by the British, poor eyesight notwithstanding. He earned his wings in 1917 and, for the remainder of the war, had flown with great success.

With Kingsford Smith out of the equation, Rendle went looking for another experienced airman to lead the crew of his twin-engine Blackburn Kangaroo. And he found a ready-made navigator in Wilkins, now approaching thirty-one. The 23-year-old Lieutenant Reg Williams, from Victoria, had spent much of the war with Rendle ferrying aircraft from England to the front in France and Belgium.

When he was recruited for the team, he had been working for Claude Grahame-White's aviation company at Hendon Aerodrome, as had the fourth member of the crew, Lieutenant Garnsey (Gar) Potts, a 22-year-old who hailed from the Melbourne suburb of Richmond. Each man was a competent flyer and had a working knowledge of aircraft engines, but the age difference between Wilkins and his fellow crewmen, not to mention his reputation and contacts, soon saw young Val Rendle willingly surrender team leadership over to the South Australian.

The Kangaroo, built by the Blackburn Aeroplane and Motor Company in the Humberside area of northern England, was a strange-looking aircraft thanks to its elongated fuselage, which jutted out some 5 metres in front of the wings. There were two open cockpits in front of the wings and another two behind — all in a line down the top of the fuselage. Rolls-Royce car and engine manufacturers supplied the twin power units, which were set on top of the lower of the two wings. Indeed, the Wilkins team were delayed for five days after an argument with engineers from the Derby-based company, who demanded to change a filter in the fuel system at the last minute.

This delay would prove costly to the team's ambitions, as would the further three days that were lost due to bad weather. So by the time they were ready to leave London, in the third week of November, several other aircraft had stolen a march.

An unofficial entrant, Etienne Poulet, had left Paris on 14 October, determined that the honour of la Belle France would be upheld by beating the Anglo-Saxons in their race to Australia. In his tiny French-made Cauldron aircraft, Poulet and his mechanic had reached India before the first of the genuine race competitors had even taken to the air. By the time Wilkins, Rendle and co. were able to take off in the Kangaroo, however, he was having trouble trying to repair an oil leak and had clocked up well over thirty days. His nationality and the Cauldron's country of manufacture meant that the £10,000 bounty was never within reach, of course, so the fact that he'd exceeded the permitted time limit would deter him not one little bit — it was the challenge that drove him on.

Captain G.C. Matthews, who had switched from the Light Horse to the Flying Corps during the war, was the first of the official entrants to leave, accompanied by Sergeant T.D. Kay, a Victorian. Their Sopwith Wallaby took off from Hounslow Aerodrome, in the west of London, on 21 October. They then ran into awful blizzards in southern Germany before being forced down 160 kilometres from Belgrade, where the pair were arrested by Yugoslav officials. They managed to escape and fly on. But the thirty days had long expired by the time they reached Constantinople. (Despite knowing that the race had already been won by a rival team, Matthews and Kay would battle on gamely until reaching Bali, where their epic journey came to an end in a forced landing that wrecked the Sopwith.)

Next to leave was Captain Ross Smith from Adelaide, a war hero who had earned a place in history for his efforts when flying Colonel T.E. Lawrence to secret destinations in the desert. With Smith was his elder brother Keith and two of his mechanics from the Middle East, Sergeants J.M. Bennett and W.H. Shiers, from Melbourne and Adelaide, respectively. They took off from Hounslow in their huge Vickers Vimy aircraft on 12 November.

The following morning, Lieutenant Roger Douglas, of Charters Towers in Queensland, and Lieutenant Leslie Ross, from Moruya on the New South Wales south coast, braved the snow to follow the Smiths out in an Alliance aircraft. Many observers suggested the plane was overloaded with luxuries, such as leather-upholstered armchairs. They had flown just 10 kilometres when the Alliance suddenly dived into an orchard at Surbiton and exploded. Douglas and Ross died in the inferno.

They weren't the only ones to die. The Martinsyde of Captain C.E. Howell and his mechanic, one G.H. Fraser, was another late

starter — on 5 December, long after Wilkins' Blackburn Kangaroo even, and just days before the winning crew would touch down in Australia. Howell's plane subsequently disappeared near the island of Corfu, in the Mediterranean. In late December, Howell's body would be washed ashore on Corfu and his aircraft found in 3 metres of water.

WITH THE FUEL system now operating to Rolls-Royce's satisfaction and the weather having temporarily lifted, the Wilkins team finally took off on Friday, 21 November. They knew they had given the Smith brothers too much of a headstart, but they were still determined to make their mark. Their spirits were especially lifted when the King's uncle, Prince Arthur, together with Winston Churchill (then secretary of state for both the War and Air ministries) and several British generals, turned up at Hounslow to bid them bon voyage. Indeed, Prince Arthur led the crowd of well-wishers in three hearty cheers as the Kangaroo, identification number C-EAOW, taxied out onto the airstrip.

The good wishes mattered not when it came to encountering the same miserable conditions that had delayed their departure. They had hoped to land in Paris, but again the elements conspired against them. They flew on until they found a break in the cloud and put down at Romilly-sur-Seine, about 100 kilometres east of the French capital. The weather closed in and kept them grounded for three days. It was then on to the cathedral city of Lyon, in the south-east of France, where once again they were victims of inclement weather and forced to wait another three days.

On 28 November, the crew of the Kangaroo were off again and heading for Monte Carlo, only to run into a violent snowstorm over the Alpes-Maritimes, near the Italian border. Suddenly, Rendle shouted to Wilkins: 'Trouble, old mate! The controls have frozen. I can't regulate the engine.' Rendle banged them with a spanner, but they were frozen so solid with ice that all he achieved was to break one of the throttles.

'Our only hope is to make for the airstrip at Fréjus,' Wilkins called back through the storm. 'It's going to be a damned hairy landing.'

Hairy it would be. Fréjus is an ancient port a couple of kilometres inland from the Mediterranean Sea, settled in the first century AD by the Roman emperor Octavian. Mountains dominate — the Massif de l'Estérel to the east and the Massif des Maures to the west. The airstrip was in the centre, but to either side there were huge ruins of the old Roman aqueduct that traverses the area. If they missed the airstrip, the Aussies could have ended up colliding with the ancient structure, with catastrophic results.

Down through the storm clouds they came, manoeuvring by switching the engine on and off, to give them the power they needed to control the aircraft without the use of a throttle. Suddenly, the primitive airfield appeared through the gloom below them. It was too close … They hit it at far too high a speed, the Kangaroo careering along the ground, off the end of the strip and straight into a hangar at the far end. Luckily there were no aircraft inside, only a few random parts of broken planes stacked at one end.

'Crikey, that was close!' said a relieved Rendle. 'I wouldn't want to go through that again.' He may not have wanted to, but he would.

The ice soon melted and the four men worked on repairs with the help of a couple of expatriate English aircraft mechanics, who had been trying to reassemble some planes that had crashed en route from England to India. The Aussies would be off again at daybreak but needed a good night's sleep. Their newfound companions promised to mount guard over the Kangaroo while they rested. The night's sleep in a local pension was more than welcome.

In the morning, Wilkins was delighted to discover there was a local cinematographer on hand to film their departure. A man after his own spirit. Instead of just taxiing out of the hangar and careering off straight into the air, the Kangaroo team decided to do everything needed for good movie coverage. One of the British mechanics swung the propeller and the engines burst into life … The four Australians waved and smiled at the camera as they waited for take-off … Then, with a roar, the plane hurtled down the strip and skywards.

It would have looked impressive. Not so a few minutes later when one of the engines spluttered and cut out. Rendle switched to the second engine and soon the first was working again, too. Briefly. Wilkins was not going to risk crossing the Gulf of Genova to Italy with a suspect engine, and after about 50 kilometres the navigator found a field in which to make another emergency landing.

The Australians began a thorough examination of the faulty engine. The problem was soon obvious: an ignition wire had been deliberately disconnected and stuck loosely to the frame of the engine. 'Bloody hell,' fumed Rendle. 'One of those mechanics has tried to kill us! What would make a man do that? To deliberately try to kill four airmen … it beggars belief.'

The flyers repaired the sabotage and then spent another few hours checking every piece of the two engines for any further deliberate damage. They found none. But Wilkins was still a worried man when they took off into an overcast sky and headed out over the open sea.

Rain lashed the plane as it flew towards Italy, drenching the four men in their open cockpits. They landed at Pisa, only to have the aircraft sink into mud as it left the runway. Hours of toil were needed for the Kangaroo to be dug out of the mire before they were able to set off again the following day. It was not only the bodies of Wilkins and his mates that had been drenched; their spirits were further dampened when they heard the news telegraphed through to the airstrip that the Smith siblings had reached Akyab, a port city in the north of Burma, having overtaken Poulet on the previous leg of the journey.

NEXT DAY, THE Kangaroo reached Rome. But everything at the aerodrome was locked up because it was a saint's day. They had to wait twenty-four hours to refuel. While they twiddled their thumbs, they received news of the arrival of Keith and Ross Smith at Bangkok.

For the Wilkins team it was on to Taranto, the busy naval port on the heel of Italy, and across the Ionean Sea briefly before hugging the Greek mainland all the way south to Crete. The foul weather continued throughout, and when they landed at Chania on Suda Bay, in the north-west of the island, the aircraft was again bogged in deep mud. Fortunately for the aviators, the airstrip was operated by the Royal Air Force, and prisoners from a nearby Turkish jail were brought in overnight to dig drainage ditches. A solid surface on which to take off for the next leg, to Cairo, was also constructed, using timber, sheets of iron and tin, rocks and bricks. Anything solid was dumped on the airstrip.

Wilkins and his crew managed to get off the ground, with their engines working overtime. But once in the air, they realised that, with full tanks of fuel, the direct route across the rugged mountains of Crete — which rise dramatically to heights of around 2500 metres — was too dangerous. Wilkins was to relate to friends later in life how they saw shepherds in the fields staring up at them in amazement as the Kangaroo skirted the coastline. 'Most had never seen an aircraft before,' he noted. 'One can only wonder what they must have thought as they sighted this strange contraption a thousand feet above them.'

Having rounded the mountains, the Kangaroo set off from Cape Krios in the south-west of the island and headed for Egypt. Wilkins was in the cockpit directly behind the wings; behind him was the mechanic, Garnsey Potts.

About 120 kilometres out to sea, Potts handed him a note: *Oil leaking from port engine.* Wilkins had hardly had time to take in the significance of this message before a second one was passed forward: *Oil crank-shaft broken. Oil now streaming out.*

Wilkins let out an expletive, quickly leaned forward and screamed at Rendle: 'Turn us around and climb! Climb while there's still some oil — we've got no time to lose!'

Nor was there time for him to explain his fears. They would be lucky to make it back to Crete, but the higher they were when the oil ran out, the more chance they'd have. Wilkins then turned back to Potts and shouted: 'Prepare for the worst, Gar. We'll manage to get up to around 2000 feet. But on one engine from that height, we'll probably manage only around 30 miles. We'll be about 45, 50 miles short. Let's just pray to the Almighty.'

Although the four men had life jackets, they could hardly have hoped to swim the 80-odd kilometres to shore. And they hadn't seen a ship of any sort since leaving the coast of Crete. In coming years, Wilkins was to explain his thoughts at that moment: 'Well, here I go again. Yet another great adventure!'

The Almighty must have heard their prayers. The plane did not lose altitude, despite the fact that it was struggling along on the single engine. From that day on, Wilkins was to shout the praises of Rolls-Royce engines, even though it was one of them that had got the intrepid flyers into this bother. They were flying into a stiff wind. While this slowed the aircraft, it did have the bonus of helping keep it from losing altitude.

'If we do make it, ditch the kite on the first beach we come to,' Wilkins shouted to Rendle.

But as Crete came slowly into view, there were no such beaches, just rugged coast rising into mountains above. They followed the coastline around towards Chania. And then another problem quickly became evident: the direction of the wind made it impossible to turn towards the airstrip. Yet if they didn't turn they would be carried out over the sea to the north of Crete.

This time Rendle barked out his thoughts: 'I'll try to restart the dead engine to push us around.'

Wilkins gave him the thumbs up.

It didn't work. Without any oil, the engine exploded into dozens of pieces of shrapnel and the blast put the aircraft into a dangerous spin. In an incredible piece of flying skill, Rendle pulled the Kangaroo out of the spin, then wrestled the biplane from its terrifying dive towards a group of houses on the outskirts of Chania. It skimmed across the roof of one house and raced across a nearby field. All of its tyres burst as it careered towards a stone wall … Fortunately — mercifully — a bank of dirt halted the plane's progress a metre or so short of the wall. There it sat, nose into the ground and the tail jauntily in the air.

The wall surrounded a mental asylum, a fact that Wilkins would joke about throughout his later life: 'We were stark raving mad to attempt the journey — so what better place to finish?'

MAD? WELL, WILKINS, Rendle, Williams and Potts all still wanted to continue and so a telegram was sent to Rolls-Royce in England asking for a new engine. While they waited they heard the news: the Smith brothers had finally arrived in Australia.

Wilkins' attempt to win the 1919 London to Sydney Air Race ended ingloriously with his plane crashing in Crete … next to a lunatic asylum.

Adding to the finality of their predicament, Rolls-Royce couldn't get an engine to them and the insurance company wiped its hands of them, too. The company's cable was to the point: 'Policy does not cover mechanical breakdown. Broken oil pipe is mechanical breakdown.' Wilkins would eventually beat the insurance company in court (with the financial backing of the Shell Oil Company), but it was a Pyrrhic victory. The insurers had to pay out on the damaged engine, but not on the plane damage caused in the crash landing. Wilkins was left around £8000 out of pocket — a huge sum of money in those days.

Meanwhile the Smith brothers had overcome difficulties of their own to win the air race. Two hundred convicts from the local jail at Singora (now Songkhla) on the Gulf of Thailand, near the border with Malaya, were used to clear a strip for the Smiths. And at Surabaya in Java, some 200 coolies were used to lay sheets of bamboo matting over the runway and physically drag the heavy Vickers Vimy out of the mud and onto the matting so it could take off again. They landed at Darwin on 10 December 1919, with just two days to spare, to win both the £10,000 and hero status around Australia.

One delighted mother in Melbourne even named her two-week-old baby after the pair. In the not too distant future, Keith Ross Miller would become a hero in his own right, both in the Test cricket arena and in the air, flying Spitfires during World War II.

As for the losing team aboard the Kangaroo, Hubert Wilkins got little publicity back home, which no doubt suited him just fine. Like Wilkins, Val Rendle continued his love affair with aviation. At one stage he hoped to fly across the Pacific in a twin-engine seaplane, until government red tape foiled his attempt. Rendle served as an officer in the RAF during World War II and died in 1962, aged sixty-five. Little is known about Reg Williams and Gar Potts after the ill-fated air-race attempt, other than that the latter returned to Australia soon after the crash and died in 1959.

# Chapter 7

# A Tale of Two Leaders

FROM THE TIME his father had fought against the effects of drought in rural South Australia, Hubert Wilkins had realised the importance of accurate weather forecasting. And this was reinforced by his experiences as an aviator and Arctic explorer. He had a grand plan for a series of permanent weather stations in both the Arctic and the Antarctic, and soon after his failure in the air race he approached the board of the Royal Meteorological Society in London with such a plan. The idea was dismissed out of hand. After all, much of the Arctic and almost all of Antarctica was unexplored — so how could one expect to set up weather stations on unexplored territory?

Wilkins then approached the Royal Navy and asked to borrow one of the Zeppelins captured from the Germans during the war, for a flight of exploration over the North Pole.

'What kind of idiot are you for contemplating such a foolhardy exercise?' snorted Admiral of the Fleet David Beatty. 'You would end up killing not only yourself but others into the bargain.'

Wilkins' next stop was a couple of wealthy English friends, to request their financial backing to have an airship personally built for him by the Zeppelin company in Germany. They were enthusiastic, so he travelled to the company headquarters at Friedrichshafen, on the northern shores of Lake Constance. There he had the first of what were to be many meetings with Dr Hugo Eckener, successor to the deceased Count Ferdinand von Zeppelin.

Initially, Eckener was delighted that he might sell an airship to the affable Australian. But he threw up his arms in horror when he heard about Wilkins' plans to fly it over the North Pole. 'Herr Wilkins, we cannot afford any bad publicity,' he told him. 'It is madness. And I can just see the headlines when the airship disappears: "Zeppelin Disaster — Zeppelin Jinxed ..." It would be the death of our company.'

'But, *Herr Doktor*, I spent three years in the Arctic,' reasoned Wilkins. 'I know that, at the right time of the year, flying conditions are perfect for an airship. The publicity would have dozens of clients hammering on your door.'

But all to no avail. Wilkins had lost his chance. And history would show how it would be left to others to pioneer the use of airships in the Arctic. The situation was frustrating for the South Australian, and there would be more disappointment in that same year of 1920 — once he turned his attention to the polar region at the opposite end of the globe.

LITTLE IS AVAILABLE regarding the background of Cambridge biologist and adventurer Dr John Lachlan Cope, the leader of Wilkins' initial foray into Antarctica. His name first appears in the history books as a member of Shackleton's ill-fated Imperial Trans-Antarctic Expedition of 1914–17, during which their ship, the *Endurance*, became locked in pack-ice in the Weddell Sea, forcing the team to abandon the mission. Like the expedition's official photographer, Frank Hurley, John Cope made it back from the icy continent to take part in the Great War, serving with the Royal Navy.

Cope certainly had the gift of the gab, and by the time he and Wilkins first discussed the latter's involvement in the venture, in May

1920, he was delighting in the publicity that plans for his British Imperial Antarctic Expedition (BIAE) had received in London and South America. The expedition was set to be a massive five-year effort involving more than a hundred people, a mother ship — polar pioneer explorer Sir Robert Falcon Scott's old vessel, the *Terra Nova* — and some twelve aircraft. A circumnavigation of Antarctica was listed as a primary aim, along with the establishment of a base several hundred kilometres inside the Antarctic Circle, from where Wilkins and another pilot would make the first flight over the South Pole. It was with these lofty ambitions that Hubert Wilkins signed on as Cope's deputy on the BIAE before departing for Australia to be decommissioned from the army.

In truth, despite all the talk, the preparations were distinctly amateurish. Cope was relying on his country's imperial greed to get his expedition under way. If everything was completed as planned, Great Britain could lay claim to almost all of Antarctica — a splendid addition to the empire. But, as it turned out, the experts were not to be fooled. The Royal Geographical Society refused to sanction the expedition and this rejection frightened off a raft of potential backers.

Wilkins was in Australia putting the final touches to his contribution to Bean's official history of the war (volume one of which was set for publication late that same year) when he received a cable from Cope. The British scientist had been unable to raise even a small percentage of the finance needed for the original plans. He had decided to abandon the use of aircraft, there would be no mother ship, and the number in the party had been reduced to just four. Wilkins exploded, and by return cable told Cope he would not be joining his party but instead would take a civil engineering job he had been offered in Adelaide. A rash of messages went to and fro across the world, with Cope begging the Australian to reconsider. Against his better judgement, Wilkins agreed to honour his original promise and arranged to meet Cope in Montevideo some months later, as planned.

When he arrived in the Uruguayan capital, in December, Wilkins found that the other two members of the team had gone on ahead with provisions for a year to a whaling station on Deception Island, just off the tip of Graham Land (the northern half of what is now known as the Antarctic Peninsula). In the meantime, Cope had run out of money and begun building up debts. The captain of the Norwegian whaling ship that was due to take Cope and his Australian deputy to join the others had even confiscated Wilkins' movie camera, as part payment of the money he was owed. Wilkins found a solution to the impasse by agreeing to film the whaling operations as publicity for the whaling magnate Lars Christensen, whose company owned the boat. Ironically, the *Endurance*, Sir Ernest Shackleton's doomed ship, had originally been built for Christensen, but was sold to the Englishman after plans to take tourists on Arctic expeditions to shoot polar bears fell through.

Arriving at Deception Island shortly before Christmas Day, Wilkins met the other two members of the team. Nineteen-year-old Thomas Bagshawe was supposed have been a geologist but had never studied the science, while Maxime Charles Lester, aged twenty-one, claimed to be a surveyor but was no more than a former second mate on a tramp steamer. After some time spent filming the whale-oil factories on the island, Wilkins was able to negotiate a passage over to Graham Land for the four men, on board a Norwegian steamer named the *Solstrejf*. Setting off early in January, they took with them supplies and a whaleboat with which to explore the various inlets along the coast.

They landed at what is today known as Paradise Harbour, on the western side of the peninsula that forms the north-western corner of the Antarctic mainland. It is the site of a Chilean base, to which the government of that South American country sends scientists for a couple of months every three or four years to ensure Chile's sovereignty over the area. It's also a popular destination in midsummer for cruise ships that take advantage of the long days, with only an hour or so of darkness, to sail leisurely around Graham Land. About twenty ships visit the area every year. International regulations decree that no vessel can carry more than 500 passengers, and no more than a hundred passengers can go ashore at any one time to mingle with the penguins. The travel brochures boast about the serenity of Paradise Harbour.

It was anything but serene, however, and far from paradise, when the BIAE quartet landed on 12 January 1921. Indeed, during the three months or so that Wilkins was to spend there, he had plenty of occasions to question the choice of place name. And the first mishap occurred just hours following their arrival.

John Cope was a failure when it came to leadership.

It was after the team had initially set up camp that Cope and Wilkins set off inland, so hungry were they for a further glimpse of this unknown continent. They soon found their path blocked by a series of massive ice-covered cliffs, rising vertically to about 200 metres in height. Foolishly, they decided to try to climb up the cliffs. Halfway to the top they were engulfed by a storm, but even with visibility down to just centimetres, the pair continued their climb. After more than four hours, they reached the top of the col.

Believing it to be too dangerous to return the way they'd come, the two explorers instead edged along the narrow ridge, looking for an easier descent or, at the very least, a sheltered spot where they could dig in and ride out the storm. The wind that whipped across the ridge was formidable, numbing the men with its intensity, but they slowly crawled onwards, tied together by several metres of rope. Everything was going as well as could be expected until, suddenly, Wilkins fell through an overhang of ice. Cope, with no firm foothold or anchor for his icepick, could not arrest the fall, and so the two men tumbled head over heels down the mountain of ice.

Unable to see properly, Wilkins feared they might be swept into a crevasse and perish — a not unlikely scenario. He bounced over a rise and into the air before finally coming to a halt with a resounding thud. The rope twisted tightly around his chest and he passed out.

To Cope, it seemed like an eternity before Wilkins regained consciousness. The expedition leader had been vainly calling the Australian's name but had received no response. 'Where the hell are you, Hubert?' he yelled again. 'You've got to help me. You've got to pull me out!'

'I-I'll be with you in a minute,' came the eventual, muffled reply. 'Just got to ... get my breath back ...'

With the fierce wind buffeting his face, Wilkins carefully worked his way back up the slope and, to his horror, found the rope had disappeared over a ledge and into a crevasse. Moving closer, he peeped over the edge and there, not far below, swinging upside down against a wall of unforgiving ice, was the hapless Cope. The rope was around the Englishman's hips and there was nothing but thin air below him — and plenty of it. The crevasse was so deep, and visibility still so poor, that Wilkins couldn't see the bottom; it was just a dark blue abyss, fading into jet-black.

Riding high on adrenalin, the Australian tore the tail off his shirt to make a second, makeshift rope, which he used to lower a heavy sheath knife down to Cope. By stabbing this knife into the wall of the crevasse, Cope was able to gradually turn himself upright. Then, as Wilkins kept a firm grip on the rope, Cope fashioned steps in the wall, with which he worked his way up to the ledge before finally hauling himself out. The pair were utterly exhausted.

'Thanks, old chap,' Cope gasped. 'I reckon I owe you a favour or two.'

Their bodies cried out for rest, but both men knew that if they surrendered now they would freeze to death. So they headed down the cliff-side, towards the harbour, cautiously negotiating their way through a minefield of crevasses.

Understandably, the experience was to haunt Wilkins for the rest of his life. 'I've never really enjoyed mountain climbing since that first experience on the edge of the Antarctic continent,' he'd say. 'Every time I see a sharp-ridged col, or a glacier with a steep descent, I'm reminded of our slide and its near-fatal ending.'

A number of other close shaves followed until, after a few months of largely uninspiring research, and with the whaling season almost at an end, the group realised they had to find a ship to get them back to South America, where they could sit out the southern winter. Leaving Bagshawe at the camp to look after their equipment, Cope, Wilkins and Lester set off in their open boat in search of whalers.

Some 40 nautical miles along the coast of Graham Land, they happened upon a Norwegian ship. But the captain was aware of Cope's poor reputation and wanted nothing to do with him.

It was a sign of how woefully inadequate the BIAE's preparation and leadership were that its team should be left to scrounge around at the end of its first summer for a lift back to civilisation. And, worse still, a storm was brewing as they set off in choppy seas.

They sailed for more than twenty-four hours without sighting a single whaler. But the storm was catching them fast. Cope and Lester were of no use to Wilkins, as they were green with seasickness, throwing up over the side of the tiny boat as it was tossed around in the broiling ocean. Wilkins was fighting a losing battle as he tried to control both the sails and the tiller by himself. Waves were breaking over the sides of the boat and it was beginning to fill with water. All of a sudden, it shuddered. The boat had run onto some submerged rocks about a kilometre out from shore.

There was a gaping hole in the hull, just above the waterline, and the rugged outline of a savage glacier lay in front of them. The trio quickly threw out much of their supplies to raise the offending gash as far above the water as possible, while plugging it with a makeshift bung and the canvas from a discarded sail.

They shot past a narrow inlet and glimpsed a whaler anchored inside — much to their horror, since there was no way they could fight the might of the storm and turn around. When recalling the episode in later years, Wilkins would present a vivid picture of the ordeal the three men were facing. 'There was a steep ice-cliff to our windward side against which the waves were breaking in tremendous fury,' he explained. 'I saw we were going to smash against the cliff. We were doomed.'

In desperation, Wilkins cut loose the mainsail. His recollection continues, with a suggestion that perhaps some divine intervention had come to their rescue:

*I don't know why the boat didn't capsize. But a well-built whaleboat is about the steadiest craft imaginable in a heavy sea. Our boat twisted like something that was alive. Or else some mysterious hand was guiding it. It steered us safely past the end of the glacier.*

*This strange force saved us from certain death. I felt this force many other times in my life. It was inexplicable, quite baffling. It was as if a ghost would walk at my side.*

An altogether more human saviour intervened moments later. Having seen the tiny boat speed past the opening of the inlet, the officer on watch aboard the whaler hastily despatched the ship's motor launch to rescue the trio. His captain, sympathetic to the explorers' plight, then agreed to pick up young Bagshawe from Paradise Harbour and take all four men north to Montevideo.

But Cope thought otherwise. Reasoning that it would be easier to raise finance for the expedition if they had personnel there in Antarctica, he suggested that Wilkins and Lester stay with the teenager on Graham Land, while he, as expedition leader, travelled on alone to South America. Lester was keen, as was Bagshawe once he'd been consulted. Wilkins was dead against the idea, however, and was eager to cut all ties with Cope as soon as possible. But he still had a casting vote in the fate of the BIAE, so he agreed to leave the two men behind, as Cope wished, on one condition: Lester and Bagshawe could remain at Paradise Harbour for a fortnight and if they were still keen to stay after that (that is, if they chose not to catch one of the final whaling ships heading home to Deception Island), he would withdraw all objections.

The two younger men were then left with plenty of provisions for an uncomfortable, cold, twelve-month stay. Instead of the tent they had used in summer, they constructed a rough-and-ready lean-to made from an upturned, abandoned whaleboat, discarded timber and canvas. The remains of this rough building are still there to this day.

When the last whaler arrived back at Deception Island, there was no sign of Bagshawe and Lester. They apparently had decided to stay. It was only when the whole fleet of whalers had set off for Uruguay that Wilkins discovered the truth. Cope had threatened the captain of the whaling station that if any whaler went near their camp, he would pressure the authorities back in London to refuse the Norwegians their licences to hunt whales in British Antarctic waters.

Cope never made good his promise to return to collect the two adventurers. They were found by a whaling crew at the start of the following summer in good spirits — and, in fact, demanded to stay until the end of the 1921–22 whaling season. This was quite remarkable, as the two young men regularly argued almost every day they were together.

For John Cope, his exploring days were over. He even had to work as a kitchen hand on a Scottish steamer to get back to Britain. 'His job was to peel the potatoes,' Wilkins would comment. 'I'm not even sure he was good at that!'

LATER IN THAT southern autumn of 1921, Wilkins left Montevideo for New York, where he set about trying to organise an expedition of his own — this time with aircraft playing an integral part. His enquiries soon attracted the attention of one John Larsen, a Danish expatriate who held the North American rights to sell the world's first all-metal plane, the German-made Junkers F-13.

Larsen called Wilkins to a meeting in his New York office late in May, during which the two men hatched a plan whereby the Australian would take two of the revolutionary aircraft with him to Antarctica once the spring set in there; more immediately, a brief foray to the Arctic was scheduled so that Larsen could indulge his fascination with Eskimos. For Wilkins, one imagines, this new association would kill two birds (that is, two polar icecaps) with one stone. But the scheme soon hit problems, and terminally so. Namely that the F-13s had a propensity to burst into flame, midair, and crash. The cause would later be traced to the unsuitability of American aircraft fuel rather than any inherent fault in the plane's design, but the damage had been done and Larsen's Junkers operation could never hope to recover from the attendant bad publicity.

All was not lost for Wilkins, though. At the same time as the Larsen venture ran aground, the explorer received a cable from Sir Ernest Shackleton, no less, inviting him to join the Irish-born Englishman's upcoming expedition to the Antarctic. After the recent BIAE fiasco, this was an opportunity for Wilkins to learn from a true leader of men. For while the failure of John Cope's half-baked foray may have led to his shame, not so the earlier abandoned expedition by Shackleton. Such were the qualities of the man and the high regard in which he was held by all.

Ernest Henry Shackleton was born on 15 February 1874 in County Kildare, Ireland, but his family moved to London when he was nine. Having tired of his studies at Dulwich College, he joined the merchant navy at the age of sixteen and qualified as a master mariner eight years later. Always good at making and keeping influential friends, Shackleton used his contacts to secure a place on the National Antarctic Expedition in July 1901, led by Royal Navy officer Robert Falcon Scott, on the ship *Discovery*.

The expedition saw a trekking party comprising Scott, Shackleton and a junior surgeon set a new record 'farthest south' latitude — 480 kilometres closer to the South Pole than anyone had come before them — but it ended unceremoniously for the young Anglo-Irishman. On the way back to their McMurdo Sound base camp, Shackleton suffered so badly from scurvy that Scott later had him sent home on the first relief ship, in March 1903. This was a bitter pill for

Ernest Shackleton's failure turned into a leadership triumph ... and that's what endeared him to Wilkins.

Shackleton, and it was followed by a four-year period away from active participation in polar forays.

He worked as a consultant for the British Admiralty and then as a journalist, before landing the secretaryship of the Royal Scottish Geographical Society. His position at the RSGS was perfect for Shackleton, keeping him within the orbit of generous benefactors and people of influence. Before long, his plans to further explore the Antarctic continent came to fruition — firstly with the successful 1907–09 British Antarctic Expedition on the *Nimrod*, and then with the notorious 1914–17 Imperial Trans-Antarctic Expedition.

Under normal circumstances, he should have had to endure an awful notoriety after the *Endurance* got trapped in pack-ice in January 1915, during the height of summer. But his epic voyage of 800 nautical miles to the island of South Georgia, at the southernmost tip of South America, had saved the lives of all of his twenty-seven crewmen and gained him the admiration of the British public.

IMMENSE ATTRACTION.

# TOWN HALL, BURTON-ON-TRENT

THE BURTON-ON-TRENT MUNICIPAL OFFICERS' GUILD
has arranged with THE LECTURE AGENCY, Ltd., of London, for

## SIR ERNEST

# SHACKLETON

C.V.O., F.R.G.S.

TO GIVE HIS

## LECTURE

ENTITLED:

# "THE SOUTH POLE"

# THURSDAY, NOV. 21 at 8

In addition to giving a popular account of his own South Polar Expedition, Sir Ernest will describe and explain the Expeditions under Capt. Scott and Capt. Amundsen.

*The Lecture will be fully Illustrated from PHOTOGRAPHS and some very striking KINEMATOGRAPH FILMS taken during the Expedition.*

THE CHAIR WILL BE TAKEN BY

# GEORGE T. LYNAM, Esq., M.Inst. C.E.
(President of the Guild.)

RESERVED SEATS, 3/- (Family Tickets to admit four), 10/6 ; UNRESERVED, 2/- & 1/-

Early Doors open at 7.30 p.m. for Ticket-holders only. | Ordinary Doors open at 7.45. Carriages at 9.35 p.m.

PLAN OF HALL & Tickets now ready at HORNE, THOMPSON, & Co.'s Music Warehouse, 184 & 185 Station St., Burton-on-Trent. Telephone No. 471. Tickets may also be had from members of the Guild, or from TOWN HALL, BURTON-ON-TRENT. WAUDE THOMPSON, *Guild Hon. Secretary.*

Late Cars will be run to Ashby

Ernest Shackleton found fundraising lecture tours easy. Wilkins didn't.

English explorer Apsley Cherry-Garrard would soon write of Sir Ernest: 'Do not let it be said that Shackleton failed. No man fails who sets an example of high courage, of unbroken resolution, of unshrinking endurance … I know why it is that every man who has served under Shackleton swears by him. Shackleton never lost a man.

He must have had some doubts as to whether he would save them. But he did, he saved them, every one.' No doubt Wilkins would have heard other glowing tributes from some of the beneficiaries of this 'high courage' and 'unbroken resolution' — men such as Cope, Frank Hurley, and Mackay and Murray from the similarly thwarted Arctic expedition under Vilhjalmur Stefansson.

Still, it had been far from easy to attract financial backers for this new venture. In the years since the *Endurance* expedition, Shackleton found that interest in his exploits had waned considerably. He owed money to many of his former crew and to those who had financed him, money he had hoped to raise through the lectures he gave twice a day at London's Philharmonic Hall. But Shackleton drew only small crowds, with the theatre often less than half full. He was also plagued by health problems, which he kept from friends, colleagues and even his surgeon, Dr James McIlroy. In addition to these woes, the 47-year-old was drinking and smoking heavily, and suffering from severe pains across his shoulders, which he euphemistically described as 'indigestion'.

Impressed by a publicity campaign in the *Daily Mail* newspaper, an old school friend named John Quiller Rowett came to his aid. The Rowetts had made a fortune back in the nineteenth century through a fleet of privateers, and now a portion of the family's coffers headed Shackleton's way. He soon purchased a vessel in Norway, the *Foca I*, which he renamed *Quest*, and began making arrangements to acquire a plane. Although the ship appeared to be in poor condition, it was encouraging that she was just four years old. And surely now, after the two recent non-starts with Cope and Larsen, and close to a decade of dreaming about it, Hubert Wilkins would finally be able to fly over Antarctica.

The South Australian agreed to join the expedition as an aviator and cameraman. And he persuaded Shackleton to give him another role,

# A reputation restored

Shackleton or Scott? Their critics today remain divided, but for most of the last century, 'Scott of the Antarctic' stood unchallenged as Britain's greatest explorer of the southern continent, with Sir Ernest almost being consigned to the role of also-ran.

The pair certainly appear to have had a testy relationship. On that first Antarctic venture in 1911–13, so the story goes, Scott fell out with Shackleton, who was generally more popular with the crew than the regulation-obsessed expedition leader. It has even been suggested that, following their polar trek, Captain Scott was simply using Shackleton's poor health as an excuse to send him packing, allegedly telling a surgeon on the *Discovery*, 'If he does not go back sick, he will go back in disgrace.'

The simmering dislike was exacerbated in 1907, when Shackleton announced he would be using the McMurdo Sound base camp for his two-year expedition on the *Nimrod*, despite a previous promise to Scott not to do so. Come January 1909, Shackleton and his three companions got to within 190 kilometres of the South Pole — a staggering 570-kilometre improvement on his effort with Scott. This achievement, together with the super-thorough scientific work carried out by his Antarctic team, resulted in Shackleton receiving a knighthood, along with a raft of other prestigious awards. Once back home, financial worries occupied much of his time, limiting future plans, but Sir Ernest hadn't given up on his quest. And neither, of course, had Robert Falcon Scott.

The latter returned to Antarctica on the *Terra Nova*, around the same time as a Norwegian team led by Roald Amundsen arrived. Scott finally made it all the way to the pole, on 17 January 1912 — only to discover that Amundsen had reached the Holy Grail thirty-five days earlier ... It was a monumental blow, but worse was to come. While returning to their base camp, Scott and his team died from a combination of exhaustion, lack of sufficient food and extreme cold.

The outside world would learn of their heroic demise the following year: one of the greats of Antarctic exploration was dead, a martyr to his country's interests in the international race to conquer the South Pole. A campaign of glorification was swiftly unleashed in Britain, and elsewhere, which saw Scott's reputation unsurpassed for most of the twentieth century.

Shackleton could never hope to compete with this, but he could aim to be the first to cross the frozen southern continent, from the Weddell Sea to McMurdo Sound, a journey of 2800 kilometres. If for all the wrong reasons, history would remember Shackleton's 1914–17 Imperial Trans-Antarctic Expedition — better known today as the *Endurance* expedition.

By 27 October 1915, having been trapped for over nine months in pack-ice, in the Weddell Sea's extreme south-west corner, the *Endurance*'s hull had been crushed so badly that Shackleton ordered his men to abandon ship and set up camp on the floating ice. The three-masted barquentine sank twenty-five days later, after which their ice platform gradually drifted north until, on 9 April 1916, they were forced to take to the lifeboats.

So began a journey that is still regarded as one of the greatest open-boat voyages in maritime history. It would take them to Elephant Island, a desolate dot in the Southern Ocean, 885 kilometres south-east of Cape Horn — from where Shackleton, ship's captain Frank Worsley and four others headed off on the 6.9-metre *James Caird* to the Norwegian whaling station at Stromness, 1300 kilometres away on South Georgia. All the while, they faced violent storms, hunger, fear and the bitter, relentless cold. And even when once on South Georgia, a 36-hour trek over a mountain range and several glaciers awaited them.

It was a stunning achievement. As British explorer Duncan Carse would remark four decades later: 'I do not know how they did it,

continued ⇲

except that they had to ...' Finally, having made it to Stromness, an exhausted Shackleton could begin raising help to evacuate his friends and colleagues stranded on Elephant Island. Every single one of them.

With triumph having thus been snatched from the jaws of disaster, Shackleton was once more the hero. But it was one thing to capture the public's imagination, quite another to hold national-icon status. In the ensuing decades, it was Scott whose name schoolchildren would be encouraged to revere and who had dozens of monuments erected in his honour.

Only in the 1990s would the world view the two men's exploits in a new light, even going so far as to completely reverse the previously held opinions. Shackleton's expedition leadership is now held up as a prime example of an enlightened, people-centred approach to management. The Boss' loyal crewmen would never have argued with that.

that of a naturalist. Wilkins had always been interested in flora and fauna since his childhood days in Australia, learning much from the Nunga people he'd got to know then, and was hoping he might turn up some previously unknown species. He also made it abundantly clear to Shackleton: 'I want you to teach me, as a master would an apprentice, how to lead a polar expedition. And, if I measure up, you will tell the people who count that I am worthy of their financial backing.'

It made sense. Every person who had ever worked alongside Shackleton, whether it be on polar exploration or in the Naval Reserve, used just one form of address. He was 'the Boss'.

When Wilkins arrived in London in June 1921, there was precious little for him to do until the departure of the expedition three months later. So he decided to use the time to gain more experience in aviation. First of all he sat for the British Air Ministry's air-navigation certificate. In preparation for the exam, he made several flights in airships, which had recently come into vogue. His mentor was Air Commodore Edward Maitland, a Great War veteran who had made the first airship crossing of the Atlantic two years earlier in the *R-34*.

Wilkins also teamed up with US naval commander Louis H. Maxfield. The Americans had been so impressed with the *R-34* that they'd financed the construction of a bigger and better airship, the *R-38*. Maxfield was in Britain to take delivery of the 215-metre-long craft. In mid August, Maxfield took Wilkins up on a training flight in the *R-34*. They flew into a storm at the end of their journey and were unable to land at the home airfield at Howden, near Hull in north-west England. For sixteen hours the pair flew around the north of the country until conditions improved and the ship was able to return to the ground. It was an ominous warning.

Wilkins was then invited to fly on the *R-38* during its final trial, after which the airship would be handed over to the Americans. The date was set for Friday, 19 August 1921. But the weather closed in over Howden and forecasters were not optimistic about it breaking. Maitland told Wilkins to return to London. 'We won't be flying until at least Tuesday,' he said. 'I'll send you a telegram the day before the flight so you'll have plenty of time to get up here.'

As fate would have it, Maitland's Monday-afternoon telegram was never delivered. The first Wilkins knew of the flight was when he saw the newspapers of 25 August, which announced that the *R-38* had taken off two days beforehand, on the Tuesday, bound for Pulham in Norfolk.

But Pulham's airship station was shrouded in fog, as a result of which officials on the ground decided that the giant aircraft should spend the night circling over the North Sea and try again early the following day. Come the morning, however, the airfield was again obscured by the pea-souper, so the *R-38* headed back to Howden.

Over the Humber River at Hull, disaster struck. Eyewitness reports claimed that the airship seemed to crumple amidships, before the front section broke away and exploded into flames. Five members of the crew in the tail section were rescued from the wreckage in the Humber River, but forty-four died in the inferno, including both Maitland and Maxfield.

Wilkins needed no reminding that, had the postal service delivered Air Commodore Maitland's telegram, there would have been a forty-fifth name to add to the death roll. It was as if that mysterious hand had reached out to save him again. And the effects were wide-ranging, as he noted: 'It was a nerve-shattering experience to all those who had put their faith in airships.' The *R-38* disaster brought the curtain down on Britain's airship experiment. It also reinforced Wilkins' idea that fixed-wing aircraft were the way to go in polar exploration.

THE *DAILY MAIL* had stepped up its promotional campaign in the weeks leading up to the departure of the Shackleton–Rowett Antarctic Expedition. By the standards of the day, it was seen as something of a major media event, to use twenty-first century parlance. The newspaper's publisher, Lord Northcliffe, was well aware of Shackleton's reputation, but he was more conscious of the charisma of Hubert Wilkins, who had been such a friend of his correspondent Bernard Grant during the First Balkan War. With Shackleton's full co-operation, the *Mail* organised a competition among the nation's Boy Scout movement, the winner of which would accompany the scientific team and ship's crew to the Antarctic as a cabin boy. In fact, two lads shared the prize, one being eighteen-year-old patrol leader James Marr, who would go on to achieve great things as an Antarctic explorer in his own right.

With suitable fanfare, the *Quest* finally set sail from St Katherine's Wharf, just down the Thames from the Tower of London, on 17 September. Huge crowds lined the banks of the river to cheer the adventurers on their way, and a flotilla of small craft accompanied the mother ship. Cadets from the Naval Academy at Greenwich saluted, before giving three hearty cheers. Nurses from the nearby Greenwich Hospital waved handkerchiefs in salute.

Once away from the well-wishers and general goodwill, however, it was as if a protective cloak had been lifted off the expedition. Contributing most to this unveiling was the condition and inadequacy of their vessel, the *Quest*. Built as a sealer, she was not much bigger than a trawler — just 34 metres long and 7 metres in beam, with a draft of 4 metres — and, most surprisingly given that she'd have to contend with pack-ice in Antarctica, her hull was made of timber. Wilkins would joke how 'The agent who bought her for Shackleton must have been drunk as a Lord at the time'. It was no laughing matter, but so many expeditions of that era were forced to use vessels that weren't entirely adequate. The cost of ships being custom-built for the task at hand was prohibitive, so expedition leaders usually took what was on offer and hoped that repairs and additions would be sufficient to ensure success.

Soon after the expedition set off, Shackleton discovered that the ship's boiler was cracked. Indeed, the *Quest* would need repairs at every port of call on the voyage south, usually because the engine's bearing kept burning out. With a capability of just 4 knots of speed, her engines were simply too weak for long ocean voyages. Plus, she was so top heavy that in big seas, such as the notorious Bay of Biscay, west of France, she lurched dangerously, making for an uncomfortable ride.

The *Quest* had to hoist a sail to get into the port of St Vincent in the Azores, because the engine wasn't working. And by the time they docked at Madeira in late October, the seasickness had got too much for the official photographer and young Norman Mooney, the second of the two Boy Scouts on the expedition, both of whom departed at this point.

A far bigger blow to the expedition's hopes, especially those of Wilkins, came further down the African coast. A significant area of the *Quest's* deck was to have been taken up with an Avro 504L seaplane, which they'd planned to pick up in Cape Town before swinging due west to Brazil. Shackleton had hoped it would be the first aeroplane to fly over the frozen continent, with Wilkins at its controls. Now, though, because of the various problems with the ship and the fact that they were so far behind schedule, he had no choice but to bypass the South African port and head straight to Rio de Janeiro. Wilkins had missed out on his dream of flying in the Antarctic yet again.

It was slow going. Wilkins had taken over as photographer after Madeira, adding to his trio of job titles. He also stood eight hours' watch on deck each and every day and oversaw the depth-sounding equipment. In fact, every expedition member found himself lumbered with more tasks to perform than those originally expected of him. Months before, Shackleton had been aware of the likelihood of this happening and had chosen his team accordingly; he knew each man was capable of branching out into fields that were new to him. Wilkins had no formal training as a naturalist, for example, but the Boss had confidence in him being able to do the job because of the way he'd adapted to so many different tasks in the past.

Shackleton's second-in-command was Frank Wild, and the sailing master Captain Frank Worsley, both of whom had filled similar roles on his previous two visits to Antarctica. Ship's surgeon Dr Alexander Macklin had also been on the 1914–17 *Endurance* expedition, along with Dr McIlroy. None of the four had to be asked twice to join the Boss on this new venture.

'He had the faculty of always being liked by everyone, and was always a good fellow,' Wilkins explained. 'He would sit around singing songs and telling stories, keeping everyone amused and entertained. No matter how things were going, he always came along with a cheerful word.'

But the joviality was a mask hiding the truth. Aboard the *Quest*, Shackleton was constantly ill. His face was pale and gaunt. At Rio de Janeiro, Shackleton had what was almost certainly a massive heart attack but, as usual, refused to be examined by Dr Macklin. The surgeon was deeply worried, especially about his patient's attitude: 'The Boss says, quite frankly, that he does not know what he will do after South Georgia [the next port of call].' They were prophetic words.

All in all, it was a dismal stopover in Rio. Again the *Quest* had had to limp into port under sail, and engineers found the tail-shaft of the engine was out of alignment and the keel twisted. Repairs would take at least six weeks. With Shackleton's blessing, Wilkins and a geologist from Montreal, George Douglas, decided to hitch a lift on a whaler going to South Georgia and spend the time on scientific research while waiting for the rest of the team to catch up.

Once the *Quest* was seaworthy, the team endured a hellish voyage south from Rio, battling hurricane-force winds. And despite his bad health, Shackleton defied his doctor's orders and stayed on the bridge for four nights in a row as the ship was buffeted by huge seas — so ferocious that on the night of 28 December the crew were forced to pour oil over the side. In his log of the journey, later published as *Into the Frozen South*, cabin boy Marr would report:

> *We hove to about nine o'clock and bags of oil were put down in front of the bows to keep down the sea, where the weight of the storm struck us. The effect was really remarkable. A large sea, which was likely to hit us, would fall flat about 15 yards off and slide away under the bows. Some six gallons of oil were used …*
>
> *The Boss told me that he had been at sea for nearly 30 years and had never seen a gale maintained so long and with such intensity.*

The *Quest* finally sailed into the harbour at Grytviken whaling station on Wednesday, 4 January 1922. Shackleton went ashore for dinner but did not stay long. He wanted to get to bed early as he had promised his team a belated Christmas/New Year party the following day, once they'd been joined by Wilkins and Douglas. So it came as some surprise to Alexander Macklin, when he passed Shackleton's cabin around 2.30 am, to find the expedition leader still awake.

'I can't sleep because of a pain in my left shoulder,' he complained. 'Could you give me a sleeping potion?'

A smile spread over Macklin's face as he joked: 'You shouldn't be taking sleeping potions. Give up the good life, and you'll sleep.'

'You're always wanting me to give up something. First it was drink, then it was cigarettes. What will be the next thing I have to give up?'

The doctor prepared a sleeping draught and handed it to Shackleton, who drank it in one gulp. Within seconds, the glass had slipped from his right hand and shattered on the cabin floor. Shackleton slumped back onto his pillow. He was dead, at just forty-seven years of age.

At first Macklin thought he'd made a mistake with the ingredients, but he soon realised it was another massive heart attack that had taken the explorer's life. This was confirmed by a post-mortem conducted on shore the following day.

When Wilkins arrived later in the morning, he was shocked to see the flag on the *Quest* at half-mast. Douglas Jeffrey, the ship's navigator, shouted to him from the bridge: 'Awful news, Wilkie. The Boss is dead. He left us just a few hours ago.'

At the time, South Georgia did not have a telegraphic link with the outside world, so it was decided to call off the expedition and return with Shackleton's body to England. At Buenos Aires, Frank Wild cabled his widow, Emily, with the terrible news. A reply came back immediately. She asked that he be buried on South Georgia.

'The Gateway to Antarctica', she called it. She also requested they continue with the expedition. 'Ernest would have wanted you to finish his work,' she wrote.

In accordance with Emily Shackleton's wishes, the team buried their Boss in the tiny graveyard overlooking Grytviken. It was a tradition that whalers who died at South Georgia were buried facing east (and their homes in Europe). Shackleton's grave faces south, towards his beloved Antarctica.

WILD TRIED TO complete Shackleton's plans, but too much time had been lost. And the ship was clearly not suited to the task. In the Weddell Sea, early in the southern autumn, they were unable to make landfall and then the *Quest* became locked in the pack-ice — just as the *Endurance* had. Like Hurley six or more years before, Wilkins took photographs to show the world their predicament.

And then an even greater problem loomed. A massive iceberg appeared in the distance. As each day passed, it was obvious that the iceberg was heading straight towards them, and it was gargantuan. Wilkins estimated it to be around 65 metres high and well over 10 kilometres long. With the floating mass looming ever closer, pushed along by unseen currents beneath the ice, the men prepared to abandon ship. There would be no heroic voyage in lifeboats this time; there was no way they could get them off the ship, as ice-drifts began piling up in front of the 'berg, pushing the ship onto a frightening tilt. The explorers clung to whatever they could, readying themselves for what they believed would be their inevitable demise.

Then that mysterious hand that seemed to follow Wilkins through life appeared yet again. The iceberg was just 60 metres from the ship when it suddenly stopped. As the crew watched in awe, it changed course and began a journey away from the *Quest*. In the iceberg's wake was a vast area free of ice. For everyone on board, who only moments before had been staring death in the face, the relief was one of euphoria and, as one, they let out an almighty cheer.

With the ship settling back into an upright position, Captain Worsley ordered the engines started, after which several crew-members hastily jumped onto the icefloe and began hauling on ropes to help propel the *Quest* into open water. Worsley cautiously steered a course west, away from the jagged pieces of ice, and then north to South Georgia. There, on 3 May 1922, as a final gesture to the original leader of the expedition, they erected a cairn high on a promontory on the opposite side of the harbour from Grytviken cemetery. As before, Wilkins recorded the event on film.

Although he would express some personal satisfaction, the Australian was naturally disappointed at the outcome of the expedition. 'We accomplished little on an expedition that ran six times over budget,' he concluded. 'We were forced to abandon our dream when the ice in the Weddell Sea proved too much for our defective vessel and accept failure before making the long trip home to England.'

This long trip home would provide an interesting footnote in the story of Hubert Wilkins. During the voyage, Wilkins revealed his extraordinary powers of mental telepathy — something he would show to the world in later experiments that proved messages could be sent halfway around the globe. Douglas Jeffrey, the navigator on the ship, was amazed at the Australian's ability to pick up radio signals in his mind. The pair conducted experiments: Jeffrey would be in the ship's radio room, listening to radio messages sent to the *Quest*, while Wilkins would be at the other end of the vessel yet able to repeat the messages verbatim. Rarely did he fail the test.

# Chapter 8

# Spies and Flies

BRITAIN WAS THE first country in the world to set up an intelligence agency. In August 1909, the British Government created the Department of Military Intelligence, which was later renamed the Secret Intelligence Service (SIS), sometimes known as MI6. Of course, by the late twentieth century it had become glamorised as the home of fictional secret agent 007, James Bond. Although there have never really been spies like the one personified by Sean Connery, Roger Moore, Pierce Brosnan et al., the intelligence agency's first director, Sir George Mansfield Smith-Cumming, did set a trend that was followed in Ian Fleming's Bond novels and the movies they inspired. Smith-Cumming only used the second half of his hyphenated surname and would sign all official documents with the letter C. Every subsequent director adopted the 'C' signature, prompting Fleming to name his fictional MI6 boss 'M'.

In the early 1920s the SIS operated out of a large red-brick mansion at 1 Melbury Road, Holland Park, a well-to-do suburb in the west of London. It was to this building that Hubert Wilkins was summoned in early November 1922. His heroics as a war photographer and his efforts in exploration had resulted in invitations to cocktail parties and dinner and luncheon dates with a variety of government and military movers and shakers in the British capital. One of these — Wilkins never revealed his name — was close to Smith-Cumming. Maybe it was C himself. Whoever he was, the high-ranking friend told Wilkins how the SIS wanted him to travel to Russia (or the Soviet Union as it was about to become) and spend six months there.

'You will take photographs, of course,' the man informed him, 'seeing as you have an international reputation for your photography. We want to know everything that's happening over there. And, with a bit of luck, we can arrange meetings with some of the Russian political leaders. Your reputation will open a few doors — and you've never been linked with us here at Secret Intelligence, so they won't suspect anything.'

The fact that Wilkins didn't have a wife or girlfriend made him the ideal choice for the job, he was told. And he had the perfect cover: officially, he would be employed by the Society of Friends to take photographs for a report on the work of their Russian Famine Relief Fund. They wanted graphic photos that would touch the hearts of the well-heeled citizens of Britain and America and persuade them to make sizeable donations to help continue feeding the starving Russians. One of the Quakers' representatives would be accompanying Wilkins, to add legitimacy to the mission. 'This employee doesn't know what you'll be doing on the trip,' the espionage man added. 'And that's the way we want it to stay.'

The assignment was interesting, to say the least. Russia had bowed out of the Great War in early 1918, long before hostilities ceased, only to become embroiled in a series of violent uprisings as the newly formed Red Army attempted to silence the various anti-Bolshevik factions known loosely as the White Army. The Russian Civil War raged for three years and by the end of 1922 had devastated much of the nation and crippled its economy. The situation was exacerbated by the crackdown on peasants carried out by the post-Tsarist government, which was headed by charismatic revolutionary leader Vladimir Lenin. Lenin was busy selling all of Russia's grain to the West (and often cheating the buyers in the process) while leaving the peasants with none to eat and nothing to sow for future crops. Estimates suggested that the famine had killed between 5 and 10 million people in the couple of years before Wilkins' planned visit.

And as ever, the political aspect added to the intrigue. The British and American governments wanted to keep an eye on what they perceived as a communist threat, and had been supporting the White Russians for that very reason. The famine gave them an ideal opportunity to infiltrate the country and find out the true feelings of the Russian workers. The American Relief Agency, under Secretary of Commerce and future US president Herbert Hoover, was active: as well as feeding some 11 million Russians every day, they were spying on the Bolsheviks. But Britain didn't want to rely on the Americans for information.

Wilkins was quite happy to use his camera as a ticket to travel around Russia. He had found in both the Balkan War and the Great War that government officials and military officers were less wary of photographers than they were of journalists; they could see what photos were being taken, but they were never sure what would be written. He was not happy with the need for a companion, however, especially when he learned that the companion was a woman.

On 7 November, Wilkins was back at 1 Melbury Road to meet her — a young American woman of Spanish descent named Lucita Squier. He found her extremely attractive, with long dark hair and an olive complexion so typical of her Latin heritage. But her fragile, tiny body worried him: he knew that hard times lay ahead for them both as they crossed Russia, and he reckoned such a frail woman would quickly fall by the wayside. Wilkins would soon find out that he'd grossly underestimated the feisty Ms Squier.

More immediately, though, he discovered that they had something in common: movie production. For the past couple of years, Lucita Squier had been working in Hollywood, scripting the storylines for silent movies. Her most recent projects were directed by the workaholic actor/director Marshall Neilan — the drama *Bits of Life* (1921) and a comedy, *Penrod* (1922). And when she returned from her Russian sojourn, she would be involved in a British detective thriller titled *A Gamble with Hearts*. She claimed to have once stood in as a double for the movie star Mary Pickford. 'At least that's what she told me,' Wilkins would say to friends. 'And who was I to doubt the veracity of her claim?'

Lucita was vital to the Australian's mission, although he did not realise it at the time. She was engaged to a Presbyterian minister-turned-journalist with socialist sympathies, one Albert Rhys Williams. Working for the *New York Post*, Williams had gone to St Petersburg to report on the public protests that led to the October Revolution; once there, he befriended several of the Bolshevik leaders, including Leon Trotsky and Lenin. He unashamedly wrote propaganda stories on behalf of Trotsky, and Lenin used him as a speaker at several seminars on the theories of Karl Marx. Lucita's paramour had a blinkered view of the Bolshevik leaders and some of the atrocities committed in their name. He once described Lenin as 'the most thoroughly civilized and humane man I ever have known'.

While in Russia, Williams had linked up with John Reed, an old socialist friend he'd known back in the United States and the author of a bestselling book on the revolution, *Ten Days that Shook the World*. Williams' own writings upon his return to America met with similar success, including the 1919 publications *Lenin, the Man and His Work* and *76 Questions and Answers on the Bolsheviks and the Soviets* (the latter sold more than 2 million copies). Reed then invited Williams to stay with him at a cottage he owned at Croton-on-Hudson, a picturesque

American socialist author Albert Rhys Williams, shown here in a white coat addressing workers in Moscow, was the conduit through which Wilkins managed to arrange a face-to-face meeting with the famous Russian (Soviet) leader Lenin.

village about 50 kilometres north of Manhattan, where Williams sat down and wrote *Through the Russian Revolution*. The editor of his book was none other than Lucita Squier, who, like Williams, was a confirmed socialist. And as they worked over the manuscript at Croton-on-Hudson, the pair fell in love and decided to get married. Williams returned to Moscow on some unfinished business, which was why Lucita was so keen to put her Hollywood career on hold and join the Quaker mission.

Most important of all, Lucita and her fiancé were to be the conduits for Wilkins to meet Lenin.

Wilkins and his companion set off for Russia the day after they met. At first they travelled by train through France, Austria and Czechoslovakia, sharing a sleeping compartment — much to the embarrassment of the straightlaced Australian. But after crossing into Poland south of Krakow and heading on to the border with Russia, they accepted any form of transport that was available. Sometimes they travelled by horseback; on other occasions they used the normal transport of the peasants of Poland and Russia: an uncomfortable and primitive four-wheeled carriage called a droshky. There were even times when they had to walk.

In Moscow a third member was added to the party. She was Laurette Citroën, the daughter of André Citroën, the French automobile magnate. Laurette had turned her back on the lifestyle of the rich and famous to work among the poor and starving masses. The trio headed off on a journey that would take them across some of the most desolate areas of the country.

Again, they started out by train, but finished up with basic transport, including camels. They slept in barns and, more often than not, under a cart in the open — no mean feat in the early Russian winter. In one barn, they were sleeping in the loft when awoken by a pack of wolves that had broken in and seized a large goat. The salivating wolves devoured the beast in a matter of minutes before retreating into the nearby forest.

On another occasion near Buzuluk, some 800 kilometres south-west of Moscow in what is now Kazakhstan, Wilkins went alone with a sackful of food to a small village that had acquired a dubious reputation as the scene of cannibalism by its starving residents. The two women refused to go anywhere near the place after terrifying stories emerged about the fate of strangers who happened upon this hamlet. Wilkins was unafraid. But as he approached, he was suddenly set upon and knocked unconscious. When he came to, he was greeted with the horrific sight of several severed human hands and feet lying next to a cooking pot on the stove. Was he to be next on the menu?

Fortunately, the villagers discovered the food he had brought and notes in Russian explaining that it was for the local population. He was instantly hailed as a hero, with the peasants kissing his hands instead of cutting them off. 'It was a close call,' he admitted long afterwards. 'My curiosity had nearly cost me my life.'

It was at Buzuluk that he received a cryptic telegram from the British Museum in London announcing that finance had been arranged for his expedition in Australia. Cryptic in that Wilkins had made no proposal to the British Museum about any expedition, to Australia or anywhere else in the world. He would look into it when he returned to London.

In the meantime he had one final task: to meet Vladimir Lenin and make his appraisal of the Russian leader for the SIS. It was late December 1922, and Wilkins had been away for less than two months, not the planned six. But after the meeting with Lenin, he would have everything his bosses in Holland Park wanted. It was an indication of the esteem in which the communist leader held Albert Rhys Williams that Wilkins had been granted an audience at all. Lenin had already suffered the first two of several strokes that would eventually claim his life. And the Moscow hierarchy were busy preparing for the gala event that would announce the official creation of the Soviet Union a couple of days later, on 30 December.

As with so many aspects of Hubert Wilkins' story, the details regarding his audience with Lenin are frustratingly slim, to the point of nonexistence. There appears to be no record of where exactly they met in Moscow, for example, let alone an account of what the two men discussed. Wilkins was certainly surprised that the 52-year-old Bolshevik leader looked much older than in his photos. But, as a lensman himself, he would have understood how photographs could be doctored and used for propaganda.

And no one knows to this day what Wilkins told the SIS chiefs about the meeting either. He would have mentioned the parlous state of Comrade Lenin's health, obviously, and late in his life he did reveal that Lenin had admitted to underestimating the strength of the proletariat's refusal to blindly accept the changes that communism brought to Russia. It seems he was very disappointed at the lack of an immediate stamp of approval from the Russian people. This lack of approval was something Wilkins had seen for himself, of course. One of the orders given to him in London was to talk to the ordinary people and gauge whether they were happy with their lot in life under Soviet rule. It was obvious to Wilkins that they weren't, and Lenin's comments only confirmed the opinion he had formed.

Hubert Wilkins is believed to have been the last person from the West to talk with Lenin. The health of the founder of the Soviet Union deteriorated rapidly after two more strokes, and he left the day-to-day running of the government to others. Vladimir Ilyich Lenin died just over a year later, on 21 January 1924. His death heralded in the darkest period in the history of Russia, under the terror rule of his successor, Joseph Stalin.

ONCE BACK IN London, and having been debriefed at Melbury Road, Wilkins sought to solve the riddle behind that mysterious telegram from the so-called British Museum (Natural History) — today, the independently governed Natural History Museum. It transpired that the museum's trustees had misinterpreted an offer he'd made when handing over specimens collected in Antarctica on the *Quest*. Back then, he had promised to help the museum at any time in the future. They took that offer as carte blanche to start organising an expedition on his behalf.

But he was still confused. After all, his experience as a naturalist during Shackleton's final foray notwithstanding, he did not regard himself as a scientist — only a man eager for knowledge. Officials at the museum in South Kensington dismissed his protests. The 'Wilkins Australia and Islands Expedition' had already been gazetted and the Treasury had allocated funds.

So Wilkins decided he would make his first trip home in almost three years, since he'd been decommissioned from the army, prior to the Cope expedition. He realised there were so many good reasons why the task should be undertaken. The museum had a large collection of Australian fauna, much of it gathered by colonial explorers such as James Cook and Matthew Flinders, but there were many glaring gaps in the collection and much of the labelling was vague. Wilkins explained in his subsequent book on the expedition, *Undiscovered Australia*, how nature had preserved types of animals there in Australia that had perished elsewhere, but how these must eventually perish as well. 'The rare mammals of Australia are dwindling rapidly, some of them which were plentiful a few years ago are already extinct, and many other species are likely to disappear in a few more years,' he warned.

Wilkins also wanted to discover whether European settlement of the continent was to blame for this situation or whether some pathological cause was partly responsible. He would travel in Queensland, working north from Brisbane, collecting animal and bird specimens from both sides of the Great Dividing Range, before moving on to some of the important islands to the north of Australia.

ALTHOUGH THE OFFICIALS at the British Museum had suggested he recruit his scientific staff in Britain, Wilkins believed he would do better by signing up people with local knowledge. He didn't realise how difficult a task this would prove to be. When his ship reached Fremantle towards the end of March 1923, he was delighted to learn that some 350 applications to join his research team awaited him. But weeks later, when he started reading them, his mood changed. Not one of them was suitable.

He had hoped to find three or four eager young students of natural history, preferably graduates, who could continue the work after his research was over. Instead, many of the applicants were simply young men seeking adventure but demanding to be paid. Several were geologists whose only aim was to search for oil. One application was from an entomologist who insisted he receive £300 a year, with increments. Wilkins described some of the enquiries as having come from 'dead-beats', others from enthusiastic amateurs. There was not one biologist who wanted to join his expedition.

Months later, Wilkins explained his disappointment to a leading university academic and was shocked by his reply. 'I personally dissuaded several promising young fellows from joining your expedition,' the professor admitted. 'There's no money to be made in expeditionary work today or even in the study of natural history. Young fellows can earn a decent living at other things. They can get well-paid commercial jobs as soon as they leave university. So there's no need for them to gain experience in the field.'

Wilkins shook his head in disbelief. He would return to this issue in the pages of *Undiscovered Australia*:

*No doubt they can get well-paid jobs and a comfortable living according to their estimation, and are quite contented with this; they have little desire to develop into highly trained investigators commanding high salaries, or indifferent to salary, to devote themselves to science. Most Australians are well off in regard to creature comforts, and many of them soon reach independent means; yet the absence of the express desire for culture and higher things, and their contentedness with the mediocre, make them perhaps the poorest rich people in the world today.*

It is no wonder Wilkins was disappointed with his fellow Australians. In the previous decade or so he had achieved more than most people would accomplish in five lifetimes. He had journeyed across the world several times, trekked hundreds of kilometres across frozen Arctic wastelands, been in the front line of major battles in two major wars (and won two awards for his bravery), and recently travelled through famine-stricken Russia and talked to Lenin, one of the most significant world leaders of all time. Wilkins was an explorer and an adventurer, forever pushing boundaries. Now, back home, he found a nation peopled by complacent consumers.

Wilkins chose Brisbane as his headquarters. There are no details of the long journey by boat and train from Fremantle. But on the way he must surely have visited surviving members of his family — his mother, Louisa, and seven of his original eleven siblings were all still alive. There were occasional newspaper stories about him, including one that described the tall South Australian as 'a fine specimen of a man'.

He did eventually find three scientists to provide the core of his expeditionary team: Oscar Cornwell, an expert on Queensland birds who had also worked in the wilds of New Guinea; Vladimir Kotoff, an expatriate Russian who had been a member of various scientific expeditions in Siberia and Manchuria; and Edgar Young, a Brisbane ornithologist with an interest in botany. Other members were recruited in each local area visited by the expedition.

Their main mode of transport was a van built on the chassis of a Model-T Ford, which doubled as a caravan in which to sleep on wild nights. Two Ford coupés were also used at various stages of the expedition. In the early days, they even used a couple of railway carriages, lent to them by the Queensland Commissioner for Railways, as their mobile headquarters. One had sleeping compartments and dining facilities; the other was a flat-based carriage in which to carry

Tucker time on 'Wilkins Australia and Islands Expedition' for the British Museum. Left to right: Wilkins, Vladimir Kotoff, Edgar Young and Oscar Cornwell.

Wilkins, with a local elder showing him the way, sets off on a 65-kilometre trek across the Great Dividing Range in Queensland.

the Fords. The carriages would be hooked up to regular trains and then left at railway stations at towns such as St George. From there the men would head out into the bush in the vehicles.

The Aboriginal people they met during their exploratory mission couldn't comprehend the work the group was doing. The only white folk with whom these nomadic people had come into contact were policemen, government surveyors and missionaries. They didn't like policemen because 'they take us away and lock us up'. And they didn't like missionaries because 'they take children away from their parents'.

The Aboriginal men would regularly offer their women to Wilkins and his team, but the propositions were rejected out of hand. A Murri chief later explained how this was a test of the group's morality. 'If you take our women, we would no longer trust you and would steal everything we could from you,' he said. 'We might sell you women, as long as we got enough — but then we would never be friends.'

At one stage, near the Moreton Telegraph Station, just south of Cape York, Wilkins wondered why he'd been receiving no co-operation from the local people as he went about collecting animal specimens. Then a friendly Murri provided the reason: they believed that once he'd got a sample of every local mammal, he would turn his attention to them — killing a couple to take their bodies off to England. 'Me fella no wantem skin and bones blong me go long that place England,' the man explained in pidgin. 'Too plenty cold, that country.'

At the top of the Great Dividing Range in far north Queensland, a blacktracker pointed to a mountain and told Wilkins: 'Plenty too much gold sit down there.' Wilkins believed it to be little more than a myth. It was only a couple of weeks later when further north, visiting the Batavia goldfields, that he realised his Aboriginal guide had probably been spot on.

Often the scientists would try the native animals as food. On Cape York, Edgar Young, the Brisbane ornithologist-cum-botanist, cooked a stew made from the flesh of a cuscus, a rare marsupial related to the possum and monkey. 'I have eaten all types of animals around the world — even frozen pieces of a prehistoric mastodon in the Arctic,' Wilkins would recall. 'But nothing was as foul-tasting and so tough as to be almost impossible to chew than the cuscus. I will never forget the awful taste.'

They returned to Brisbane from Cape York by boat in December 1923. During the voyage, Wilkins asked the steward on the small ketch for a few bottles of whisky. Others on board expected a party. When they peered into Wilkins' cabin, however, they were sorely disappointed. They discovered him pushing young snakes and rats through the neck of each bottle, into the whisky. That way the alcohol would preserve them for future dissection, to examine the bodies' physiological make-up.

'A bloody waste of good whisky,' one of his fellow passengers snorted.

WILKINS ALSO SPENT considerable time in the Northern Territory. After a few weeks in Arnhem Land, Wilkins gained the confidence of the local Aboriginal people he had befriended there. The Yolngu warmed to him because, as they put it, he was unlike other white men, who treated them as servants. They wove grass into ceremonial bracelets for him to wear, showing he had been accepted as a member of their tribe.

They also explained to Wilkins how murder was widely accepted among the Yolngu people. 'If you kill a man in his sleep you have done something you can boast about and laugh over, for the man should have been more cautious,' Wilkins wrote in his report on the research. 'But, if your enemy knows that you wish to kill him, you

Wilkins snapped this evocative photograph of an indigenous inhabitant of Groote Eylandt, in the Gulf of Carpentaria, sitting on Sir Hubert's briefcase.

must not take unfair advantage of him. If you can dispose of your victim in such a way that no violence is visible, the death will be attributed to evil spirits. Later on, when you gradually let it be known that you were responsible for the deed, your reputation will increase.'

Wilkins was amazed when members of the tribe confided that cannibalism was commonplace. Murder victims could be eaten by anyone, he learned, but there was a strict code for the consumption of other bodies. 'Only men may eat young babies,' Wilkins reported. 'The flesh of young girls is retained for the exclusive use of the old men of the tribe. Women may not eat young boys, but anyone may eat grown-up men and women.'

Wilkins was introduced to a man named Narragudji, whose stillborn child had been eaten by six other members of the tribe. The bones were then wrapped in paperbark and grandly presented to the mother of the child. The expedition leader photographed Narragudji and his wife to illustrate the man's reminiscences.

There were other stories that Wilkins said were too ghastly to repeat, stories of cannibalism that could not be dismissed as mere 'sordid flights of imagination or ancient myths', he insisted. 'The incidents related happened during the months of September and November 1924. The cannibals still roam the bush, unconscious of having committed a criminal act, and fearing only the disapproval of the white man.'

While in Arnhem Land, Wilkins became aware of one of the most disgraceful episodes in Australian history: the massacre of scores of Yolngu by a mob of white vigilantes, for no other reason than to satisfy a blood lust aroused by an unsubstantiated rumour. What made it even more sickening perhaps was that it occurred not in the wild colonial days of the eighteenth or early nineteenth century, but most recently.

On 26 March 1923, a Queensland Government ship, the wooden-hulled steamer SS *Douglas Mawson*, had set off from Burketown, in the south of the Gulf of Carpentaria, bound for Thursday Island. She was never seen again. Two days into the voyage, the steamer ran into a tropical cyclone and sank. A few weeks later, rumours began circulating like wildfire in the white communities of Queensland and the Northern Territory. It was claimed that there had been twenty survivors, eighteen men and two women named Willett, who had all made it ashore in Arnhem Land — although why the ship had been anywhere near this stretch of coast was never explained by those spreading the rumours. The men were alleged to have been speared to death and eaten, while the Willett women were spared and taken as concubines.

A punitive expedition was mounted. It involved two policemen, two blacktrackers and seventeen white vigilantes. They arrived at Elcho Island, in north-western Arnhem Land, aboard the SS *Huddersfield*, just as Wilkins and his team reached the same port. Wilkins volunteered to join the group, but his offer was promptly rejected. The vigilantes were in no mood to allow a scientist from England to witness what they had in mind, even if he was an Australian by birth. It's not known just how many Yolngu were slaughtered by the group in the next six months as they headed south to Caledon Bay, midway between the Gove Peninsula and Groote Eylandt. Hundreds, maybe — no one will ever be sure. A royal commission was held, behind closed doors, and the record of its proceedings has inexplicably disappeared since.

The lynch mob in this sad episode would not have known that, earlier in his recent explorations, Wilkins had been shocked to learn of a similar massacre, in Queensland. It was at Mount Wheeler, between Rockhampton and Yepoon, and was likewise discussed in his report to the British Museum:

> *Years ago, a sergeant of the police, enthusiastic in his duty of quelling Aboriginal disturbances, developed a blood lust and sought to carry on a wholesale slaughter in support of the theory that no matter how good a black fellow may be, he is better dead. During a raid on a tribe, and to impress others in the neighbourhood, the sergeant and his troops drove two or thee hundred — it is curious to notice that a hundred or so does not seem to matter in the estimate of numbers of victims in a tragedy — Blacks, men, women and children, up the sloping sides of Mount Wheeler and over the precipitous sides, to be dashed to pieces on the rocks below.*

What made the Mount Wheeler incident all the more appalling was that the police sergeant apparently chose this method of slaughter to avoid having to 'waste' ammunition.

IT WAS EVENTUALLY time for Wilkins to bring down the curtain on his expedition, having spent two years in his search for specimens.

Sometime in mid 1925, he and his team set out from Caledon Bay for Thursday Island, weathering a cyclone on the way. The locals greeted his arrival with amazement.

An acquaintance ran up to him and exclaimed: 'Thank God, you're alive!'

'Of course I'm alive,' Wilkins replied. 'What made you think I wasn't?'

'Well, you've been lost for months. The Federal Government was talking about sending out a search party for you.'

'Anyone who knew me well would have realised I was safe. I've never been lost, in fact — although newspapers have had me dead a few times!'

It was then off to Brisbane, Sydney and Melbourne before sailing 'home' to Britain. Wilkins took with him almost 6000 specimens. Many of the animals and insects had never been seen before by scientists. There were also several dinosaur bones and a multitude of fossils. The museum named two of the previously unknown animal species after Wilkins — a short-legged lizard and a rock wallaby.

And there was an unexpected legacy, as explained by the museum's director, Sir Sidney Harmer: 'Captain Wilkins concentrated his attention principally on the mammals and birds, as they stood in the gravest danger of extinction; but he never missed an opportunity of collecting other natural history specimens, and when he came across the Aboriginal inhabitants in northern Australia he secured an important ethnographical series.'

Wilkins arrived in London to a damp autumn and had just a six-week break in which to tie up loose ends. He handed in his report, much of it having been dictated to a stenographer on the voyage back. He explained to one of the museum trustees that it was really only the bare bones of a manuscript on the expedition, and that he intended to write it up properly when he found some time.

'Don't worry,' came the reply. 'There's enough here for a book.'

And there certainly was. Illustrated by forty-four of the hundreds of photos he had taken, *Undiscovered Australia* was published in 1928, first in Britain and then in the United States. It was ironic, considering Wilkins' pioneering aviation experience, that the US publisher was George Putnam. In the coming years, Putnam was to meet and eventually marry Amelia Earhart, America's most famous aviatrix, who regularly made headlines until she vanished over the Pacific Ocean in 1937 during an around-the-world flight.

*Undiscovered Australia* was highly controversial, especially after newspapers in Britain, the United States and Australia concentrated on Wilkins' brief reference to cannibalism among the Aboriginal people of Arnhem Land. He had expected this could happen, but Wilkins' determination to be thorough and accurate in his reporting outweighed any realisation that some would use his words to justify their own prejudices.

But that would be three years away. Returning to October 1925, all that remained was for Wilkins to hand the British Museum his final expense account for this, the very first expedition under his command. It came to £2010 — just £10 more than his original estimate.

# Chapter 9

# Blame It on the Fokkers

AMERICAN EXPLORER ADMIRAL Robert Peary is credited with being the first to reach the North Pole, in 1909, although some experts today suggest he fell short of the elusive Holy Grail of Arctic exploration. He had been ferried north by Captain Bob Bartlett, skipper of the ill-fated *Karluk* on the Stefansson expedition. But despite Peary's efforts and those of others, such as Roald Amundsen — the Norwegian explorer who laid claim to being both the first to navigate the Northwest Passage and the first to reach the South Pole, in December 1911 — the world's knowledge of the polar regions remained quite meagre for many years.

Peary also reckoned he had found solid land in the Arctic Ocean. In June 1906, while looking out from Cape Colgate in Canada's Northwest Territories, over the frozen wastes before him, he was amazed to see what would become known as Crocker Land. 'North stretched the well-known polar pack,' he wrote. 'And north-west it was with a thrill that my glasses [binoculars] revealed the white summits of a distant land.' Peary estimated it was some 190 kilometres offshore. He named it after one of his financial backers, George Crocker. An expedition to the area by the American Museum of Natural History in 1913–18 failed to find the mysterious Crocker Land, however.

Three decades earlier, American whaling captain John Keenan had 'discovered' another island, north-east of Point Barrow in Alaska, which he called Keenan Land after himself. And in 1908, the disgraced explorer Frederick Cook, whose claims to have reached the North Pole before Peary were proven false, saw two islands in the same general area, which he called Bradley Land.

These and other supposed discoveries were marked on maps and atlases with dotted lines, signifying their unconfirmed status. But when Hubert Wilkins' plans to fly over the Arctic started to come together, once his Australia expedition had drawn to a close, he sincerely hoped they did exist. For years he'd wanted to prove the worth of a weather station in the Arctic, which he believed could help meteorologists around the world forecast droughts and floods. A weather station needed solid ground. And the further north, the more important it would be.

By 1925, Wilkins had decided the time was ripe for exploration of the Arctic by air. Midway through the year, Amundsen, with the financial backing of American billionaire Lincoln Ellsworth, had tried using two flying boats to travel across the roof of the world. Although the expedition had almost ended in disaster, the planes were serviceable. Wilkins later tried to buy the aircraft off Amundsen, but to no avail. He was forced to look elsewhere.

In these groundbreaking early years, aviators were part of a close-knit community. Most of them knew each other personally, and if they hadn't met, they were well aware of the other's reputation. So it was with Wilkins and that pioneer of aviation Anthony Fokker.

Born at Kediri, Java, in 1890, Anthony Herman Gerard Fokker was the son of a Dutch tea planter. Fokker was just four years old when the family moved back to the Netherlands. At school he showed an inventiveness that was to make him one of the most famous names in aviation. He was only twenty when he designed one of the fastest aircraft in the world, and when World War I broke out, his services were snapped up by the German Government. He is known to have designed at least sixty different aircraft, the best known being the DR-1 triplane made famous by the flying ace Baron Manfred von Richthofen. Fokker also perfected a synchronised machine gun, able to shoot through the aircraft's propellers — within forty-eight hours of him turning his attention to the task.

After the war he migrated to the United States, where he constructed aircraft for commercial use and for the burgeoning group of devil-may-care flyers who were keen to set every conceivable record for endurance and undertake flights into the unknown regions of the world. Given his enthusiasm, it was quite natural for Wilkins to befriend the design genius. 'He was a true supporter of my efforts to fly in the Arctic and Antarctic,' the Australian would enthuse to anyone who would listen. 'He understood there were so many frontiers to be challenged by aviators.'

Although considerable money changed hands between the pair, Wilkins was nevertheless able to purchase at bargain-basement prices the two Fokker aircraft he needed for himself and a second flyer. Anthony Fokker realised the value of the publicity that could be gained from Wilkins' venture. The two aircraft were a high-winged Fokker VIIa monoplane and a three-engine Fokker VIIb, which Wilkins named respectively the *Alaskan* and the *Detroiter*. The latter was an experimental aircraft and, at 23 metres long, the largest Fokker ever built. No one was sure how it would handle the Arctic.

The money for the expedition came from the North American Newspaper Alliance, especially one of its flagship titles, the *Detroit News*. The *News* even had thousands of schoolchildren sending their dimes and nickels to a fund set up to help finance Wilkins' expedition. It was tough on the Aussie aviator: he knew he could not let down the kids who supported him with their pocket money.

The NANA hierarchy had approached Vilhjalmur Stefansson with the aim of him leading another Arctic expedition but, remembering the discussions he and Wilkins had had while sitting out the 1915–16 winter on Banks Island, Stefansson put forward the Australian's name as a more suitable candidate. Stefansson also recommended to Wilkins a daring North American aviator named Ben Eielson as the man to share his adventure.

Carl Benjamin Eielson was born in North Dakota in 1897, the son of Norwegian immigrants. Another to become entranced by the possibilities of flight while in his youth, he was at college studying law when the United States joined the Great War, but by the time he had signed up for action and begun his pilot training, the war was over. Nevertheless, having earned his wings, he was commissioned as a second lieutenant in the US Army Air Service before being discharged back into civilian life, on the very same day, in March 1919.

'Taciturn' was probably the best description of this self-effacing adventurer, who was aged twenty-eight — almost ten years younger than Wilkins — when the two first met in late 1925. A man of few words. One who listened rather than talked. And that was the type of person Wilkins preferred to have on his expeditions. 'It's all very well for a bloke to be a laugh a minute,' the Australian would explain. 'But after a few weeks cooped up together in the wilds of the Arctic, the jokes soon wear thin. You can't laugh when you're stranded in the middle of nowhere and facing a fortnight's trek across the ice and snow to safety ... Those are the times you need a mate who has a cool head under pressure.'

Eielson had a cool head: calm, unruffled, steadfast, resolute. All that and more.

# Brother to the Eagle

Such was Ben Eielson's affinity with the primitive aircraft of the 1920s that Eskimos in Alaska called him 'Brother to the Eagle'. When he was at the controls, it seemed as if he, not the plane, was soaring through the air. Few others in that intrepid band of pioneer aviators had the same innate ability to understand the art of flying.

To see Eielson with his feet firmly planted on land, one would not have realised this. He was broad-shouldered, standing a little under 6 foot tall, and beginning to lose his hair at an early age; he didn't stand out in a crowd. Meeting him face to face, one might have wondered why so many of his friends would swear by him.

Although noted for his ability to say little, when it was necessary he could be an eloquent speaker. And once out of the army, it was his persuasive arguments that convinced a group of businessmen in Dakota to bankroll him in the purchase of a war-surplus plane. As well as teaching some of them to fly and taking the others up for joyrides, Eielson was able to hire himself out as one of the growing band of barnstormers — the fearless young pilots who put on exhibitions of stunt flying at agricultural shows around the country.

By 1921, the proceeds from these activities had allowed him to enrol at Georgetown University's law school in Washington, DC, where he befriended a congressman from Alaska. Through their association, Eielson realised that Alaska was the place for young men like him and so, despite having not completed his studies, he soon moved to Fairbanks as a teacher. News of his prowess as a flyer preceded him, and before long Eielson had a DH4 aircraft at his disposal and was flying passengers and goods to remote mining camps in the Alaskan wilderness.

His efforts showed the advantage that aircraft had over

primitive dog sleds, slicing journeys that previously had taken weeks down to a matter of hours. In the autumn of 1923 he flew to Washington and convinced US Postal Service chiefs to give him a contract to fly mail between the central Alaskan towns of Fairbanks and McGrath. He charged the government $2 a pound, half the amount the dog-sled operators had been demanding.

Eielson made his first airmail flight in February 1924, covering the 400-kilometre trip to McGrath in just three hours. The overland journey took three weeks. A few months later, he received a letter of congratulations on his efforts from no less than the president of the United States, Calvin Coolidge. But the knives were out. The dog-sled operators had been using all their influence in the national capital to torpedo Eielson's business, and a minor crash was the straw that broke the camel's back. The Postal Service used the crash as an excuse to cancel his contract.

At the time, it seemed like a real setback for Eielson, but it would turn out to be a blessing. Had he still held the airmail contract, he would have been unable to accept Wilkins' offer the following year — an offer that would eventually make the two flyers the toast of world aviation.

EARLY ON IN the new year, 1926, the two Fokkers were dismantled and transported by sea from San Francisco to the Alaskan port of Seward, and thence by train the 600 kilometres north to the territory's capital of Fairbanks. Situated less than 200 kilometres south of the Arctic Circle, this was an ideal spot for the expedition's southern base. Wilkins and Eielson would transport their gasoline drums from Fairbanks up to Point Barrow, the northernmost settlement in the world, from where they planned to carry out a series of flights in search of uncharted islands near the North Pole. In addition, they hoped to make a daring flight across the top of the globe to

Spitsbergen, an island situated around 600 kilometres north of Norway. It was a flight no one had ever made. In fact, most aviators reckoned it was so dangerous that no one had even contemplated attempting the journey.

The first task was to reassemble the two planes at Fairbanks, after which, on 11 March, it came time to honour the sponsors. The *Detroit News* had assigned the NANA's Alaskan correspondent, Palmer Hutchinson, to provide colour stories for their readers, and a gala christening of the aircraft was duly organised. Along with a horde of pressmen, there were preachers from three Protestant denominations (Methodist, Church of England and Salvation Army), a Catholic priest and even a representative of the Theosophical Society. According to Wilkins' account of events as told to Lowell Thomas, to appease the temperance views of a couple of the ministers, each of the Fokkers had a bottle of aircraft fuel cracked over a propeller instead of the traditional champagne.

With the official business concluded, Wilkins pulled Hutchinson aside to give the reporter a tip designed to help him steal a march on the other journalists and photographers present. He would be making a test flight later in the day, the Aussie told him, and Hutchinson should be sure to attend, to cover the event for the *Detroit News*.

While heading for the crude runway to start the flight, however, the *Detroiter* got stuck in a snowdrift. The support crew began pushing and Hutchinson apparently felt he had to help also; showing his inexperience, the American positioned himself just in front of one of the wheels and started pulling. Wilkins and the others failed to see the danger in time, and as the plane lurched forward, Hutchinson was caught by one of the propellers and killed instantly. It was a tragic waste of a life and the trial run was immediately abandoned. Strangely enough, Tom Lanphier, a veteran US Army aviator who'd joined the expedition team, almost suffered the same fate the following day, but he only had his flight jacket torn to shreds.

These two incidents were just the first of several setbacks that had Wilkins believing the Fokkers were in some way cursed. Within a week, the *Alaskan* had crashed with both Wilkins and Eielson on board. Neither man was seriously hurt, but the plane lost its undercarriage and propeller and the engine was a write-off. The next day, Wilkins and Lanphier took up the *Detroiter*. It was the first time the plane had been in the air. On take-off it slewed to one side and narrowly missed hitting a spectator; later, while coming back in to land, it stalled and crashed, almost in the same spot as the *Alaskan* had been wrecked. All three engines had been torn off and the undercarriage was wrecked beyond repair.

The expedition was over before it had even got off the ground, so to speak. It took only three weeks to repair the *Alaskan*, which was then used to ferry fuel to Point Barrow. But work on the *Detroiter* was to take a lot longer — leaving not enough time to beat the autumn fog and blizzards later in the year.

All was not lost. On the first of thirteen ferrying flights in the *Alaskan*, Wilkins made a significant discovery regarding John Keenan's unconfirmed find of the 1880s. A tailwind had sped the Fokker's journey north and, with plenty of fuel in the gas tank, Wilkins decided to check out the mysterious Keenan Land before putting down at Point Barrow. Scouring the area, he found that the so-called giant island had been no more than a figment of the old whaler's imagination, a polar mirage. A further bonus was the fact that Wilkins' trip from Fairbanks to Point Barrow had taken less than five hours compared with the two months the advance team of dog sleds had needed to cover the same distance on the ground. Had he not indulged himself with the brief detour in search of Keenan Land, the travel time would have been a couple of hours less, of course.

The Eskimos at Point Barrow were amazed by their first sighting of an aircraft. One told Wilkins: 'When I first heard the loud noise and looked up into the sky, I thought it was a giant duck. But once it came down to the ground it looked more like a huge whale with wings.'

A second achievement of note occurred on a later trip, when weather forced the *Alaskan* off course and over the Endicott Mountains, which maps of the time had rising to just over 1500 metres. But as the plane, weighed down with all the drums of fuel, struggled over one of the ridges, the wheels touched the ground — the altimeter showing the Fokker to be at around 9000 feet, meaning that particular mountaintop had to have been around 2750 metres. The maps were duly changed.

And there had been another important moment earlier on in the expedition, if only from the point of view of watching history being made, albeit by others. On the morning of 13 May 1926, while waiting for some clear weather to enable him to take off from Point Barrow, Wilkins was astounded to see, through a break in the clouds, a silver airship come into view. He had to pinch himself to make sure he wasn't dreaming. In the middle of the Arctic wastelands, a semi-rigid dirigible?

He had heard in radio broadcasts from Fairbanks that attempts were being made to sail an airship over the North Pole, but he never really expected to see it. Everyone at Point Barrow ran onto the airstrip to get a better view, and they all waved frantically in the hope that those on board would see them.

It was a historic flight — a joint American–Italian–Norwegian expedition to fly from the settlement of Ny-Alesund on Spitsbergen, the largest island in what is now the Norwegian-ruled Svalbard archipelago, to Alaska. Bankrolling the venture to the tune of $100,000 was 45-year-old Lincoln Ellsworth, the surveyor son of a billionaire American coalmine owner and banker. On board was Roald Amundsen and, in his honour, the airship was named after the famous polar explorer's country of birth, *Norge*. Commander of the dirigible was a self-promoting Italian army officer, one Colonel Umberto Nobile. The two men loathed each other but their animosity never hindered their success. They had set off two days earlier and had already traversed the polar icecap.

As Wilkins and his team watched in awe, the *Norge* made its way through a mottled sea of white clouds before disappearing from view some 40 kilometres south of Point Barrow. It was later learned that those on board did not see either the settlement or Wilkins' crew. They also missed a reporter from *The Times* of London whom they were supposed to pick up near Point Barrow. He saw them, but they blindly sailed past. Wilkins sent a story about the sighting by radio to the *Detroit News*, whose parent company syndicated it to other NANA newspapers around the world. The poor old scribe from *The Times* was scooped.

Still, for Hubert Wilkins, solving a couple of the world's cartographic riddles and serving as his sponsor's breaking-news aviation reporter were no substitute for real success. And given the hoopla of the expedition launch back in March, the loss of Palmer Hutchinson and an astronomical repair bill for the two troublesome Fokker aircraft, the North American Newspaper Alliance was impatient for success.

As expedition leader, Wilkins stood by his team. But, after another crash involving the *Alaskan*, he had no other choice than to call a halt to their efforts for the year and head back to California to await the spring of 1927. For him, spring couldn't come soon enough.

# Chapter 10

# A Trek Across the Arctic

TUESDAY, 29 MARCH 1927 was the morning that one of the two Stinson aircraft of Wilkins and Eielson flew further north than any flyers had ever dared. The Stinsons were replacements for the Fokkers, in which Wilkins had gradually lost faith. On the same day, the two airmen became the first in history to land on an icefloe. And, in doing so, the pair barely escaped with their lives.

The whole episode had begun the previous month in Fairbanks, after Wilkins had spent the best part of half a year involved in public fundraising for the expedition and attempting to placate his financial backers in Michigan. Although the *Norge*'s success in May 1926 had appeared to nullify a central aim of his own venture, the Amundsen-led team had provided precious little in the way of scientific discovery. That remained a prize that Wilkins' team could hope to collect.

Once back in the chilly climes of Fairbanks, central Alaska, he and Eielson were joined by a fearless young pilot named Alger Graham. And yet another, Joe Crosson, agreed to help out in the preliminary stages. Like Ben Eielson, Crosson had established a reputation for daring while flying in supplies to remote mining camps in Alaska and adjacent areas of Canada, and bringing injured men and women back for hospital treatment in Fairbanks.

Two Stinsons, Detroit-made (of course) and with Eielson and Graham at the controls, ferried supplies to Point Barrow. It was everything they needed for the work that Wilkins had planned for the upcoming summer, culminating — he hoped — in the first trans-Arctic aeroplane flight, across the frozen Arctic Ocean to Spitsbergen.

Crosson, meanwhile, had volunteered to fly in a journalist from the North American Newspaper Alliance, who would file reports on the flyers' Arctic adventures, whetting the voracious appetite of an American public enthralled by the derring-do of the young pioneers of the air. The reporter got unexpected first-hand experience of the wilds of the Arctic Circle, as Crosson became the first aviator to fly so far north … in a plane with an open cockpit.

It was fine and clear on 29 March when Wilkins and Eielson took off in their Stinson, although a blizzard was looming in the distance. As they headed north, the two adventurers could see below them a vast expanse of icefloes — rough icefields that were anything but ideal for a landing if one became necessary.

When they were some 1000 kilometres north of Point Barrow, the aircraft's engine began to splutter. Eielson tried every trick he knew to ease the engine back into action as he quickly turned the plane around for the safety of the Arctic outpost. But it soon became evident that his efforts were in vain. He was going to have to land the Stinson on the only thing available: an icefield floating above some 6000 metres of icy water.

The plane descended, with the pair looking for a place to make their emergency landing. As it did so, the propeller began to lose power. Finally, leaning forward in the navigator's seat, Wilkins pointed to a spot. 'There, there!' he shouted at Eielson. 'Don't worry, it'll be plenty thick enough to take us.'

Of course, Wilkins had absolutely no idea whether it was thick enough. But he wasn't about to tell his colleague that.

Eielson put the plane into a dive, to get the propeller moving faster, and it suddenly sprung to life. The spluttering had stopped. The American was all for continuing towards Point Barrow, but Wilkins argued against it. 'No, no, put it down, Ben. We'll check the engine and make sure it's all okay.'

As he spoke, the engine stopped again and the aircraft was forced to glide down onto the ice. It was a perfect landing — the first ever on an icefloe in the Arctic Ocean.

After an hour's work on the engine in the sub-zero temperatures, Eielson had it working and they took off. But within two minutes, it had died again. They made a second forced landing and Eielson carried out further repairs, lasting almost three hours. The temperature had dropped to around 25 degrees below zero and frostbite had started to attack Eielson's fingers. And as he worked, he could see an Arctic blizzard bearing down on the pair.

Eventually they were off and heading south once again, this time into the teeth of a gale. They were flying in clear sky above the blizzard, but the wind was as strong as it was in the murky mess below them. The Stinson should have been flying at around 160 kilometres an hour; instead, on full power, their speed was closer to 65 kilometres an hour. It soon became evident that their fuel, being consumed as it was in great quantities as the plane battled the gale, would not be enough to get them back to land. Their one hope was to get near enough, pray for solid ice on which to land, and walk the remaining short distance to civilisation.

They then realised that it would be no short distance.

They were around 100 kilometres from land when the fuel ran dry. Moments later the engine stopped. The altimeter showed they were at 5000 feet. It was around midnight, but being spring near the

North Pole, there was still a semblance of light — at least, above the clouds there was. Wilkins and Eielson knew that below, in the storm, it would be pitch-black.

The Stinson plunged through the clouds for what would be a virtual blind landing on an icefield of indeterminate smoothness or thickness. For that matter, they could end up in a watery grave, as there were often areas where no ice at all lay over the ocean.

When the altimeter showed they were getting close to sea level, Eielson levelled the aircraft and the pair braced themselves for a rocky landing. As the Stinson touched down, the left wing clipped an unseen object and swung the plane around in an arc before it ploughed into a snowdrift.

Eielson and Wilkins turned and looked at each other in the dim glow of the cockpit lights, and their relief instantly manifested itself. They broke into hysterical laughter — they were alive! — even if they were also stuck on a frozen ocean with a possible fortnight's trek ahead of them across the icy wastelands.

Once it was light enough to see their surroundings, the two men learned how close they'd come to having an awful crash. The wing had clipped a small ridge of ice and swung the Stinson onto a smooth patch; had it not, they would have ploughed straight into a massive ice ridge ahead that would surely have wrecked the plane and caused serious injury, if not death, to the intrepid flyers. Yet again, that unseen hand …

The radio had gone dead, damaged in the crash landing, so there would be no help from Point Barrow. And there was to be no walking for a while either. The blizzard blew up harder than ever, and for five days it swirled around the plane as the pair curled up inside their sleeping bags, dozing and occasionally eating small meals from the emergency rations on board: nuts and raisins, biscuits, bars of chocolate, and pemmican (a type of cake made by mixing a paste of dried meat, fat and dried fruits). For drinking water they would put a container of snow inside their sleeping bags and let their body heat do the rest.

After they'd been cocooned in the cabin for just under a week, the storm finally abated. It was time to press out in search of civilisation, but first there was more bad news to come. Wilkins worked out from his sextant readings that during the storm their icefloe had drifted further out to sea — they were now around 160 kilometres from land.

Improvisation being a prerequisite of the job, they fashioned a couple of sleds from pieces of metal they'd ripped from under the aircraft. Soon after setting off, however, they realised the makeshift sleds were as good as useless in travelling over the ice and abandoned them. Instead they packed the scientific instruments that would help them plot their way to safety, together with about 15 kilograms of food, into their sleeping bags, which they then used as backpacks.

Hubert Wilkins, rugged up in his typical Arctic attire.

The going was slow. Sometimes the ice was so slippery, they had to crawl on their hands and knees. At night they would build an igloo — like a number of other survival techniques he adopted, a craft Wilkins had learned from the Eskimos while on the Stefansson expedition a decade before. Eielson could offer only limited help in this essential activity, since the frostbite he'd suffered while repairing the engine had left his hands close to useless. He was also unable to assist as Wilkins went through a complicated routine before turning in each night: the Aussie would remove all the snow and frost from their clothes and fill their boots with soft material to ensure they kept their shape.

On one occasion, Wilkins fell through the ice. After dragging himself out of the water, he took off his wet clothes and 'dried' them on the loose snow, which blotted up the excess fluid. At the same time, he danced around in the nude, banging his arms against his body and legs to keep them warm and the blood circulating. Eielson was to later reveal that, when he saw this incredible exhibition, he was convinced Wilkins had been broken mentally and that they were doomed. The younger man knew that, with his frostbitten hands, he could not survive on his own.

In mid April, after almost two weeks of staggering across the ice, and often in a zigzag fashion to avoid patches of clear, unfrozen water, they suddenly saw smoke in the distance. It turned out to be coming from a trading post at Beechey Point, 200 kilometres west of Point Barrow. As Wilkins and Eielson made a last, laborious trek towards the smoke, some Eskimos appeared, rushing across the ice behind a couple of sleds dragged by dog teams.

The pair had been saved.

IT TRANSPIRED THAT when the two airmen did not return from their 29 March flight, Alger Graham had flown up and down the coast dropping messages to wandering Eskimos, asking them to keep an eye out for Wilkins and Eielson. The trading post at Beechey Point had been alerted in this way. Graham had also spent many days flying out over where the Stinson was believed to have gone — but it was a long shot, since it would have been nigh on impossible to spot the two flyers from the air.

The trader was shocked by the arrival of Wilkins and Eielson. They had long been given up for dead.

The first task was to address the problem of Eielson's frostbite. Originally the fingers had been swollen and bright red; now they had turned a deathly white. The frostbite was complete. It seemed to laymen like Wilkins and the trader that Eielson's fingers would have to be amputated. He was in no condition to make the long overland journey to Point Barrow and proper medical care, especially as yet another blizzard was brewing. They were convinced that gangrene had begun to set in, and if unchecked, it would eventually kill him.

Wilkins and the trader discussed it with Eielson. Of course, there was no anaesthetic available, so the plan was for him to drink as much whisky as possible. Then, once he was suitably drunk, the other two would remove the affected digits using fishing knives.

'I won't be able to fly again, but at least I'll be alive,' a grim-faced Eielson offered as one of his would-be surgeons opened the bottle.

But then, just as the American was getting himself well and truly drunk and the trader was honing his fishing knives until they were razor-sharp, the three of them heard the sound of an aircraft. At first, Wilkins thought his ears were deceiving him. But the sound got louder. He rushed outside just in time to see Alger Graham landing the second Stinson on the ice, next to the trading post.

Graham had been on his way from Fairbanks to Point Barrow when the blizzard pushed him off course. He'd intended to weather the storm at the trading post and was delighted now to discover the new arrivals, but Eielson's frostbite forced a rethink. The three flyers climbed into the plane, and this time Graham made it to Point Barrow, where the local doctor conducted emergency surgery, amputating just one finger. The other digits were left in the hope that further medical treatment could save them. It did, and Ben Eielson survived the ordeal to fly again.

While he recovered, Graham and Wilkins made several flights north in an attempt to salvage something from a second, bitterly disappointing year, but any exploration was severely limited. They had also hoped to find the abandoned Stinson, refuel it and bring it back to Point Barrow. Low clouds prevented any sightings, and to this day no one knows what eventually happened to the plane. Is it still floating around in an icy esophagus? Or has it sunk beneath the icefloes? It's regrettable that the plane can never go on show in a museum, for the historically curious to pay homage to the first aircraft to land on the frozen Arctic Ocean.

It was obvious that the flyers would again have to postpone their plans. The dream would have to wait for yet another year. And for the second year running, the expedition leader was heading south in an effort to keep the dream alive.

THE REACTION OF his backers in Detroit can't have come as too much of a surprise to Wilkins: the North American Newspaper Alliance was pulling out of the expedition. *Detroit News* readers could only take so many stories of adversity without a suitably happy, triumphant ending. Ownership of the team's aircraft was passed on to the Australian himself, and the NANA picked up the tab for any outstanding expenses incurred thus far, but for all intents and purposes, Hubert Wilkins was now on his own.

On the subject of his aeroplanes, Wilkins was already casting a long, disapproving eye over the inventory. His friendship with

Anthony Fokker was all well and good but the aircraft manufacturer's VIIa and VIIb were the wrong machines for flying around the Arctic. For them to operate effectively for scientific purposes, especially the three-engine monster they'd dubbed *Detroiter*, there had to be five or six people involved, including three or four in the air. Where could Wilkins get a team that size, and how could he afford to pay their wages? The aircraft were also insatiable when it came to burning fuel. Anthony Fokker and his team designed great aeroplanes, but it sure cost a lot to run them. Friendship or not, Wilkins' two Fokkers had to go.

Then there were the Stinsons. One was somewhere out on an icefloe in the Arctic Ocean. And the other was not as suitable as Wilkins had at first thought.

He already knew which plane he wanted as a replacement — a revolutionary new aircraft that he'd first sighted in the skies over San Francisco, one balmy August day in 1927. In the twenty-first century, people rarely look twice as a plane flies overhead. But in the 1920s everyone, especially aviators like Wilkins, sat up and took notice.

He shook his head in disbelief at the graceful aeroplane he was seeing for the first time. He telephoned the obvious point of landing, San Francisco's Crissy Field, in an effort to discover the identity of the plane.

'It's out of this world,' he told the airfield manager. 'It has a single cantilevered wing. There are no struts. And it had to be flying at around 120 miles an hour.' The speed was quite incredible — close to 200 kilometres an hour.

'No way,' came the reply. 'No kite like that exists.'

Until then, most aircraft were cumbersome biplanes, with wires and struts to keep the wings parallel. Even the newer monoplanes were awkward and bulky. The aircraft that Wilkins saw was so different, with its sleek, streamlined fuselage, and fast ... so fast.

The answer was the same at each field Wilkins managed to telephone. But such a plane *did* exist — he'd seen it. Wilkins was determined to find it and that afternoon got a mate to drive him to every airfield in the San Francisco area.

They eventually found the mysterious aircraft at Oakland. It was the prototype of a new Lockheed plane; the manufacturers had called it the Vega, after the bright star in a galaxy some twenty-five light years from our own.

Wilkins couldn't believe his eyes. He turned to his friend and the superlatives poured from his mouth: 'It's like nothing I have ever seen before — not even in my wildest imagination. It makes the Fokkers and Stinsons we've flown look like the clumsy work of children. It is as if God has designed this plane for Ben and me …'

Maybe not God, but a 32-year-old American named Jack Northrop, an aircraft designer decades ahead of his time. His first effort came shortly after the war, and was the Loughead S-1 (later renamed Lockheed for ease of spelling by the two Loughead brothers, who owned the company). It had a surfeit of revolutionary features, such as folding wings, a moulded plywood fuselage, and wing flaps — the last being something universally accepted today, but unique back then. It was too expensive, however, and the money spent on its construction forced the brothers out of business. For a while at least.

Although Northrop was now working for another aircraft company, he had designed the Vega in his spare time. Allan Loughead reckoned it would be a winner and, snapping up the opportunity to get back in the action, agreed to build it at his small shop in Hollywood. The Vega prototype had only been completed the day before Wilkins saw it, and that flight around San Francisco Bay was its first.

It was at the Oakland airstrip to take part in a race known as the Dole Derby. James Dole, head of the famous Hawaiian pineapple company, had offered $35,000 for the winner of a race from California to Honolulu. Despite the fact that the 3800-kilometre ocean crossing had recently been completed by two US Army pilots, so denying the derby much of its prestige and any historical importance, interest in the race remained high. This, Wilkins had to see.

Newspaper magnate William Randolph Hearst had backed the Lockheed Vega. It was at his insistence that the plane be christened *Golden Eagle*, a name that, according to Hearst, had a patriotic ring to it.

Several of the entrants in the derby crashed before the day of the race, two of them with all on board killed. Hoot Gibson, the star of Hollywood western movies and a daredevil flyer in his own right, was one of the lucky ones: he survived, even if his Dole hopes didn't. But there were still eight entrants that lined up in the fog on the airstrip at Oakland on the morning of Tuesday, 16 August 1927. Some 90,000 excited spectators were on hand to cheer them away.

*Golden Eagle* was the favourite because of its sleek looks, which were enhanced by its metal fuselage. All but one of the others was made of cloth. The Vega had been given the aircraft licence number NX-913, a detail that led a reporter to ask one of its two-man crew, former World War I flyer Jack Frost from New York, whether he was superstitious. 'Hell, no,' replied the navigator. 'Why should I worry about one more thirteen in my life?' A grin spread over his face.

The sun burst through the fog at around 11 am, and fifty minutes later the starter flagged away the first plane, *Oklahoma*, which lumbered into the air and headed off to the west. The next two entrants never even made it off the ground.

Wilkins was on hand to watch the *Golden Eagle* take off. And he wasn't disappointed. It roared majestically into the air and raced off towards the ocean. The ease of its take-off compared with the struggle of its opposition — which variously spluttered off the runway and returned home soon after, or never made it away at all — confirmed in his mind that the Vega was the plane for his Arctic adventure.

Despite the obvious inferiority of the aircraft, it was *Woolaroc* that got to Hawaii first. Flown by wartime ace and movie stunt flyer Art Goebel and an army lieutenant by the name of William Davis Jr, the crossing had taken twenty-six hours and seventeen minutes. *Golden Eagle* and another plane, *Miss Doran* (named after its pilot, a 22-year-old teacher the press had dubbed 'the Flying Schoolmarm'), disappeared, never to be seen again.

The race was a publicity disaster, with ten lives lost either before, during or after the event. And for the fledgling Lockheed, the disappearance of *Golden Eagle* almost spelled the end. It was Hubert Wilkins who ultimately saved the company. Unconcerned about the Dole Derby tragedy, he told Loughead and Northrop he wanted the second Vega they were planning to build.

Next, the Australian passed on the good news to his Arctic partner. Ben Eielson was perturbed by the disappearance of the prototype over the Pacific, but Wilkins assured him by mail: 'Forget the Dole Derby. This *is* the plane for us. It is perfect for our needs.'

True to his character, Eielson's reply was brief and to the point: 'I'll leave it up to you. If you decide we should have the Lockheed Vega, I'll fly it.'

First, however, Wilkins had to unload one or both of the Fokkers to raise the money to buy the new machine. And, as luck would have it, he didn't have to look too far for a solution.

One morning there was a knock on his door at the Hotel St Francis in San Francisco, where he was staying. He opened it to find two well-tanned young men beaming smiles at him. It needed just one word from the more garrulous of the pair for Wilkins to recognise he was a fellow Australian.

'G'day!' the first stranger said. 'I'm Charles and this is Charles, too. We're looking for a plane and we reckon you've got the one we want. What d'you say we have a chat about it?' Charles Number Two nodded in silent agreement.

The pair were Charles Kingsford Smith and Charles Ulm.

Kingsford Smith was known for his devil-may-care attitude in the sky. It was this that had cost him a place in the 1919 London-to-Sydney air race, and it was the same attitude that saw him volunteer as an aerial stuntman for Hollywood movies. He almost lost his life in one effort, where he tried to hang upside down from the undercarriage of his aircraft. But he had passed up a possible chance to fly in the Dole Derby — even to the thrill-seeking Queenslander, the race was foolhardy.

'Smithy' explained that he needed the three-engine Fokker for an attempt to become the first to fly the Pacific. While Wilkins was eager to offload the *Detroiter*, he couldn't do so unless there was sufficient funds coming his way. His Arctic expedition was a self-financed effort now, after all.

New South Wales Labor premier Jack Lang had previously offered Kingsford Smith up to £3500 in financial backing, but Lang had just lost an election and his mind was elsewhere as he geared up for another joust for state leadership. Before long, Sidney Myer stepped in to help. The Belarus-born Australian department store owner and philanthropist lived for much of each year in San Francisco since remarrying and had heard about the aviator's financial needs.

Kingsford Smith bought the plane, which he renamed *Southern Cross*. History shows how he, Ulm and Americans Harry Lyon and Jim Warner achieved fame in 1928 by flying it from Oakland to Honolulu, on to Suva in Fiji (setting a new world record for long-distance flying of 5025 kilometres) and thence to Brisbane, in a time of eighty-three hours.

Wilkins regularly dined out on their success. 'It wasn't the right plane for me in the Arctic,' he would explain to Hollywood celebrities and American scientists at dinner parties. 'I thought it was jinxed. But it certainly did the trick for Smithy and his mates. It became one of the immortals of world aviation history.'

Later in life, though, Wilkins found it ironic that this aircraft was more famous in the land of his birth than he was, even though his exploits were as groundbreaking and, arguably, more dangerous than those of Kingsford Smith's flight across the Pacific.

EIELSON WAS FACED with further doubts when he first set eyes on the new Vega.

Lockheed had rushed ahead with the construction of two planes that were ready for testing in early 1928. A test pilot took up the one purchased by Wilkins, gave it a thorough workout and landed with no problems. Wilkins did not have time to discuss its performance, however, because he had to meet Eielson at the train station. By the time the pair returned to Oakland, the second Vega was being put through its Department of Commerce licence testing by another pilot. Wilkins and Eielson watched as the flyer made a landing that was far too fast: the impact with the runway smashed the landing gear and the plane spun almost uncontrollably off the runway.

The pilot was unhurt, but unimpressed, leaping out of the cockpit and shouting his harsh, uncompromising critique of the Vega at the gathered Lockheed staff and government officials. Wilkins shook his head in disbelief. Eielson was noncommittal.

'I think I'll try out our plane and find out for myself,' the quiet American said after a while.

Eielson took it up for about an hour, putting the aircraft through a series of complicated moves. As he came in to land, he was blinded by the late afternoon sun and almost hit some powerlines, but was able to avoid them at the last second. Such was the manoeuvrability of the Vega.

More test flights were made over the next fortnight — including one in which the engine cut out because of an airlock in the fuel lines. Eielson was able to make a successful crash landing with only minor damage to the undercarriage. He and Wilkins made a minor adjustment to the engine design, to prevent any further airlocks, and the landing gear was strengthened.

As spring came on and the time to leave for Alaska approached, Eielson was taking the Vega up twenty or thirty times a day, getting to the stage where he almost became part of the aircraft, aware of every single nuance in the way it performed. If anyone watching from below needed an explanation of the American flyer's 'Brother to the Eagle' moniker, here it was. And soon the whole world would acknowledge his skill.

# Chapter 11

# Across the Top of the World

NOT FOR THE first time in his life, people questioned Hubert Wilkins' sanity. Although a bare minimum of fanfare accompanied his preparations compared with the frenzied coverage of the previous two years, whenever he did talk about his plans for April 1928 — to fly the Lockheed Vega from Point Barrow to Spitsbergen — the experts shook their heads in disbelief.

Spitsbergen is the largest landmass in the Svalbard archipelago, in the Arctic Ocean. The Norwegian island covers about 40,000 square kilometres, making it a large target for the explorers. They would not be plotting a course directly over the North Pole from Barrow, of course, because the varying magnetic fields would cause too many problems with their navigation. As it was, even by travelling to the south, they couldn't fly in a direct line. They would have to make up to twenty-five or more changes in course during the stressful flight.

But it was the ice and snow over which Wilkins and Eielson would fly that worried polar explorers and aviators alike. Roald Amundsen put it bluntly: 'Hubert, what you are trying to do is beyond the possibility of human endeavour.' Others were angry, believing that if Wilkins perished, they would find it so much harder to get sponsorship for their own Arctic exploration.

From Wilkins' point of view, the major problem concerned navigation. To plot their course by compass, the Australian would have to make adjustments about once every hour. A mistake of just 1 degree would see the aircraft missing Spitsbergen completely. Although he'd have use of the radio to systematically check his navigation and keep in touch with members of the crew in Point Barrow and Spitsbergen, he and Eielson would be flying over the Arctic Ocean — there was no land to verify his calculations.

The two aviators and their aircraft arrived in Fairbanks on 26 February. After a fortnight of test flights around the area, they were ready to head for Point Barrow. They had painted the plane bright orange and replaced its wheels with broad skis. Wilkins reckoned the colour added to the Vega's personality, not to mention ensuring that it would stand out if they needed to be rescued. He'd also had engineers build two windows into the floor to assist him both in mapping the geography of the region below and in the difficult task of navigating during the journey. In addition, the Australian planned to use the 40-by-40-centimetre panes to take photographs that could then be sold to newspapers (including, hopefully, the *New York Times*) and magazines.

The pair flew to Point Barrow on 19 March. Dog sleds pulled the plane to thick ice on the settlement's lagoon and every Eskimo in the area was employed to help clear a runway 2 kilometres long and 5 metres wide. Twice they had to start again after snowfalls undid all their good work.

And three times the Vega failed to make it off the ground because it was too heavy. On one occasion, the tail hit the pile of snow at the end of the runway, spun the aircraft around 180 degrees, and sent it careering into a huge snowdrift.

'Hell, that was close,' said Wilkins, picking himself up off the floor of the cockpit.

Hubert Wilkins and Carl Ben Eielsen with the Lockheed Vega they flew across the Arctic.

After each failed attempt, he and Eielson jettisoned more and more provisions until they were down to the bare essentials, including a couple of rifles. If they were forced down, they might need the firearms to kill animals for food.

Wilkins had planned the take-off for the first two weeks of April because weather reports of the previous decade had shown them to be the most suitable. But thanks to the various setbacks, the window of opportunity was swiftly disappearing. Eventually the historic flight got under way at 10.15 am on Sunday, 15 April 1928. It was touch and go, though, because the Eskimos refused to work on a Sunday and the snow was blowing onto the runway. Finally, the bright orange Vega, bearing its identification number X3903, thundered down the icy runway and struggled off the ground, snow swirling angrily around it. Wilkins was sure they were going to crash into the bank of snow at the end of the runway, but he had one of the great flyers in history at the controls.

'He pulled the joystick back and she lifted smoothly into the air and away from Point Barrow,' he was to recall of Eielson's successful take-off. 'This time we were really on our way over the top of the globe. We were about to wing our way where no man had flown before. The feeling of exhilaration was overwhelming.'

Now came the hard part. The two men's lives depended on Wilkins making the right calculations every fifty minutes or so. He had to concentrate on the charts at his disposal — not certain by any means in those early days of aviation. He had to take readings with a sextant, hoping that the sun (and later on, the stars) was visible. Then there was the wind; its strength and direction had to be taken into consideration at all times.

Wilkins would also watch through the customised floor of the plane. He was looking for proof or otherwise of the existence of islands or undiscovered land in the Arctic Ocean. As it turned out, he proved there wasn't. Among the equipment that had been discarded to lessen the weight of the aircraft was a heater. He wasn't too concerned about this loss, as the Vega was a great plane — so airtight that the temperature never dropped below zero degrees Celsius inside, even though at times it would be a numbing minus 25 outside.

Some 1100 kilometres into the flight, the aircraft encountered swirling dark clouds, so dense that visibility was nonexistent. Eielson tried to get down under them, but to no avail. He tried to climb above, and also failed. For more than 200 kilometres he flew blind, trusting in Wilkins' navigation. Then suddenly, they were out in clear skies again.

For another 1000-plus kilometres they flew over more icy ocean before encountering yet another storm. But Wilkins was able to make out a mountain peak on Grant Land, just after the halfway point in the epic journey, and he could therefore confirm that his navigation was spot on. Then it was on towards Greenland, flying through a heavy snowstorm, unable to see anything outside.

After a few more hours of flying, there was clear weather again — although now the pair sighted a massive blizzard ahead. They were tired, the natural effects of such intense concentration over a long period of time. But after travelling almost 4000 kilometres, they were so close to their target. Less than 200 kilometres to go.

'Do you want to land on the icefloe, have a rest and sit it out?' Wilkins shouted to his pilot. But the noise of the engine was too loud for him to hear.

So the Australian hastily scribbled a note and passed it over to Eielson: *We can land and wait till it's over or continue on and face the storm at Spitsbergen.*

Eielson gave a reassuring smile. Although Eielson knew it would be blind flying again, he also realised that if they went down, they may never be able to take off. And he didn't fancy another trek across the Arctic wastes of maybe 300 kilometres to find a settlement.

On they flew. Fingers weren't crossed; both men were convinced they would reach their destination. Each put his life in the hands of the other and was happy with that decision.

They tried to circle the storm by turning north, and got to within 500 kilometres of the North Pole while doing so, before turning south again. The snowstorm had engulfed Spitsbergen, however, and there was no alternative but to take it head on. Wilkins' knowledge of weather and cloud formations was of utmost importance here, particularly since the radio, which he'd been using extensively throughout the flight, had just given up the ghost. Although he hadn't been able to acquire a detailed map of the area, he had studied basic ones of the island, and was thus able to direct Eielson to its western side. Even so, Wilkins couldn't be sure where the main settlements of Green Harbour and King's Bay were, and he and Eielson could see no more than 100 metres in front of the plane.

'We'll take a chance, Ben,' he shouted. 'Let's get down under the clouds and fly low above the ocean until we can find somewhere to land.' Eielson gave him the thumbs up and put the Vega into a low descent.

Suddenly he shouted: 'Oh, hell! We're too low.'

They were heading straight into the ocean. Eielson pulled out of the dive just centimetres above the water, the waves drenching the plane, covering it with an icy sheen.

It was impossible to see through the cockpit window now, so Wilkins opened it, stuck his head out into the numbing cold, and directed Eielson using hand signals. Through the gloom, the Australian could see what looked like a solid runway of ice ahead and signalled to his pilot accordingly.

Eielson eased the Vega down, hoping for the best. Miraculously, he found a patch of smooth snow. Wilkins later described the moment: 'She settled down like a tired bird onto the soft snowy surface, and the wind was blowing so terrifically that we hardly travelled 30 feet [9 metres] after the skis touched the snow. We must have sat there for some time, breathing heavily in our relief to be once more on Terra Firma. We looked at each other and smiled our satisfaction.'

Ironically, they had landed in a place known to locals as Dead Man's Island. But they were alive and kicking, after a flight that had taken them twenty hours and twenty minutes across the top of the world.

Of course, it wasn't over yet. They hadn't even reached a populated settlement. And, with a blizzard raging around the aircraft, they wouldn't do so for almost a week. Nor could they contact anyone, with the radio having packed up — a situation that prompted the pair's supporters to fear the worst. There was nothing the two men could do but to curl up in their sleeping bags and wait for the storm to blow over.

On 21 April, a Saturday, the clouds cleared. The pair crawled out of the Vega and began the long task of clearing the snowdrifts that had engulfed the aircraft. The wind had been kind in blowing the snow away from the ice in front of the plane. But Wilkins had to push the plane to get it started while Eielson manned the controls, and twice in doing so was left behind on the ground.

'Fair go, mate!' he laughed when Eielson returned. 'I know the plane's a lot lighter without me, but I don't fancy staying behind in this God-forsaken hole.'

Eventually, Wilkins used a piece of driftwood while sitting in the open door of the cockpit — as he put it, 'rather like a Venetian gondolier uses his pole' — and they were both airborne.

Almost immediately they sighted the masts of a wireless station and recognised Green Harbour. In their roundabout flight, they had covered some 4200 kilometres across unforgiving ocean and terrain.

NEWS OF THE duo's feat was soon flashed across the globe by wireless, after which the messages of congratulation poured in. But it would be a while before the two heroes were to make it out of Green Harbour. There was no aircraft gasoline at the settlement, so the aviators had to wait for almost three weeks until an icebreaking steamer, the SS *Hobby*, was able to get close enough to take the orange Vega on board. Once again they had to dig the plane out of the snow, after which they flew it the 35 kilometres to the *Hobby*, where, on 10 May, it was manhandled onto the deck. There was just a cupful of gas left in the aircraft's tank.

The *Hobby* had to force her way through more than 200 kilometres of pack-ice before reaching open sea and heading for the port of

Tromso, in northern Norway, where she docked in the early hours of Tuesday, 15 May. Next they headed south to Bergen, where they hurried out to buy dinner suits and spruce up for an official celebration being thrown by King Haakon VII.

A few days later, there was an official parade through the streets of the capital, Oslo, finishing at the home of Roald Amundsen. The conqueror of the South Pole apologised for daring to doubt the pair's dream and described their effort as the greatest by anyone in the history of aviation. Amundsen also arranged for a special cake to be baked, decorated with a map of the Arctic and the course taken by the aviators in their historic flight. It was to be his last public appearance. Within a month Amundsen would be dead, at the age of fifty-two. Despite the animosity between the pair, he had leased a Latham 47 seaplane to go and search for his old colleague Umberto Nobile, who had crashed the *Italia*, the sister dirigible of the *Norge*, on the way back from a trip to the North Pole. Amundsen, four French crewmen and a fellow Norwegian disappeared over the Berent Sea on 18 June. None of the men were ever found.

Wilkins and Eielson's celebrations did not end in Norway but continued across Europe. Germany's Luftwaffe scrambled two squadrons of Messerschmitt fighter aircraft to provide an escort for the passenger plane that took them from Oslo to Berlin. Wilkins looked out the window and shook his head, before turning to Eielson and noting: 'The last time I had anything to do with the Luftwaffe, they were shooting at me as I dangled from an observation balloon over the trenches in France. How time changes everything.'

At Flughafen Tempelhof, the aerodrome in the German capital, they were welcomed by, among others, a much-decorated fighter pilot, member of the Red Baron's squadron and close friend of Adolf Hitler — a man by the name of Hermann Goering. That very week Goering had been elected to the Reichstag as one of twelve new

Nazi Party members. A few years later he was to become commander-in-chief of the Luftwaffe and one of the architects of Germany's journey into World War II. Goering took it upon himself to host a series of parties in Berlin feting the two Arctic heroes and basking in the associated kudos.

It was then on to Paris, where Wilkins heard he had been awarded a knighthood in the King's Birthday Honours list. On 4 June, he received the telegram asking if he would accept the tribute. Remembering the pride that John Monash had shown when Wilkins photographed him receiving his knighthood from King George V while serving on the Western Front a decade earlier, the Australian had no hesitation in sending the reply-paid telegram of acceptance. Ten days later, Wilkins would be at Buckingham Palace in London, where the same monarch would touch him on the shoulder with his sword, to symbolise the ultimate royal honour.

Before leaving Paris, though, he and Eielson endured another round of high-profile engagements. Among the lavish parties was one thrown by the US ambassador, Myron Herrick. A year before, he had hosted a similar soirée for Charles Lindbergh, after the latter's historic solo flight across the Atlantic; indeed, such was Herrick's enthusiasm for aviation that he would later write the foreword to Lindbergh's book, *We*.

It was a star-studded guest list, including President Gaston Doumergue of France and countless French military officers. One officer approached the two Arctic heroes, but was interested only in the North American. 'Monsieur Eielson,' the Frenchman began, 'permit me to introduce my wife. She wishes to give you a kiss.' And she did so.

Once the couple had excused themselves, Wilkins turned to his comrade and said, 'Why was I not so lucky?' But he was to be lucky in love much sooner than he could ever have imagined.

THE VICTORIAN TOWN of Walhalla lies in the Great Dividing Range about 180 kilometres east of Melbourne. In the late nineteenth century it was a thriving settlement, with a population of around 5000; there were ten licensed hotels, several dance halls, three breweries and seven churches. There were also three suburbs, including one with the wonderful name of Happy Go Lucky, built on the steep mountain slopes that surrounded Walhalla. Most of the residents were miners drawn to the area by one of the richest goldfields in Australian history.

The Long Tunnel Company, which owned the biggest mine in the area, introduced electricity into the excavation in 1884 and a telephone into the mine seven years later. There were also two electric streetlights outside the mine, erected just five years after the first such innovation in the world. But it was not through any feelings of civic duty that the company decided to erect the lights. It was to deter the locals from, under the cover of darkness, stealing the wood that was needed to feed the furnaces which generated the power. Ironically, despite being among the leaders of the world in the 1880s, Walhalla was the last town in Victoria to be linked to the state's electricity grid. Only in 1998 did the twentieth century finally catch up with the twenty-odd remaining residents of the hamlet.

It was at Walhalla that Suzanne Evans was born, in 1901, at a time when the township was starting to disintegrate. As the gold seam started to run dry, more and more miners departed. And as the population dwindled, so too did the number of pubs, shops and churches.

Suzanne showed exceptional musical talents as a child. By the time the teenager left to study at Melbourne's Conservatorium of Music, Walhalla was well into its decline to a virtual ghost town. But Suzanne was to cherish the memories of her childhood in Walhalla for decades to come. She also enjoyed her time at the Conservatorium.

Later in life she told friends of the excitement of meeting the famed Australian diva Dame Nellie Melba, who gave some inspirational advice to the student when she made a visit to the Conservatorium. 'Dame Nellie encouraged me to head for Europe to advance my singing career,' Suzanne remembered.

Having adopted the stage name Suzanne Bennett, the stunning brunette with a prominent beauty spot on her left cheek left Australia in early 1924 but never made it to Europe. During a stopover in New York, she was offered a part in a Broadway musical; she accepted, and fate took over. Four years later, she was still in the Big Apple, which is how she came to be part of the Hubert Wilkins story in July 1928.

A few days before the Norwegian American Line's SS *Stavangerfjord* was due to berth in New York, with Wilkins and Eielson on board, officials at the Australian Consulate contacted Suzanne. At the time, the 27-year-old beauty was starring in the Broadway show *The Cyclone Lover*, co-written by later Hollywood star Charles Bickford. It was her seventh show since making her New York debut in May 1924 in the musical revue *Innocent Eyes*. There had since been a couple of box-office flops, none more pronounced than *Nic Nax of 1926*, which lasted only for thirteen performances. *The Cyclone Lover* was not much better, eventually closing after just a month and thirty-one shows. It was performed at the Frolic Theatre, a venue made famous by director Florenz Ziegfeld and his long-running 'Folies' revues.

The Australian authorities wanted Suzanne to join their consul on a tugboat that would go out and rendezvous with the *Stavangerfjord* as it sailed into New York Harbor.

'But why would anyone want me to meet these two men?' she wondered aloud.

The official looked at her in amazement. Didn't she read the front pages of the *New York Times*, which had carried several stories about the pair of celebrated explorers? 'We thought it would be nice if Wilkins was welcomed here by a fellow Australian,' replied the bureaucrat. It would just be a couple of single Aussies having a chat and getting photographed together, he added. Harmless fun, and good PR.

Suzanne agreed. On the morning in question, she arose after just a couple of hours' sleep following her stage show, to rush to The Battery, the area described as 'the Cradle of New York' because it was where the first Dutch settlers arrived in 1623. There she boarded the tug *Malcolm* for the trip past the Statue of Liberty and out to greet the ship carrying the Australian explorer and his pilot. She was surprised by what she thought was the rudeness of Wilkins. Twelve years her senior, he smiled at her as she presented him with a bouquet of flowers, but then turned away to talk to the Australian consul.

One of the group mentioned to Wilkins that Miss Bennett was an Australian, too.

'Yes,' came the cold reply. 'I meet them all around the world.'

Suzanne must have wondered how this man with the curt disposition could have attracted such attention. After all, he was hardly good-looking. He was prematurely balding with dark, brooding eyes and, without the beard that he'd grow during his trips of exploration, his jutting jaw stood out like a beacon. One arm was crooked, the result of an injury suffered in the Arctic, and he shuffled rather than walked, thanks to the problems with his feet and ankles that had the AIF medico in London ruling him unfit for military service. But Suzanne would have had to admit there was a certain, inexplicable charisma about the man.

A press boat took them ashore, but they had to bide their time before landing as news came through that the mayor was running late for the planned welcome at City Hall. So the boat circled the Hudson River to while away the time. A photographer tried to catch the pair in an animated pose. Wilkins was uncomfortable about this intrusion until he heard the photographer's accent: he was another Aussie. The three of them laughed and talked about their times back in Australia. As Suzanne recounted: 'The ice had been broken. I realised Hubert wasn't rude or even just aloof. He was shy. Here was this hero who was uneasy with his fame.'

After the official ceremony, where Mayor Walker handed Wilkins and Eielson the Keys to New York City, it was off to the famous Waldorf-Astoria Hotel, on the site of what is now the Empire State Building, for a reception. Suzanne needed some sleep before that night's performance, so she excused herself before the lunch. Wilkins told her he would have liked to dine with her that evening, but plans had already been made to entertain him. He asked for her telephone number so they could keep in touch.

'Why don't you ring me at midnight,' she said, without thinking how such a suggestion might sound.

'I will,' was his reply.

And at the stroke of midnight, the phone rang. She had known it would. After the show, she had rushed back to her apartment and changed into clothes that one would wear on a late-evening date. She even bought an orchid to wear on her dress. In the meantime, the Australian officials had filled Wilkins in on Suzanne's background.

As she later described it: 'On the stroke of twelve, the Australian explorer called on the Australian actress. My famous compatriot whisked me away to the St Regis [Hotel, in Manhattan]. There we did what the song said — danced 'til three in the morning. He was a good dancer, too. I mentioned it, which pleased him.' Hubert Wilkins may have dragged his feet when walking, but it was a different story on the dance floor.

Wilkins then headed off with Eielson for a two-month lecture tour of the United States. When he returned, Suzanne had started in another forgettable Broadway production, *Guns*. And he went to see her on stage for the first time. After the show he invited her to supper, where, at only their third meeting, Wilkins asked her to marry him.

'Yes, yes, yes,' she said. It was a genuine case of love at first sight and a union that would only be broken by his death many, many years later.

# Chapter 12

# Lessons in Geography

.

SUZANNE BENNETT IMMEDIATELY knew their relationship would be like no other. Within two days of her accepting his proposal of marriage in September 1928, Wilkins was off on his next adventure. Although, he didn't actually call any of his exploits 'adventures', it should be noted. 'Adventures are generally the outcome of ignorance or incompetence,' he once observed. 'An adventure often means a task not done, a condition unforeseen. Provided you know of other people's adventures, adventures may be avoided.'

Suzanne had wanted him to stay longer and for both of them to learn more about each other before he left for Montevideo. But, as she would realise over the next three decades, her explorer was of a restless disposition. The fact that he would head off to remote parts of the world for long periods didn't mean that he loved her any less. And there was no way she would ever have been able to keep pace with him.

'But I followed his movements on the map,' she pointed out. 'And I had mail from all over the world. All of this meant quite a geography lesson — from an expert geographer. So it was for 30 years. Hello. Goodbye. Hello again. Goodbye again. But before the final goodbye there were so many happy times.'

LIFE FOR SIR Hubert Wilkins was happy in more ways than one following his success in the Arctic. Professionally, he was at the top of his game and receiving an avalanche of plaudits from all over the globe. Wilkins would be at pains to correct the general perception that he had received his knighthood for that one highly publicised flight from Point Barrow to Spitsbergen. 'Actually I was knighted for my work in both science and exploration over the previous fifteen years,' he said. That distinction was clearly important to the Australian. Within a week of his knighthood in June, he was given the highest award possible from seventeen different scientific bodies around the world, including the Royal Geographical Society of London and the American Geographical Society. And within less than a year, different publishers rushed out two books he had written about his explorations, *Flying the Arctic* and *Undiscovered Australia*.

Media magnate William Randolph Hearst backed several of Wilkins' adventures.

The historic flight across the roof of the world had also attracted welcome attention from potential sponsors, notably the media tycoon William Randolph Hearst. In early July, with the Arctic heroes fresh off the ship from Europe, Hearst had immediately sent the managing editor of his chain of newspapers, T.V. Ranck, to Wilkins with an offer: a staggering $40,000 for exclusive rights to stories from Wilkins' upcoming expedition to Antarctica. There was a bonus of $10,000 if the Australian made it to the South Pole.

To Wilkins this was manna from heaven. He had already been turned down by the Australian Federal Government of Stanley Bruce, despite support from his home country's political liaison officer in London, Richard Casey, a future government minister and governor-general. Casey, who like Wilkins won a Military Cross during the Great War, had met the explorer when their paths had crossed in France. There were suggestions that the government's rejection of Wilkins' request for funding was made on the recommendation of polar explorer Sir Douglas Mawson, a fierce critic of the South Australian.

So Wilkins got his financial backing from Hearst — even more than he had asked from his own people. He was unconcerned about the bonus offer; all he wanted to do was make flights of exploration over the frozen continent. And he was unfazed by the penchant of Hearst's headline writers to portray his venture as a race to the pole between him and US Navy admiral Richard Byrd. With another pilot, Floyd Bennett, Byrd had claimed to have been the first to fly over the North Pole, on 9 May 1926, but today there is extreme doubt about this claim because of his inability to provide credible navigational proof. Indeed, it has even been suggested that the pair, once out of sight of their home base in Norway, had merely circled for almost sixteen hours before returning to triumph. Back in 1928, though, Byrd still basked in the glory of his supposed feat, and Bennett's death early in the year ensured that the navy flyer had the

## Was Mawson jealous?

The relationship between Hubert Wilkins and Australia's most celebrated Antarctic explorer, Douglas Mawson, could at best be described as frosty. Mawson was disdainful of Wilkins' lack of a university degree. He saw him as no more than an enthusiastic amateur with absolutely no academic clout to give credence to his ideas. And, truth be known, there was probably more than a whiff of jealousy.

One can only wonder whether the paths of the two men ever crossed before Wilkins made an international name for himself. Back in 1905, when Wilkins was attending the University of Adelaide, Mawson was a lecturer in geology at the same academic establishment while studying for his doctorate. Mawson was already eyeing the great white continent to the south and was to go on to reach the South Magnetic Pole as a member of Shackleton's triumphant British Antarctic Expedition of 1907–09 before leading two expeditions of his own, in 1911–14 and 1929–31.

The two Australians met in London in June 1928 when Wilkins was in town for his appointment at Buckingham Palace. Wilkins was still pushing his idea that there should be meteorological stations across the Arctic and Antarctic to help forecast the world's weather, and he wanted Mawson to be the first leader of what he had dubbed the International Weather Monitoring Service. The older man dismissed the idea out of hand, describing Wilkins' plans as crazy. 'Wilkins knows nothing about science,' he sneered.

Had he read some of Wilkins' reports, he would have soon realised how wrong he was. But Mawson continued to deride the gifted 'amateur' until his death in October 1958. Yes, the international community of explorers and pioneers were a tight bunch as a rule, but it seems that petty rivalries exist in the most enlightened of worlds.

sole word on the subject when it came to first-hand accounts. Now Byrd was determined to complete the set and be the first to fly over the South Pole. With a seemingly limitless budget, he had prepared a massive assault team of fifty men, a ship, three aircraft and a hundred dogs.

But his preparations were well behind those of Wilkins. The Australian had gathered together a small team of five other men, including trusted pilots Ben Eielson and Joe Crosson, a wireless operator and a couple of mechanics. He had two Lockheed Vega aircraft: the one used to cross the Arctic, now named the *Los Angeles*, and a second they had named *San Francisco*. Each plane honoured cities where the Hearst media empire had begun. Learning from the mistakes of Shackleton, Wilkins had already deposited the wages of each team-member in their respective bank accounts.

They sailed out of New York on the SS *Southern Cross*, bound for Montevideo, on 22 September 1928. Soon after leaving, Wilkins was summoned to the radio room. 'We have a surprise for you,' the wireless operator grinned. Suddenly the short-wave radio receiver crackled and he heard the voice of his new fiancée. She was singing a love song for him. Wilkins was lost for words.

Ship radio rooms would see the expedition leader running the full gamut of emotions on this trip. Later on during the long journey south, Wilkins would receive word that his mother had passed away not long after he and the team had left New York. Well into her eighties, Louisa Wilkins had only seen her youngest boy a handful of times perhaps since he'd first left Australian shores in 1911. But George Hubert was a dutiful son and regularly wrote letters home before and after embarking on his ventures — even if he tended to brush over the more life-threatening aspects. No doubt he would have loved for her to have met Suzanne, this vivacious young woman who had captured his heart in a matter of days. Still, he could console himself that at least Louisa had lived to see him become a knight of the realm and conquer the Arctic.

In the Uruguayan capital, Wilkins and his men joined the 14,000-tonne SS *Hektoria*, a former White Star liner (SS *Medic*), which the previous year had been bought by Norwegian whaling magnate Nil Bugge and converted into a whaling factory ship. Some of the first-class cabins had been kept in their original opulence — so the Wilkins team would have a pleasant voyage to Deception Island and a comfortable stay through the southern summer.

'What a difference from the tough life we experienced in the Arctic, eh?' Wilkins remarked to Eielson. 'Let's enjoy it while it lasts.'

Their cabins would be a welcome sight at the end of each day during the planned five months of exploring the polar wilderness from the air. A stark contrast to the wet, cold nights at Paradise Harbour in 1920–21. Wilkins had learned well from the Cope expedition. He also liked the history of the ship: on the return leg of her maiden voyage to Australia in 1899, the *Medic* had transported Australian troops and horses to South Africa for service in the Boer War.

It was a tough journey south, calling in at the Falkland Islands on the way. The men stayed just long enough on the British colony to celebrate their leader's fortieth birthday, on 31 October, before continuing through the harsh South Atlantic waters. The *Hektoria* then encountered thick pack-ice around 300 nautical miles north of their destination. But this was a solid ship, unlike the poor old *Quest*. She forced her way through the barrier of ice, the five tiny whalers that escorted the expedition flagship following like ducklings in pursuit of their mother.

Eventually the forbidding, towering peaks of Deception Island loomed large on the southern horizon. The *Hektoria* steamed into the caldera of the dormant volcano and Wilkins whispered a prayer of thanks. But he knew that, despite the perils that lay ahead, this trip had been well planned and he'd left as little as possible to chance. Which was just as well, because immediately upon arrival he had to rethink his plans.

When he was there with John Cope, there had been a solid ice coverage of the bay, some 2 metres thick and secure enough to enable an aircraft to take off and land (had Cope managed to acquire one). But this summer was warmer and the layer of ice was less than a metre thick. Although Wilkins had brought pontoons in case they had to convert the two aircraft to seaplanes, he hadn't counted on the whole area being populated by albatross-type birds. Obviously they had never seen an aircraft before, and when Eielson made an attempt to take off, the birds decided to fly in formation with the *Los Angeles* and were sucked into the propeller, almost causing a crash.

They had no choice but to clear a runway on the land. Each member of the team worked with picks, shovels and wheelbarrows on the only flat area on the island, removing rocks and stones and smoothing over the jagged terrain as best they could. On the morning of 22 November, they decided the runway was smooth enough to use and Eielson took up the *Los Angeles* for a brief reconnoitre of the island from the air. The following day, Crosson made a similar flight in the *San Francisco*. Now they had their runway, but there was one problem: it was too short to allow a safe take-off with a full load of gasoline.

Wilkins was still hoping that the unusually warm weather would break, that a cold change would ensure the ice in the caldera would be thick enough to provide a secure runway. Sure enough, there was a cold snap and Wilkins found an area that would safely take the weight of his aircraft. Both the Vegas took to the air without incident and flew out through the mouth of the harbour. But when Eielson tried to land, he found the ice was so slippery that he careered onto thin ice. The wheels broke through the surface, the *Los Angeles* tilted on its nose and the engine disappeared under water, with the plane left balancing precariously on the edge of the hole. Eielson climbed cautiously to safety. Meanwhile, Crosson had seen what happened and didn't risk landing the *San Francisco* on the ice, but headed for the runway instead.

The ship's crew were joined by a band of eighteen whalers, who ventured out onto the ice hoping to pull the stricken Vega back out of harm's way. With each passing minute, the plane was sinking further into the water, and the men spared no effort as they toiled against the clock — several of them falling through the ice and having to be rescued. Eventually the whalers were able to attach ropes to the tail and ease several planks under the wheels. Slowly, ever so slowly, the *Los Angeles* was pulled from its would-be grave.

The whole episode had taken eighteen hours of nonstop heavy labour. But the aircraft, the third hero of the Point Barrow–Spitsbergen triumph, had been saved. Now the mechanics got to work; they had to fix the damage the salt water had done to the engine.

Wilkins then borrowed one of the whalers' small boats to check out the nearby islands, to search for a possible flat area on which to build a long runway. But it was all to no avail. They would have to improvise by extending the existing runway over two hills. It was not perfect, but beggars can't be choosers — and nor could Hearst-bankrolled knights of the realm. The crew and some of the whalers worked for almost two days straight clearing the extra area. Once finished, it was decided not to wait any longer. History beckoned.

On the morning of Thursday, 20 December 1928, Eielson and Wilkins made their mad dash down the improvised runway. Up over one hill, down the slope on the other side, veering up a second hill, followed by a flat-out race down towards the harbour. Eielson managed to get the *Los Angeles* into the air with only a few metres to spare before the shore.

Eielson didn't even bother to circle the base, instead heading due south. On board was enough gas to make a flight of some 2300 kilometres, cruising at 200 kilometres an hour. There was an air of excitement. Of course there was: they were off to become the first men to fly over the Antarctic continent. If anything went wrong, they had enough rations to last them two months — and an 800-kilometre trek. They also had a high-powered, short-wave radio transmitter, built by the San Francisco firm of Heintz and Kaufman, which could be used for long-distance communications as well as a radio beacon. When a message wasn't being sent, Wilkins would clamp down the Morse code key and the wireless operator on Deception Island could know the exact course of the aircraft. The company had made a special aluminium carry-case to house the device, with the result that the transmitter weighed a total of just 20 kilograms. Charles Kingsford Smith had used an identical transmitter when he'd made his epic flight across the Pacific in Wilkins' old Fokker seven months earlier.

The pair first flew over Bransfield Strait, then around the tiny Trinity Island, with the highest of its three mountains rising to about 1800 metres, before heading to Graham Land, where eight years before Wilkins had diced with death on the ice-cliffs. It was a return visit he was overjoyed to be making:

*This time, I had a tremendous sensation of power and freedom —*
*I felt liberated — when we were approaching Graham Land by air.*
*The contrast was most striking between the speed and ease of flying in*
*by plane and the slow, blind struggles of our work along the coast a*
*few years before. It had taken us three months on foot to map 40 miles*
*[64 kilometres]. Now we were covering 40 miles in 20 minutes, and*

*I had scarce time to sketch the principal terrain and shoreline features in my notebook before the scene had entirely changed and I was drawing a crude map of the next section of this area. No one had climbed to the Graham Land plateau summit, and I was thrilled to realise that for the first time, human eyes — our eyes — were going to see it.*

It had generally been assumed that the summit was 2000 metres or so above sea level. But the Vega had been cruising at that height and had to climb to around 2700 metres to clear it.

They continued on, flying south along the eastern coast of the Weddell Sea. There were no charts for this area and no human had ever seen it before that day. As landmarks emerged, Wilkins sketched them and used the sun to plot their position. They eventually turned west to follow the coastline. They soon discovered what they thought was a channel that appeared to prove Graham Land was not a peninsula at all, but an island. Wilkins named the body of water Stefansson Strait, after his Arctic mentor. It was to be years before Wilkins realised he had made a mistake: 'Stefansson Strait' was, in fact, just a couple of deep fjords.

They flew over island after island — at least, as with the strait error, what appeared to be islands — before reaching what was truly the Antarctic continent. He named the vast plateau that loomed before them Hearst Land.

By then, they had used up half of their fuel and an angry storm was developing. Before heading for home, Wilkins opened a hatch in the floor of the Vega and dropped a Union Jack flag and a note claiming this newly discovered land on the frozen continent for Great Britain. He had been asked to do so by the governor of the Falkland Islands. With insufficient fuel to attempt to go around the storm, they headed straight into it and endured a rocky ride on the way home.

Then, just ten hours after taking off, they were back above Deception Island. There was a tiny break in the storm clouds, through which Eielson spied the harbour. He guided the aircraft into the gap, spiralling down through extreme turbulence that threatened to tear the plane apart. The runway was shrouded in fog, but it held no fear for the Brother to the Eagle. He headed straight into the murky gloom and brought the *Los Angeles* to a bumpy halt.

Their progress had been remarkable, as Wilkins was to muse: 'We had left at 8.30 that morning, had covered 1300 miles [2080 kilometres] — nearly 1000 miles of it over unknown territory — and had returned in time to cover the plane with its storm hood, go to the *Hektoria*, bathe and dress, and sit down to our eight o'clock dinner as usual.'

He also suggested that Lady Luck might have been flying with them that day. For, within an hour of them landing, the storm was so violent that they would have been unable to land. And the hurricane-force winds continued for another three days.

Two days before the new year, Wilkins and Eielson made a second flight south, looking for a suitable site to establish a base in which to make further explorations of Antarctica. But none was revealed. Wilkins decided they had done as much as they could have hoped for, and radioed the Falkland Islands to charter a boat from the Royal Mail Steam Packet Company (forerunner to the Cunard Line) to collect them from Deception Island. They would be back for more when the summer months returned, late in 1929.

FOR THE SECOND time in eight months, the press and general public alike were marvelling at the exploits of Wilkins and his mercurial pilot, Ben Eielson. Hearst's reporters wasted no time, and spared no sensationalism, when passing on news of the latest triumph once Wilkins' report had been sent as usual from the *Hektoria*. But acclaim came also from unexpected quarters. Although committed to supporting Richard Byrd as a sponsor, the *New York Times* was lavish in its praise of the Australian's efforts. 'Captain Wilkins has done what few men of his generation have been permitted to do,' an editorial ran in late January 1929. '[He] has changed the face of the known earth.'

Meanwhile, Admiral Byrd had finally arrived at his base in the Ross Sea, on the far side of the continent. He was angry that Wilkins had become the first man to fly over Antarctica. But he would take some consolation in being the first to fly over the South Pole, in November that year — something that really had never been on the Australian's agenda.

# Chapter 13

# Winning the Girl
but Losing a Friend

THE *R-38* DISASTER over Hull in August 1921 didn't stop Wilkins from making further flights on airships. Seven and a half years later, with time on his hands before the change of seasons in the Antarctic, he was quite amenable to a suggestion by William Randolph Hearst to join the *Graf Zeppelin* on its inaugural around-the-world flight. Besides, you didn't knock back a request from the man who was sponsoring your polar exploration. The only thing was that it was happening so soon after Wilkins' return from the southern continent.

The *Graf* was an impressive machine. Powered by five 550-horsepower engines, the airship was 237 metres long and the equivalent of nine storeys high. It was the brainchild of Count (or Graf) Ferdinand von Zeppelin, who unfortunately didn't live to see it fly. The LZ127, to use the dirigible's identification number, had made its maiden flight in September 1928, just before Wilkins set out for Antarctica.

The airship voyage was scheduled for the middle of May the following year, a mere two months after Wilkins and Eielson had returned to another hero's welcome in New York City. It would mean

Wilkins meeting up again with Dr Hugo Eckener, who had knocked back his request to purchase a Zeppelin for a flight over the North Pole nine years earlier. Hearst had put up half the money needed for the *Graf* flight, in a typically flamboyant attempt to boost the circulation of his chain of newspapers, and he wanted his team of correspondents to cover the journey from start to finish. Hearst had only one demand of Eckener and the crew: regardless of the Zeppelin factory being based in southern Germany, the official circumnavigation would begin and end at Lakehurst, in the state of New Jersey. Thus Wilkins would have to first cross the Atlantic by boat to take up his seat on the airship, only to then fly straight back on the dirigible as it headed for the US East Coast to start the circumnavigation. It left him with precious little time for his other commitments, let alone seeing Suzanne.

Among the others on board would be the legendary tabloid reporter Karl Henry von Wiegand (German-born but raised in the United States) and his lover, fellow journalist Lady (Grace) Drummond-Hay; both were veteran Hearst journalists. Von Wiegand was suspicious of Wilkins. After all, the 55-year-old German-American had an enormous ego and didn't want to share the limelight — except with his paramour. Such was von Wiegand's self-opinion that in his dotage he would explain to young journalists that it was he who decided to charter the *Graf Zeppelin*. He would also tell of how Adolf Hitler was such a close acquaintance that, as the Führer was hurrying to Paris in 1940 to accept the surrender of France, he made a detour to Brussels so that von Wiegand could interview him for a Hearst feature story. And when Japan invaded Manchuria in 1931 he covered the war from both sides: 'I'd go in the morning to the Chinese front. At noon I would call a taxi-cab and drive over to the Japanese front. Very simple really!'

Before leaving New York, Wilkins was honoured by the Explorers Club, an elite group of adventurers. It had been formed in 1904 and its membership was exclusive, to say the least. Wilkins accepted an invitation to become only the sixteenth member in the quarter-century of the club's existence.

VON WIEGAND AND Lady Drummond-Hay were based in Europe and met Wilkins for the first time when he arrived at the home of the Zeppelin airship company, Friedrichshafen, beside Lake Constance on the border between Germany and Switzerland. Wilkins expected, with good reason, to get the cold shoulder from von Wiegand. But he got in first and explained that Hearst only wanted him to write about the technical side of the flight, and that he would be shooting newsreel footage. Von Wiegand's attitude apparently changed. 'He proved to be a prince of a colleague,' Wilkins would say later. 'He never showed anything but a spirit of cordial good-fellowship and was always ready to help me.'

The *Graf* sailed away from Friedrichshafen at dawn on 16 May 1929. The journey started perfectly: flying quietly over an ever-serene Lake Constance, then down the Rhône Valley in France to the Mediterranean, where Herr Doktor Eckener changed course and headed west for Spain.

Just as the passengers were about to sit down for lunch, there was a setback. One of the five engines had stopped. Assuring his guests that there was no danger, Eckener announced that he would have to head back to Germany. The airship was flying back up the Rhône Valley when a second engine cut out ... and a third, and then a fourth. There was now just one engine working — and struggling against a 65-kilometre-an-hour headwind.

A chimpanzee bound for a zoo in New York decided that this was the moment to escape into the area above the gondola that housed the gas bags. Frantic crew-members chased her along the girders until she was finally caught.

Eckener addressed the passengers again. 'We might have to abandon ship,' he said calmly. 'You will all go into the area below the gas bags. If we have to make a forced landing, it would be too dangerous to stay here in the gondola. When the ship hits the ground we will rip open the envelope of the airship and you will escape through the torn fabric. Meanwhile we are radioing the French authorities to see if we can land at an old airship field nearby.'

The field was at Cuers-Pierrefeu, about 20 kilometres north of Toulon. Dusk had just descended when the *Graf* arrived there. A senior officer from the airship, Captain Ernst Lehmann, parachuted to the ground to direct a team of French soldiers in the intricate art of airship landing procedures. A safe landing was achieved and the *Graf Zeppelin* was hauled into the hangar that had housed the *Dixmude* during the war. Meanwhile the passengers were placed under house-arrest at the aerodrome while engine repairs were carried out. The local authorities were unsure of how to handle the team of journalists on board.

In a replay of his and Bernard Grant's adventures in 1912 in western Turkey, Wilkins and another reporter, a young American named Frank Nicholson, decided to make a break for it. Twice they sneaked away and were caught by the local gendarmes. On the third occasion, the pair ran into a local whose mother happened to be an Australian. She took them to the nearest telegraph office, where the operator agreed to send their stories to their respective newspapers. But Wilkins' plans were thwarted by the local mayor, who got a sniff of what was going on and wouldn't allow the stories to be sent until he had proper translations of each of the yarns. By the time they were eventually sent, they had missed their American deadlines.

In Wilkins' case, this official intervention meant little; the Hearst sub-editors back in New York had pieced together local reports of the drama, beaten the story to within an inch of its life and added his byline. They would never have been game to put von Wiegand's name on a story he hadn't written, but Wilkins wasn't an employee, so he got the notoriety. The story told of panic and terror; the standard safety measures that Eckener had outlined were changed to last-ditch attempts to escape death.

Eckener himself was furious, even after he was shown the original report. He thought it was Wilkins' way of getting back at him for his refusal to sell the Australian explorer a Zeppelin almost a decade earlier. The company director hadn't wanted bad headlines back then, and he certainly disliked having them now.

Despite these fireworks, Wilkins would describe the flight back to Friedrichshafen as the most beautiful he had ever experienced. 'I shall never forget the wonderful view of the mountains in the Alps at night followed by the lights of Geneva and Zurich,' he said. 'And the splendor of the dawn over Lake Constance was indescribable.'

It was to be at least two months before Hugo Eckener would have the *Graf* ready to set out again on its epic flight. In the meantime, Wilkins had to make a hurried trip back to New York. He had received a cable from Suzanne explaining that she'd fallen seriously ill with rheumatic fever. A childhood disease, it often reoccurred in sufferers after they reached adulthood. Suzanne had previously been stricken with the fever when she was at school in Walhalla.

In her cable, Suzanne said she didn't want to be a burden on him and suggested they call off the wedding — but Wilkins would hear of no such thing. For the next month he spent every waking hour at his fiancée's bedside as he helped nurse her back to full health.

Once this was achieved, and having received word from Eckener about the airship's similar recovery, he headed back to Europe. Stopping off in London, the Australian tried his luck at getting the British authorities to lease him an airship to use in the Antarctic later in the year. Okay, so the *Graf* had had problems, but his opinion after watching the *Norge* fly over Point Barrow was that dirigibles could easily navigate the polar weather. If the British naval chiefs shared his enthusiasm, they failed to show it.

EVENTUALLY, ON 1 August 1929, the *Graf Zeppelin* headed off across the Atlantic, without incident. Except for the discovery of a young stowaway several hours after the airship had left Friedrichshafen. Eckener was determined that no such extra passenger would be on the airship when the official circumnavigation started and arranged for guards to keep watch on the airship at Lakehurst. He used only three of the five engines on the trip across the Atlantic to ensure there were no problems, but would put all five to the test when the airship backtracked over the same ocean during the first leg of its official voyage. 'Serenely uneventful' was the way Wilkins described the 55-hour trip to New Jersey. It was a compliment, but one imagines he must have been starting to tire of the sight of the grey Atlantic waters.

The *Graf Zeppelin* leaves Lakehurst Airfield in August 1929 at the start of its round-the-world flight, with Wilkins on board.

Having arrived at the large field about 80 kilometres south of New York City, it was time to take on the full list of passengers. Added to the crew of forty-one on this historic voyage were twenty guests, many of whom were journalists. Tickets cost $12,000 — the amount an average American would earn in ten years. There was a multi-millionaire named William Leeds, who had previously financed unsuccessful attempts to fly across the Atlantic in fixed-wing aircraft; US Marine commander Charles E. Rosendahl; US Navy observer Lieutenant Jack C. Richardson; Dr Geronimo Megias, the personal physician to King Alfonso XIII of Spain; and Baron Heinz von Perckhammer, a Prussian nobleman who was taking photographs for a German media chain. Also on board was a shadowy figure from the Soviet Union, known only to fellow passengers as Comrade Karklin. He was there to ensure that Soviet national sovereignty was not infringed. How would Karklin have reacted had he known that Wilkins had once worked as an MI6 spy in Russia, and had even spoken to Lenin in that capacity? On the other hand, perhaps he knew.

The Australian would recall how an American woman offered him $30,000 not to turn up on the day the *Graf* was due to leave Lakehurst, so that she could take his place on board. She was obviously unaware that Wilkins could not be bought for a few pieces of silver. The exhilaration that exploration brought was his reward.

Lady Drummond-Hay was over the moon about the cast for this media blockbuster. She gushed in print: 'Ours is a little republic of democracy where professors, kings' physicians, millionaires and officers and crew dine and fraternise in the most amicable harmony.'

The *Graf* lifted off from Lakehurst on the morning of 7 August. It made a short pass over the centre of New York City and then headed out into the Atlantic. Wilkins was surprised at how the airship made so little noise. 'We hardly heard the engines except when we were leaning out of the windows,' he noted.

The Zeppelin flew over Paris without stopping, before returning to its home base on the shores of Lake Constance. The voyage then went into limbo for five days at Friedrichshafen while Eckener did a thorough check of all five engines. Ahead lay the toughest assignment: the flight to Tokyo, which, at 11,000 kilometres, was to be the longest nonstop flight ever attempted by anyone in history. Two new passengers boarded for this leg — a Japanese newspaper journalist and a Japanese naval officer. The former Hollywood actress Anna May Wong, at the time domiciled in Europe, was granted a private tour of the airship, and an admirer unsuccessfully offered many thousands of dollars to have her join the voyage.

In the early hours of 15 August, the *Graf Zeppelin* left Friedrichshafen and headed north-east, past Nuremberg and Leipzig to Berlin, where Eckener made a low sweep over the Brandenburg Gate and Alexanderplatz. They then continued east to Danzig (now Gdansk) and on to Lithuania. Once over Soviet territory, Comrade Karklin 'ordered' Eckener to change course and head for Moscow — an outrageous request that the airship captain duly ignored. Wilkins was already quite unimpressed with their Russian shadow:

> *He was supposed to translate official messages and weather reports from Moscow. But he could speak nothing but Russian. He was all but useless. He would pick out the English or German letters one by one and transliterate them into Russian characters. He would brood over them for a while and emerge with some kind of meaning. But it was rarely correct. We were getting weather reports from Moscow but he would take three hours to translate them. Why was he on board? One could only speculate.*

The *Graf* crossed the Ural Mountains, just north of the city of Perm. For the next few days it would fly over Siberia. Much of the area was still uncharted, so Eckener navigated by dead reckoning, just as a ship's captain would do on the vast oceans of the world. Wilkins described the experience: 'If we didn't know it was impossible, we might almost think the Zeppelin had flown to the moon or Mars. This view [of Siberia] is positively unearthly.'

It was bitterly cold also. Lady Drummond-Hay noted:

*We have a million cubic feet of gas but no heat. Merciless cold [is] driving through the canvas walls of this flying tent. I have visualized myself gracefully draped over a saloon window ledge romantically viewing the moonlit sky. The men have reminded each other not to forget evening jackets and boiled shirts in their baggage. We have drawn ourselves lovely pictures of dining elegantly in mid-air with Commodore Eckener at the head of a flower-decked table. But leather coats, woollies and furs will be our evening dress; hot soup and steaming stew more welcome than cold caviar and chicken salad.*

When they passed tiny hamlets, terrified Russians would duck for cover, frightened by this strange contraption drifting by in the sky. 'We could see frantic mothers grabbing their children and fleeing into their houses,' Wilkins remembered. 'Peasants would jump out of their ox-wagons and run behind trees.'

One of these hamlets was Verkhne-Imbatskoye, on the Yenisei River, where Eckener was able to verify that his navigation had been correct. The *Graf* headed on to the Tunguska region, where Eckener hoped to find evidence of the intriguing Tunguska Event. At about 7.30 am on 30 June 1908, there had been a massive midair explosion, the equivalent of a hydrogen bomb, that flattened an estimated 80 million trees across some 2000 square kilometres of the Siberian countryside. It was detected by seismic stations as far away as London. At the time, it was thought to have been caused by a meteor, and

Eckener hoped to find the meteor's crater. But after a day of searching he gave up and continued the journey east. Today scientists believe the Tunguska Event was the result of the air-burst of an asteroid about 8 kilometres above the surface of the earth. The asteroid is believed to have been around 80 metres in diameter.

It was then on to Yakutsk, on the banks of the 8-kilometre-wide Lena River. In the Tsarist era, this fur-trading town had been the location for one of Russia's most notorious concentration camps. During the Great War, German prisoners of war had been detained in the gulag and hundreds died. Eckener had decided to pay homage to his fallen countrymen. He flew the airship low over the town's cemetery and dropped a wreath, which landed on a corner-post of the graveyard's fence. Wilkins made sure to capture the poignant moment on film.

Ahead now was Eckener's greatest challenge: the awesome Stanovoy mountain range, in the far east of the vast country. Most of the snow-capped peaks were uncharted, and no one knew just how high they were — perhaps 2000 metres. It was believed that there was a pass through the forbidding mountain range, at a height of around 1500 metres. Eckener went looking for this elusive pass.

It appeared without warning, and he edged the airship into the gap, which quickly turned into a deep canyon with almost vertical cliffs on each side. The floor of the pass got higher and higher, however, and Eckener was forced to head the Zeppelin ever upwards. As he did, the walls edged closer and closer until there was less than 50 metres on either side of the giant airship.

Suddenly, at 2000 metres and with the *Graf* just 40 metres above the canyon floor, the airship emerged at the far side of the mountain range. There was an audible gasp of relief from the passengers, as Eckener flung his arms in the air and shouted, 'How's that for flying an airship? What a thrill!'

The captain's skills were indeed impressive, and Wilkins was full of respect for the old man from Kiel. The Australian spent much of the flight ensconced on the *Graf*'s bridge, watching Eckener at work.

Ahead in the far distance now, they could see the Sea of Okhotsk, which fronted the Pacific Ocean. Eckener turned the ship south-east. It was dawn when they arrived over the island of Hokkaido, in Japan's north. It was then on to Tokyo, which they reached in the early afternoon of 19 August, landing at the Kasumigaura naval base with the help of some 500 sailors.

Several hundred thousand Tokyo residents had walked the 30 kilometres from the city to see the historic arrival. They clapped and shouted, '*Banzai!*' — a term that Westerners would be less comfortable with over the ensuing decades, but one that here demonstrated the Japanese public's ultimate respect for Hugo Eckener's achievement. And it was quite a feat: 11,000 kilometres of nonstop flying from Lake Constance to Tokyo, over a handful of days.

The round of parties that followed during the short stopover, including tea at the Emperor's Palace, reminded Wilkins of the way he and Eielson had been feted after their flight across the top of the world. He also made a series of radio interviews and befriended several top Japanese bureaucrats — contacts that were to prove invaluable a decade later when he was back in the secretive world of espionage. Wilkins discovered that, while there had been no headline-grabbing flights by any Japanese pilots, the aviation industry as a whole was as up to date as its counterparts in the United States, Britain and Europe, with thriving production of Mitsubishi, Kawasaki and Nakajima aircraft. The Japanese would eventually prove their expertise to the rest of the world when they entered World War II.

Eckener, who had turned sixty-one just days before undertaking the long flight over Russia, was not well and so called a halt to the

# Beware the yellow press

The exploits of Hubert Wilkins were tailor-made for the newspaper empire of William Randolph Hearst, one of the architects and finest proponents of so-called yellow journalism. Hearst knew money talked, and Wilkins needed money to finance his polar sorties. In return, the magnate received a regular harvest of headlines and the prestige that came from being associated with a fearless and successful explorer.

William Randolph Hearst was born in San Francisco on 29 April 1863, the son of Senator George Hearst, a rough diamond who'd made a fortune as a prospector during the California gold rush of the late 1840s and early '50s. Young William was never afraid to ruffle feathers and was expelled from Harvard University for presenting several professors with personally inscribed chamber pots. Having first worked as a reporter on *The World*, the famous New York daily owned by Hungarian immigrant Joseph Pulitzer, in 1887 he persuaded his father to give him a local newspaper, the *San Francisco Examiner*, and his path to greatness was set.

Hearst turned the *Examiner* into a carbon-copy of *The World*, which was renowned for its jingoism, sensationalism and titillation, with huge headlines and flamboyant illustrations. By 1895, Hearst decided to take on Pulitzer on his home turf by purchasing the *New York Journal*, so beginning a bitter circulation war. He commissioned stories from some of the most famous of America's writers, Mark Twain and Jack London among them, and set about poaching Pulitzer's top journalists and contributors. One of these defectors was illustrator R.F. Outcault, whose cartoon character 'the Yellow Kid' lent part of its name to the derogatory term still used today for unprofessional or unethical journalism. Certainly, both newspapers regularly published reports of events that never happened.

There's a famous story concerning an alleged exchange of cables between Hearst and artist Frederic Remington, who had been sent to Havana in 1897 to provide illustrations for pieces about the Cuban Revolution. All was calm when Remington arrived in the capital, so he wired his publisher: 'There is no trouble. There will be no war. I wish to return.' Hearst cabled back: 'Please remain. You furnish the pictures and I'll furnish the war.'

With the success of the *Journal*, Hearst turned his attention to media outfits around the United States. He would eventually own twenty-eight major newspapers in New York, Los Angeles, Chicago, Washington, Detroit, Atlanta, Seattle and beyond, and eighteen magazines, including *Cosmopolitan*, *Good Housekeeping*, *Town and Country* and *Harper's Bazaar*. Later in life he also bought several radio stations.

But quantity is one thing, quality quite another. It was Hearst who once said: 'News is something somebody doesn't want printed. Everything else is advertising.' As hard as it was to imagine a man like Wilkins — someone who'd risked life and limb on the battlefields of Europe in the pursuit of an accurate record of events — being on the payroll of the yellow press, both he and Hearst were giants in their field and gained plenty from this marriage of convenience.

festivities, ordering the crew and passengers back on board. There was a slight hiccup when the Japanese ground crew inflicted some damage on the main gondola; hurried repairs were carried out and the eighteen crewmen involved, having lost face, pledged to commit harikari if the *Graf Zeppelin* failed to complete its circumnavigation of the world. Then there were three false starts, when Eckener was forced to turn back because of major storms. Finally, on 23 August, the hydrogen–filled giant of the sky left Kasumigaura for the last time and headed east across the vast expanse of ocean between Asia and America's West Coast.

The Pacific crossing passed without further incident, mostly with the airship engulfed in fog. At one stage Eckener manoeuvred the craft to have it pulled along by the tail of a typhoon. While sailing in the storm's wake, it reached speeds of around 160 kilometres an hour.

Late on the afternoon of 25 August, the *Graf* made a dramatic appearance over San Francisco. As it flew through into the bay, past where the completed Golden Gate Bridge would stand eight years later, the setting sun reflected off its silver body. 'Hundreds of planes flew out to escort us,' Wilkins recalled. 'There was a splendorous haze of golden light over the mountains and the sea and the craggy piles of buildings on the hills of San Francisco.'

With darkness descending, Eckener turned the *Graf* south towards Los Angeles. The passengers shivered. Was it because of the cold August night, or the realisation of what had been achieved? As they passed over the Hearst family ranch at San Simeon, where the now-famous tourist landmark Hearst Castle was under construction, Eckener dipped the nose of his airship in a symbolic gesture to the voyage's benefactor. Sadly, the whole ranch was in darkness.

It was a different matter when they approached Los Angeles. It seemed as if every light in the City of Angels was blazing. Eckener was amazed. He circled the metropolis so that everyone on board could soak up the atmosphere. No one was interested in sleep now, gazing down instead on the stunning light show until the first rays of dawn took over.

As the airship descended on Mines Airfield, the new aerodrome being constructed south-west of the city (and today's Los Angeles International Airport), a broad smile broke out over Dr Eckener's face. '*Meine Damen und Herren*,' he announced, 'we have set a record for crossing the Pacific — seventy-nine hours and three minutes.' His words were met with a clinking of champagne glasses and a hearty 'Three cheers!' echoed around the main lounge.

Early that evening of 26 August, Hearst threw a lavish party at the famous Ambassador Hotel, on Wilshire Boulevard. Anyone who was anyone in Hollywood turned up to rub shoulders with the current world heroes. The Mexican movie star Raquel Torres turned heads; she was the toast of Tinseltown, having starred in the recent *White Shadows of the South Seas*, the first talkie synchronised for both dialogue and music. Monte Blue was also prominent at Hearst's party. A protégé of director Cecil B. DeMille, during the silent movie era Blue played romantic leads opposite stars such as Lillian Gish, Gloria Swanson, Clara Bow and Norma Shearer. Torres and Blue had earlier made a special visit to the Ambassador to meet Wilkins.

As for the true hero of the hour, Dr Hugo Eckener, he was somewhat embarrassed at all the fanfare. He didn't enjoy formal dinners and cocktail parties, but he had to turn up because he was the main after-dinner speaker. Wilkins also said a few words, forcefully pushing his favourite topic — the need for a worldwide weather forecasting system. It would all make sense, even to Hollywood party-goers, once his ideas were adopted by a world more focused on international co-operation than the xenophobic one-upmanship of that era.

At midnight all those involved in the round-the-world voyage headed back to the airfield for the final leg of the epic journey. Eckener was worried about a rise in air temperature, which could hamper the lift-off. To lighten the load, he had crew-members toss overboard excess food and any furniture not in use. Six disappointed members of the crew were also offloaded and sent on to New York by train.

Eckener then addressed the sailors whose job it was to push the airship away from the mooring mast once it was released from its tether: 'I want you to give us the biggest push you can muster. Every little bit will help.' The words of encouragement appeared to do the trick. After a mighty heave, the dirigible was away. But once it was about 4 metres from the ground, it stopped rising. The thousands of people on the ground, watching the *Graf* lit up by a bank of searchlights, held their breath.

'Give me full speed!' Eckener shouted to his engineers. 'As much thrust as you can give me!'

The nose rose, but as the ship drifted forward, it was obvious that the rear gondola was likely to become entangled in the high-tension electricity wires lying in the airship's path. Should they touch, there would be an incredible explosion, which would surely kill all those on board, and probably hundreds in the crowd below as well. Then the master airman pulled a remarkable stunt. Eckener ordered a sudden shutdown of all power and the forward water ballast to be dumped (as it turned out, all over the onlookers). This forced the rear of the aircraft to buck like an angry bronco. As it did so, the rear gondola leaped over the electricity wires; and when the engines were turned on again, the mighty *Graf Zeppelin* was free to sail off safely into the night.

With the ballast gone, there was no water on board now. In Wilkins' words: 'So all the way across the United States, still thirsting under its Prohibition Law, we drank champagne in lofty disdain of water and the law. We washed ourselves in eau de cologne.'

The *Graf* flew slowly eastwards, over the continental divide of the Rocky Mountains, swerved south into New Mexico, and then back to Texas, where some high-spirited cowboys fired guns at the passing airship. On it went to Kansas City, Chicago, into Canada briefly and then to Cleveland, at midnight on 28 August. There, in Ohio's lakefront city, they saluted the American dirigible *Los Angeles*, moored at the local airfield where the ten-day National Air Races and Aeronautical Exposition had opened five days earlier. 'Wild

Indians could hardly have made more noise than Commander Rosendahl and Lieutenant Jack Richardson at the familiar sight,' Lady Drummond-Hay observed.

On the morning of 29 August, the *Graf* flew over Manhattan before landing back at Lakehurst, having established an around-the-world record of twenty-one days, five hours and thirty-five minutes. And if only flying time was counted, the journey totalled twelve days and eleven minutes. Eckener's airship had travelled 31,500 kilometres. All in all, it was an extraordinary achievement.

A plane was waiting at Lakehurst Airfield to whisk Eckener off to Washington, DC, for a private meeting with President Herbert Hoover. With him was Dr Otto Carl Kiep, counsellor of the German Embassy. According to *Time* magazine, 'As soon as courtesy visits could be paid, Dr Eckener rushed by motor to Dr Kiep's home where *gemütlich* he snuggled into a featherbed and slept from twilight to dawn, his first careless sleep in three weeks ...' The next day, Eckener flew back to New York for a ticker-tape parade through the central business district. Returning the gesture from two days before, the *Los Angeles* flew overhead as a tribute to the *Graf Zeppelin*.

As for Wilkins, he kept well clear of all the festivities. He had arranged for Suzanne to meet him at Lakehurst when the airship arrived, and within two hours the couple were on a train to Cleveland. Ostensibly, it was because he wanted to see the National Air Races and pick up a Caterpillar tractor for his next expedition (there would be no manual construction of airstrips in the future). In fact, he had a much more important task to fulfil.

The following day, Friday, 30 August, in the small office of a Cleveland justice of the peace, Sir Hubert Wilkins and Suzanne Bennett were married, well away from the publicity and back-slapping that the shy groom abhorred. Apparently, Wilkins was so

Sir Hubert Wilkins
and his devoted wife,
Suzanne.

nervous that his hands shook uncontrollably and he was unable to put
the wedding ring on Suzanne's finger — so she put it on herself.

There was no time for a honeymoon right now. That would have
to wait. Within three weeks, Wilkins would be off again, back to the
Antarctic.

As THE TIME approached for Wilkins to resume his endeavours in the
extreme south, he was called to a meeting with T.V. Ranck, Hearst's
editorial manager.

'How much for exclusive stories on this year's expedition,
Sir Hubert?' Ranck asked him. 'The same again? Will $40,000 be
enough?'

'I don't need any more money,' Wilkins replied. 'I accepted
Mr Hearst's offer as a one-off. As far as I'm concerned, the $40,000 was
for exclusive rights whether I spent one summer in the Antarctic or a

dozen. My planes, equipment and instruments are already at Deception Island. All I need is the money to get me and my team to Montevideo and for our stay on the *Hektoria*.'

Ranck shook his head in disbelief. He was used to dealing with people who held out for every cent they could get.

Wilkins had been busy as he prepared for the second leg of his Antarctic expedition, during which he planned to continue charting the coastline and in doing so, find locations for future settlements that could be used to further his dream of global weather forecasting. While in Britain earlier in the year, he had arranged for the Colonial Office to lend him one of their research ships, HMS *William Scoresby*, named after a renowned nineteenth-century English whaling captain and polar explorer. The Colonial Office also paid £10,000 towards the expedition costs. To demonstrate the official nature of his endeavours, Wilkins was working under a royal charter. Although it wasn't something to which the British would necessarily admit, they were fiercely protective of their sovereignty over much of Antarctica and would be suspicious of Byrd's efforts on the southern continent, just as the Americans were apprehensive about what Wilkins was doing.

This time he would have two new pilots for his pair of Lockheed Vegas. After returning to North America in March 1929, Ben Eielson had been asked by the powerful Aviation Corporation of America to set up Alaskan Airways through the merger of several small air companies. As general manager, he had duly hired Joe Crosson as his top pilot. Not wishing to leave his Australian friend in the lurch, however, Eielson recommended Parker 'Shorty' Cramer as his replacement. A 33-year-old former barnstormer, Cramer had twice crashed while trying to open up a new route from North America to Europe. On the first occasion, in 1928, he and co-pilot Bert Hassell had come down in Greenland and were found several weeks later, having walked 120 kilometres through snow and ice. The following year, Cramer and Robert Cast had come down on the north coast of Labrador and had been forced to make a similar trek to safety. Wilkins was impressed by the American's vision and strength of character in overcoming the elements to survive these two hiccups.

For his part, Crosson suggested that Wilkins contact a friend of his, fellow Canadian bush flyer and aviation engineer Alward (Al) Cheesman, to see if he could recommend someone as a second pilot. Cheesman, in fact, asked if he could come himself, and took six months' leave from his regular job as assistant to the legendary aviator Harold 'Doc' Oaks at the new Western Canada Airlines.

The team duly arrived on the *Hektoria* at Deception Island at the end of November, but during the first flight south, with Cheesman at the controls, Wilkins was horrified to discover that the edge of the Antarctic icepack had retreated some 1000 kilometres from where it had been a year earlier. This lack of ice meant they'd be unable to establish a base within flying distance of Deception Island. He did, however, have plan B: the *William Scoresby*. But she would not arrive for another three weeks.

Wilkins was then dealt a personal blow, when he was informed by radio of the disappearance of Ben Eielson in the Arctic. A fur-trading schooner, the *Nanuk*, had become trapped in the ice off Cape North in Siberia; on board were fifteen passengers and $1 million worth of furs. Alaskan Airways was hired to rescue the passengers and cargo, so Eielson and his mechanic flew from Teller, a staging point north-west of Nome, Alaska, across the Bering Strait to the stranded ship. They returned with two passengers and 450 kilograms of furs before heading back to the ship on 9 November. When Joe Crosson arrived at the *Nanuk* the following day, he learned that Eielson had never arrived. Immediately one of the biggest searches ever conducted in the Arctic got under way.

It was to be seventy-seven days before the remains of Eielson's plane were spotted, buried in snow nearly 150 kilometres from Cape North. There was no trace of Eielson or his mechanic, Earl Boland, and a further twenty-four days went by before their bodies were found. Apparently the pair had been thrown from the plane during the crash and the bodies were then buried in the heavy snow. Eielson was just thirty-two years old.

Wilkins was understandably shattered when he heard of the discovery the following February. 'Together we had sighted more than half a million square miles of the earth's surface that no other human eyes had ever seen,' he wrote in tribute to his friend and fellow pioneer. 'We had flown over unknown coastlines and seas and had added literally hundreds of terrain features to the charts and maps of the known world. Eielson will live in the history of exploration as long as men fly over the earth.'

WHEN THE *WILLIAM Scoresby* arrived in mid December, they loaded the *Los Angeles* (the Vega, not the dirigible) onto her deck and sailed to Port Lockroy, on the western coast of Graham Land, a harbour regularly used by whalers. Today it is one of the most popular destinations for tourists on cruise ships, with its main building having been converted into an Antarctic museum.

Wilkins and Cheesman attached pontoons to the *Los Angeles* so it could be used as a seaplane, and headed out in search of a stretch of flat ice from which they could take off with a heavy load of fuel. Far to the south, they found a narrow bay that looked suitable. Returning to Lockroy, the aircraft was then loaded back onto the ship, which steamed off in search of this discovery.

The area was home to thousands of giant Emperor penguins. These big birds fascinated Wilkins: 'It was a weird journey in the Antarctic silence, with the glittering icebergs towering around us, and the multitudes of gnome-like creatures watching us from the ice floes.'

It took a day to find their way to the bay they'd selected. Once the *Scoresby* had been moored to the stretch of ice, the Vega was readied for action by replacing the pontoons with skis and lowering it onto the ice. To cut down on labour when hauling gasoline from the ship to the plane, Wilkins' team had brought a specially adapted Austin car with them; it had eight wheels that were linked by chains to provide extra traction. The sailor responsible for the customised Austin became part of history as the first man to ever drive a car in the Antarctic. But its usefulness was short-lived, for by 10 am that day, the ice began to melt. The primitive snowmobile was hastily lifted back on board the ship.

Then suddenly there was a shout from one of the sailors: 'Look out — the plane's starting to sink!' Without delay, Wilkins and Cheesman attached ropes to the *Los Angeles* and the team began hauling it back towards the ship and hoisting it aboard. It was an uncomfortably close call.

Late in the afternoon, Wilkins had cause to think again about the mysterious hand that always seemed to be there to rescue him. He had intended flying south that day. Had he done so, he would not have had time to get back to the *William Scoresby* before it was lashed by a violent storm that lasted three days. Such was its ferocity that all the pack-ice around the ship was broken into small pieces. Any emergency landing would have seen the plane disappear into the depths of the ocean.

The *Scoresby* steamed further south in search of either solid ice or smooth water from which a flight could be made. After a few days, on 29 December, the explorers found a suitable anchorage north of Charcot Land, an area that may or may not have been a small island, such was the guesswork of contemporary maps of

Antarctica. Wilkins decided to try for another flight. The pontoons were put back on and the *Los Angeles* lowered over the side. While he and Cheesman prepared to take off on the icy water, the plane bounced around as it rolled in the swell and was buffeted by a strong Antarctic wind. Eventually Cheesman roared the engines and they were airborne. Wilkins described the take-off in dramatic words:

> *The plane picked up speed, springing from wave to wave like a hunted kangaroo. The pounding of the pontoons on the water sounded like artillery fire, and the light plane seemed to buck on the sea like a thing run wild. There was a shift to a rapid tattoo, as if someone were beating on giant drums beneath us, then the thrill of soaring smoothly upward, leaving the waves and the* William Scoresby *behind and below us.*

There were storm clouds to the north of the ship, but they didn't unduly worry Wilkins, as the Lockheed Vega headed south for Charcot. Then, after the two aviators had been flying for less than an hour, they began to encounter the first signs of an impending blizzard. Within minutes, visibility was down to no more than a couple of metres. Cheesman dropped altitude in an attempt to get under the violent squall, but to no avail. He was having trouble even keeping a straight course, such was the buffeting. Wilkins knew there were high mountains on Charcot Land, so he ordered Cheesman to turn back. The two men were disappointed, but as the plane swung around in an arc, they suddenly saw the mountains — another couple of minutes and they would have smashed into the snow-capped peaks. Wilkins was now concerned about finding the ship in such weather. Lady Luck was with them again, however, as out of the gloom the *Scoresby* suddenly loomed large.

The ship sailed further westwards, into the Bellingshausen Sea, part of the southern Pacific Ocean, and on most days they were able to make a flight. They soon proved that Charcot Land was indeed an island, and not part of the Antarctic mainland as Frenchman Dr Jean-Baptiste Charcot thought when he'd discovered it in 1910. Wilkins dropped an official document claiming the area for Britain. Today the body of water discovered by the Australian between Charcot and Alexander Island is known as Wilkins Sound; most of it is taken up by the Wilkins Ice Shelf, which covers an area of about 150 by 100 kilometres.

The expedition leader was also able to locate and map dozens of other islands. Beyond Peter I Island (discovered nine years earlier and named after the Russian emperor), the icepack turned to the south. It was from there that the duo made their final flight. As the days passed, the *William Scoresby* was routinely pummelled by storms and raging seas. They tried several times for another flight, but on every occasion were forced to abort their take-offs.

Eventually, with just enough fuel to get the ship back to Deception Island, Wilkins called a halt to their exploration in January. Much valuable charting of the icy wasteland had been effected during this second, and final, Antarctic venture, and he had given more food for thought to scientists about the need for research into weather and climate. To this end, Wilkins had found a score of possible sites for future weather stations. As a *New York Times* editorial noted: 'Like all great men, he knows when to take the last desperate chance and win; he is wise enough to skirt the edge of the abyss without falling in.'

As the *Scoresby* was being refuelled at the whaling station, the second Lockheed Vega was loaded aboard. Wilkins and his team then sailed north to Buenos Aires, where the two aircraft were sold to provide a kitty for the Australian's next venture. His days of exploration from the air were over.

Wilkins was famous enough in the United States for advertisers to seek his endorsement.

ONCE HE'D RETURNED to the United States, in March 1930, Wilkins was able to pay his last respects to Eielson. The *Alaskan*, the single-engine Fokker they had flown in their first sortie in the Arctic, had been in storage in Seattle for the past three years. Wilkins decided to donate it to a committee that had been set up to provide a lasting memorial to the deceased aviator. Today it has pride of place in the Carl Ben Eielson Museum, established at his boyhood home in Hatton, North Dakota.

# Chapter 14

# 2000 Leagues Under the Ice

NINE MONTHS AFTER their wedding, Hubert and Suzanne Wilkins finally got to set out on their honeymoon. They had originally planned to sail across the Atlantic on the new ocean liner SS *Europa* with a good friend, the British playwright George Bernard Shaw, and then spend six weeks in Switzerland as guests of Lincoln Ellsworth at his luxury castle, Schloss Lenzburg. But at the eleventh hour, Hearst intervened, asking the couple to go on the *Graf Zeppelin* from New York to Friedrichshafen instead and each write their own version of the flight. The holiday at Ellsworth's Swiss castle would follow as planned; it was just the mode of transport that had changed for the not-so-newlyweds. They flew from Lakehurst on 2 June 1930. As the Zeppelin set a course for Europe, Suzanne remarked on how the giant steamships ploughing out of New York below them looked like toy boats in an enormous bathtub.

Eckener was captaining the *Graf* as before, and Wilkins spent many an hour with him at the airship's controls. As they approached their destination, the couple chatted with Eckener over coffee in the grand saloon. They were over the beautiful Rhône Valley in France at the time.

'The trip has been very uneventful, *Herr Doktor*,' Suzanne noted with a smile. 'There has been no excitement. It's not like my husband's life at all.'

'Ah, but my passengers would prefer it that way,' Eckener said, returning the smile.

It was a premature observation for, within minutes, the *Graf* was flying into a heavy storm, lurching and dropping several hundred metres. Everyone was thrown across the saloon, with coffee cups and afternoon tea plates smashing against the wall, and milk and coffee drenching the luckless passengers. The pilot only managed to gain control when the airship was metres from crashing into the ground. So much for the lack of excitement.

As a result of this episode, Wilkins refused to fulfil Hearst's request for a feature story on the trip. 'If we write the truth, no one will ever again fly in an airship,' he told Suzanne. She protested but quickly acquiesced when she realised his mood. 'That was the only time in our lives together that he was ever angry with me,' she would say much later.

Lincoln Ellsworth met the Wilkinses at Friedrichshafen. The three of them then took a boat across Lake Constance before motoring the 150 kilometres to Lenzburg, west of Zurich. One of the oldest castles in Switzerland, dating back to the eleventh century, Schloss Lenzburg had been purchased in 1911 by American billionaire coalmine owner and banker James Ellsworth and passed on to the latter's only son on his death, in 1925.

On the first morning in their new surroundings, Wilkins was contacted by two young German engineers who wanted him to go up in an aircraft they had designed themselves and made in their back yard. Wilkins was keen to get at the controls, and Suzanne insisted she come, too. 'If anything goes wrong, I want to be with you,' she told him. 'Early widowhood in a foreign country does not appeal to me.'

Lady Wilkins is believed to have shot this photo of Sir Hubert while they were on their honeymoon at Schloss Lenzburg.

For the rest of the time during those early summer months, the honeymooners relaxed, enjoying long walks together up and down the hills around the castle, taking in the cool mountain air. On one occasion, though, Suzanne went off alone for a hike in a nearby forest and got lost; a search party found her, cold and miserable, at 3 am the next day.

The couple also made the most of the tourist attractions on offer, including the funicular railway up spectacular Mount Pilatus. Wilkins was particularly excited that day. Suzanne thought it was the stunning vista of hundreds of snow-capped mountains that had set her husband's adrenalin rushing. It was only when they were coming back down the mountain that he explained the real reason for his exhilaration: he had decided on a new venture in exploration. This time it was to take place in the northern polar region ... and it would be under water.

WILKINS MOVED IN exalted company. Hollywood stars and leading newspaper columnists gravitated to him, eager to see what made such a man stand out from the rest. They in turn introduced him to other creative people, all masters of their craft.

One such person was the Italian-born American sculptor Antonio Salemme, who was still to become famous when his path crossed with that of Hubert Wilkins. It was in 1930 that the two men got together. Salemme wanted to delve into Wilkins' psyche and suggested he pose for a sculpture — a bronze bust.

Salemme had previously hit the headlines over a life-size nude bronze sculpture of his good friend Paul Robeson, the ex-football star turned world-famous baritone and Shakespearean actor. The Italian-American had created the piece in 1924, calling it *Negro Spiritual*. But when he wanted to exhibit it in an exhibition at the very staid New York Union League, the board of the club refused to show it — even after Salemme placed a plaster fig-leaf over Robeson's overly large (but physically accurate) penis. The furore over the sculpture was to resurface years later when Lady Mountbatten, wife of Britain's Lord of the Admiralty Viscount Louis Mountbatten, sued a London newspaper for suggesting that she'd had a clandestine affair with Robeson. Among Salemme's other well-known works was a bust of US president John F. Kennedy. The sculptor was still active until his death at the age of 102 in May 1995.

Did Salemme really get to fully understand Wilkins as he fashioned the explorer's bust in his Greenwich Village studio? Suzanne thought he had, as the bust clearly illustrates the Australian's characteristic calm. 'Antonio once asked Hubert if he was afraid he might never return from the unknown icy north,' Suzanne explained. 'My husband merely smiled and said he was always afraid … that was part of the business.'

The fear would most certainly have been there during the upcoming Arctic mission. While the Wilkinses were at Schloss

Lenzburg, Sir Hubert had spent hours in deep conversation with their host. Suzanne had left them to it, knowing they shared such a passion for the polar regions. Ellsworth had flown with Roald Amundsen on his expedition to the Arctic in 1925, when they had got further north than any flyers in history, and they were together again on the historic voyage of the airship *Norge* in 1926. Now, four years later, Ellsworth was swept up by Wilkins' enthusiasm to become the first to venture underneath the Arctic icecap. Not only did the billionaire hand over a sizeable cheque to help finance the Australian's expedition, but he gave Wilkins one of his personal lucky charms: a horseshoe from a steed ridden by Ellsworth's wild west hero, Marshall Wyatt Earp.

Wilkins had first discussed the possibility of using a submarine in polar exploration with Vilhjalmur Stefansson in 1915. The Canadian had been keen on the idea, even though contemporaries dismissed it as the fanciful dreams of someone who had been reading too many Jules Verne novels. Buoyed by Stefansson's support, Wilkins continued to see himself in the role of a latter-day Captain Nemo and was now ready to put the idea to the test. The plan was to adapt a submarine for the task of crisscrossing the unexplored areas of the Arctic Sea, between Alaska, the northern Siberian coast, the North Pole, Greenland and Spitsbergen.

His peers, even a few of his enlightened colleagues at the Explorers Club, were quite sceptical. But Wilkins was able to answer their every question.

The men in his crew would freeze to death, offered one. Ah, but a submarine travels in water, the Australian reasoned, so it couldn't be any colder than water.

And what about the possibility of running into an iceberg under water? There weren't any icebergs in the Arctic Basin, Wilkins reminded his colleagues, only in the Atlantic Sea; there were icefloes and icecaps, but no icebergs.

But the ice would be hundreds of feet thick, surely — how would they ever get down that deep? Away from the coast, he was able to assure them, the ice was rarely thicker than 3 metres, and he had no plans to travel near the coast.

It would be too dark to navigate properly, another doubter suggested; they were sure to get lost. Wilkins would have chuckled at this objection no doubt. He'd been able to find Spitsbergen after flying some 4000 kilometres at speeds of up to 160 kilometres an hour. In the submarine, he would be travelling at less than 16 kilometres an hour and coming up at regular intervals to check his position.

But how would he come up through the ice exactly? To this question, Wilkins could point out that there were plenty of areas free of ice, and, if he wasn't able to find one at a particular time, they'd simply drill a hole through the ice from below.

But still the nay-sayers shook their heads and mumbled thoughts of doom and gloom. It was this very way of thinking that Wilkins delighted in overcoming as much as he did challenging the elements and pushing the boundaries of science. Besides, he'd had his plans ridiculed in the past, hadn't he?

He might not have enjoyed the unanimous support of his peers or the press, but the Australian had lucked in when it came to acquiring a vessel for the expedition. Earlier that year, on 22 April, the major naval powers — America, the United Kingdom, Japan, France and Italy — had signed the London Naval Treaty in a bid to halt the arms race that had been raging for some time. The agreement stipulated that no new ships were to be built until 1937 and a number of existing ships, including submarines, were to be scrapped. Wilkins was thus able to lease one of these obsolete subs from the US Navy for a nominal figure of just $1 per year. Under the terms of lease, the vessel would be scuttled once his expedition was over.

The original plan was to use an early-model submarine, the *Defender*, built in 1907. But this idea was abandoned when the more state-of-the-art USS *O-12* became available. Designed by naval architect Simon Lake, the man the Americans had dubbed 'the Father of the Modern Submarine', and launched in 1917, the *O-12* had been decommissioned in 1924 and placed in reserve at the Philadelphia Navy Ship Yard. At 53 metres long and weighing 570 tonnes, Lake's submarine could travel 7000 nautical miles on the surface without refuelling; when travelling under water, she needed to surface every 130 nautical miles to recharge her batteries. A real bonus was the two giant lights that would allow Wilkins to examine the underside of the ice while looking through the sub's retractable periscope.

The 64-year-old Lake had gone into partnership with a former submarine commander named Sloan Danenhower, who would skipper the *O-12* on the Wilkins–Ellsworth Trans-Arctic Expedition, leading a crew of twenty. Danenhower was the son of American Arctic explorer John Danenhower, who became a celebrity as one of the survivors of the ill-fated *Jeannette*. The latter ship was trapped by ice in the Bering Strait for two years before being crushed, in June 1881, forcing an eleven-month trek and voyage to eventual safety for him and a few of the crew.

Lake would make the necessary modifications for the bold venture at his shipyard at Bridgeport, Connecticut. One of Wilkins' requests was the attachment of a mechanical probe that would scrape along the bottom of the icecap to show how much clearance the submarine had. Others included the fitting of special shock absorbers on the bow in case the vessel ran into some rogue ice, and the addition of drills that could cut through 4 metres of ice. Cutting a hole in the ice would provide the fresh air needed to recharge the vessel's batteries.

The *O-12* was soon found to be far from shipshape, however, much to the expedition leader's dismay, and the modifications took considerably longer than expected. Eventually, though, the submarine was ready to be relaunched, with Suzanne performing the ceremony at the Brooklyn Naval Yard on the morning of 24 March 1931. Wilkins had renamed her the *Nautilus*, after Captain Nemo's ship. Hearst, who had stepped in to co-finance the expedition with Ellsworth, brought Jean-Jules Verne, the novelist's grandson, over from France especially for the event. Amid the photos splashed over Hearst's various newspapers, Verne would be quoted as enthusing: 'This almost surpasses anything my grandfather dreamed of.' Hedging their bets somewhat, a navy band played both 'God Save the King' and 'The Star-Spangled Banner', as well as 'La Marseillaise'. And because Prohibition banned alcoholic beverages, instead of the traditional bottle of champagne being broken over the bow, Suzanne swung a champagne bucket filled with ice-cubes.

Wilkins' old friend Hugo Eckener was another special guest, although it was hoped he'd be playing a rather more active role during the months to come. In a highly ambitious move that had his doubters in uproar, Wilkins planned to surface at the North Pole and rendezvous with Eckener's *Graf Zeppelin*. The pair would then exchange bags of commemorative mail in a symbolic exhibition of man's mastery of the Arctic. If the aims of the expedition were beginning to sound epic, it came as no surprise to find that Paramount Pictures had also come on board with financial backing in return for exclusive newsreel footage of the trip.

The sheer scope of the *Nautilus* venture was the grandest of Wilkins' career thus far, as was the amount of time spent planning the mission — so much so that a full year had already passed since his return from the second leg of the Antarctic expedition. While this allowed Wilkins to finally celebrate a birthday with Suzanne (his forty-second), it also meant he could choose his team with the utmost care. Having quickly discarded requests from the usual cranks and

# Under the North Pole?

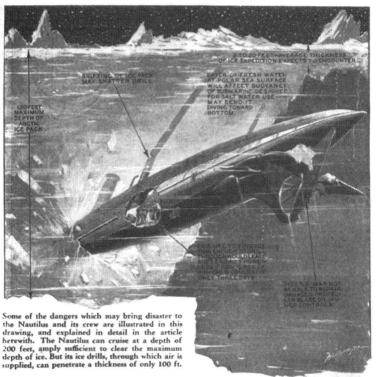

Some of the dangers which may bring disaster to the Nautilus and its crew are illustrated in this drawing, and explained in detail in the article herewith. The Nautilus can cruise at a depth of 200 feet, amply sufficient to clear the maximum depth of ice. But its ice drills, through which air is supplied, can penetrate a thickness of only 100 ft.

ter which will snuff out the *Nautilus* and all aboard it. Yet every resource of science, every mechanical precaution which ingenuity can devise, is incorporated in the *Nautilus* to protect the submarine from anticipated dangers. The detailed drawing on page 48 shows the arrangement of the novel devices which make the *Nautilus* the most unique submarine in all history. Most of these devices—ice-cutting drills, sled runners, diving chambers, etc. —were designed by Simon Lake, veteran submarine inventor.

What are the dangers which will imperil the expedition? Some of the most obvious are these:

The *Nautilus* may get caught beneath ice

so thick that its 100-foot drills could not bore through it; consequently the submarine could not get air, without which the men would perish. Air is also essential to run the Diesel engines used to recharge the batteries which drive the sub under water. For eight hours out of the 24 the sub must lie on the surface recharging the batteries.

The bow of the *Nautilus*, reinforced with concrete though it is, may be damaged by collision with obstacles sufficient to spring a leak and flood the interior.

Batteries may be discharged more rapidly than calculated, leaving the submarine powerless.

A preview of Wilkins' submarine project in *Modern Mechanics and Inventions* magazine.

publicity seekers, among those he selected were the 42-year-old Norwegian oceanographer and meteorologist Professor Harald Sverdrup, who had worked with Amundsen, and another renowned polar scientist, Bernard Villinger.

On 4 June 1931, the *Nautilus* sailed out of New York en route to the English port of Plymouth. 'Our hearts beat high as we churned away from American soil,' Wilkins recalled of the moment. 'But little did we know that the Atlantic crossing would be the most dangerous part of the expedition.'

There was a problem on that first day, when Danenhower put the submarine through a test dive to 80 metres and the *Nautilus* got stuck hard in mud at the bottom of Long Island Sound. As he and other

The crew of the *Nautilus* before setting off on their vain attempt to sail under the North Pole. Wilkins is in the centre in a hat.

senior members of the crew pondered ways of releasing the vessel, she miraculously freed herself. Still, if an omen was needed, this was it.

Real trouble raised its ugly head on 13 June, when the *Nautilus* was about 1500 nautical miles out to sea. A storm was brewing and Lieutenant Commander Danenhower demanded full speed from his mechanics to try to outrun it. But the sea began tossing the submarine around dangerously. Suddenly the starboard engine stopped, having suffered a cracked cylinder; then, after the crew had changed the fuel line from an empty oil tank to another, the port engine started spluttering. Apparently a sea valve used for diving had broken and sea water was leaking into the adjacent fuel tank, causing an erratic feed to the engine. Then some wiring in the motor collapsed and sparks were soon flying around the engine room, threatening to set the submarine on fire. Danenhower was left with no alternative but to close down all equipment and radio an SOS. It was a humiliating start to the mission.

The American battleships *Arkansas* and *Wyoming* raced to their aid. The latter manoeuvred close enough in the huge seas to attach a line and then began towing the *Nautilus* to Ireland.

After three days behind the *Wyoming*, the storm was still buffeting the submarine. One vicious wave crashed over the vessel's bridge and swept quartermaster Edward Clark and assistant engineer Raymond Drakio clean off the conning tower. Fighting for their lives, both men managed to hold on to the slippery surface of the submarine deck and slowly crawl their way back to the tower, where they opened the hatch and dropped down inside to safety.

On 22 June, the two ships rendezvoused with the Irish tug *Morsecock*, which took over the task of towing the stricken sub. Four days later they reached the port of Cobh in County Cork, Ireland. When nothing could be done there to fix the problems, the *Morsecock* towed the submarine on to Devonport in Plymouth Sound, where the repairs were carried out in the Royal Navy dry dock over a number of weeks.

Midway through this frustrating period, on 15 July, Wilkins played host to the Prince of Wales (later King Edward VII and, after he abdicated, the Duke of Windsor). 'I cannot imagine his thoughts on our standard of neatness,' the Australian later mused. 'We were, after all, a scientific party in an experimental craft equipped for our work, not the spit-and-polish type of crew and ship the prince had usually seen.'

Of greater concern to Wilkins, though, was how behind schedule they had fallen. He couldn't hope to meet up with the *Graf* later in the month at the present rate.

On 28 July, the *Nautilus* finally left England. She arrived at Bergen, in south-western Norway, at 5 am on 1 August, where no doubt Wilkins and Danenhower would have learned that Eckener's airship had completed its Arctic voyage and was already back at the hangar in Friedrichshafen. More repairs were instituted there at Bergen, and at their next port of call, Tromso, in the far north of the country.

On 15 August, the *Nautilus* arrived at the Spitsbergen port of Longyearbyen. The fuel tanks were topped up and a general maintenance check completed before the final leg of the journey to the Arctic ice got under way, at about 3 pm on 18 August.

Four days later, the submarine was among the pack-ice some 600 nautical miles from the North Pole. At last it was time to begin the experiment for which they had all prepared. In ideal conditions, Danenhower attempted to submerge the *Nautilus* ... but nothing happened. Assuming that something must have become lodged in one of the two diving rudders, he sent senior diver Frank Crilley — a man who had won the US Medal of Honor for making the deepest dive in history — into the icy water to investigate.

Crilley was lowered between several pieces of floating ice. After a few minutes under water he surfaced, blissfully unaware of the danger zeroing in from behind him. Those on board saw it only too well: a massive piece of ice was drifting over towards the hull and

A dramatic photo of the Arctic icecap shot by Wilkins.

Crilley looked likely to be crushed in the middle. Quartermaster Clark and another crewman, chief radio operator Ray Meyers, immediately leaned over the deck and dragged the bewildered Crilley to safety, seconds before the ice slammed into the *Nautilus* with a bone-shaking crash.

The diver was handed a large glass of rum to calm his nerves before giving his report, which was every bit as chilling as the incident that had just occurred. Both diving rudders had disappeared, he told Commander Danenhower, although the steering rudder was completely intact.

*Disappeared.* How could this have happened?

It was inconceivable that the two diving vanes — solid steel plates bolted to the frame of the submarine — could have broken away at the same time without damaging the steering rudder, located between them. The only answer was sabotage. Considering the raft of setbacks,

227

it seemed that one of the many discontented crewmen on board had deliberately set out to disable the vessel.

Logic dictated that they would have to abort the mission. Only one member of the team wanted to continue; as a younger man, he'd experienced betrayal in North Africa and blatant sabotage in the South of France, and he'd never let them distract him from his goal. After some time spent alone pondering his decision, Wilkins returned to the bridge and spoke to Danenhower: 'We've come this far. At least we should try to get under the ice. That's what the whole expedition is about. To make no further attempt would be to admit complete failure.'

Some reports suggest that Wilkins had been forced into a corner after receiving a radio message from Hearst, who had ordered him to continue — the explorer had been paid to dive under the Arctic ice and head for the North Pole, and dive under it he would. This would not have been out of character for the media magnate, who put headlines above all else, even human lives. But later radio communications call these claims into question. Whatever the case, Wilkins had the final call. The buck stopped with him, and many would question the wisdom of his decision when the lives of his expedition team and the ship's crew were at stake.

Danenhower set a northerly course and on 28 August the *Nautilus* reached her furthest point north, 81° 59' N, less than 500 nautical miles from the pole, but fog closed in before they could attempt to get under the ice.

By 31 August, the fog had cleared. It was D Day for the *Nautilus*. 'Okay, here we go. Flood the main ballast,' Danenhower roared to his crew.

While the vessel gradually sank lower into the water, he and Wilkins watched the waterline rising through the conning tower's mini-portholes. Then there was an almighty crunch as the *Nautilus* headed forward under the icefloe. Wilkins described the sound of the ice smashing against the submarine as being like that of continuous thunder, and the vessel trembling as if caught in a massive earthquake. To everyone bar the awe-struck Australian, it was a terrifying moment.

The ice was about 5 metres thick but the light still penetrated the frozen canopy above the submarine. 'Stop the motors!' shouted Danenhower. 'Let's savour this moment. We can now look at something no man has ever seen before.'

With the *Nautilus* holding station at a depth of some 11 metres, members of the crew took turns at gazing through the portholes at the wondrous sight. The underside of the icefloe was rough, but generally flat. Occasionally there were small peaks protruding and tiny valleys heading upwards. And the colours changed as clouds passed overhead, blocking out the rays of the sun.

Wilkins was entranced as he gazed at the icefloes during the brief dive. 'They were of every shape and size and every conceivable form — minarets, domes, majestic cathedrals and geometric blocks,' he marvelled. 'And all in beautiful, crystal-clear blue water.'

Without the diving rudders, and with the main ice drill having been found to be malfunctioning (suspiciously so) some days before, Danenhower dared not risk heading further under the ice. All he could do was use the steering rudder to reverse out.

'Full astern,' he ordered.

And slowly but surely, the submarine inched its way back and upwards. Soon bright sunlight was bursting through the portholes — they were on the surface again.

The official log of the *Nautilus* suggests that several other dives were made in the next couple of days, with film being taken by the official photographer, Emil Dored, and by Wilkins himself. Officially, however, at least one member of the crew claimed there was only the one dive, on 31 August, and that all the film was shot at that time. Whichever version is the truth, Wilkins had achieved his aim of

The *Nautilus* surfaces on the edge of the Arctic icefloe.

venturing under the icecap. 'No further dive could equal the thrill of our first Arctic plunge,' was his verdict on the experience.

On 5 September, Hearst radioed a plea for the team to return. To prove to the general public he had the safety of the *Nautilus*' crew at heart, Hearst published the text of the radio message on the front page of his various newspapers. 'I feel continued concern about the welfare of yourself and your crew. I most urgently beg you to return promptly to safety,' the message read in part. 'We are all alarmed about the dangers you are incurring which seems to us needless. Will you not please come back now.' Such tugging at the heartstrings did wonders for newspaper sales.

In fact, Wilkins had called a halt to the proceedings just the day before, but the damage inflicted on the superstructure during the dive had left the sub with a radio that could only receive incoming signals. The *Nautilus* was duly turned around and they began their return journey south. In the hope that a message might get through, the expedition leader radioed Hearst in reply with the words: 'Our Arctic trip is over.'

Four days later, the submarine arrived back at Longyearbyen. Wilkins headed straight on to London and into the welcome arms of his wife, after which the couple caught a steamer bound for New York. Already the Australian realised he was facing an administrative nightmare when it came to tying up the many loose ends of the expedition. Meanwhile the submarine, buffeted by early winter storms, limped her way to Bergen, from where the crew returned to the United States aboard the SS *American Banker*. All wages were paid immediately from Wilkins' personal bank account.

On 20 November 1931, a flotilla of ships accompanied the *Nautilus* as she was towed out of Bergen. At noon that day in a nearby fjord, she was scuttled in water 350 metres deep. More than seven decades later, she remains a popular dive site.

The *Nautilus* hadn't made it to the North Pole, but she had proved that it was possible for submarines to dive under the icecap. Ironically the first vessel to reach the pole would be the nuclear submarine USS *Nautilus*, in August 1958.

WILKINS RECEIVED A lambasting in the US press and a particularly frosty reception from William Randolph Hearst when he arrived home late in the year. The media boss was angry that the expedition hadn't resulted in the headlines for which he lusted, and at a meeting with the explorer, he refused to pay outstanding monies. It was especially poor treatment for the man who had always been a good servant to Hearst, and who had more than once shown that his ego, public image and personal financial considerations came a combined, distant second to the importance of scientific exploration. This would be the last time the two men ever spoke to one another.

Hearst wasn't the only one to renege on payment. Paramount refused to come through with the final payment on its contract to take newsreel pictures of the voyage. The company chiefs gave as their lame excuse the 'obvious' fact that Wilkins never really intended to go to the North Pole. Added to his woes was a bizarre demand for $10,000 from the US Shipping Board for not returning the *Nautilus* to New York — even though the very same organisation had ordered that the submarine be scuttled in Norway. A planned lecture tour of the United States was cancelled thanks to a concerted campaign of vilification by American tabloid reporters. Earlier in the year, having been shut out of the story by the exclusive coverage granted to the Hearst and Paramount empires, many of these journalists had either ridiculed Wilkins' plans or at best given them short shrift; now they relished the news that the expedition had fallen well short of its objectives.

Wilkins had been relying on the income he could generate on the lecture circuit, especially as he owed his good friend Lincoln Ellsworth a princely $20,000. But he received an unexpected Christmas present from the billionaire when Ellsworth wiped the debt. He told Wilkins the money was his to use however he wished, other than to pay off debts on the submarine. 'I do not want Danenhower or Lake to profit by it,' he added, intimating that the two navy insiders would surely have been aware that the *O-12* was a dud. Did Ellsworth have an ulterior motive? Future events suggest that he most certainly did.

Some years later, when the dust had settled, Wilkins would write to Hearst detailing his plans to try again with a submarine built from scratch to special specifications. He intended to name the vessel the *Poseidon*. Wilkins also sent the media tycoon some recent photographs of Hearst Land, the Antarctic plateau he had named in the American's honour. Hearst sent a terse reply: 'It is a very pleasing plateau, but it does not seem a very good location for oranges. I think I prefer California as a homeland.' Wilkins never made another attempt at reconciliation.

## Citizen Hearst

There's something about those that achieve greatness in their chosen field of endeavour that inspires biographers, historians and storytellers for decades, even centuries, to come. From the first half of the twentieth century, this would certainly apply to the likes of Shackleton, Amundsen, Lenin, Hearst, Lindbergh and many others with whom Hubert Wilkins came into contact. But woe betide anyone who shone a harsh biographical light on William Randolph Hearst during his lifetime.

In 1903, the year the then forty-year-old newspaper publisher took a seat in the US Congress, Hearst married Millicent Willson, a New York chorus girl half his age. The couple had five sons, even though for much of the time the marriage was a sham, with Hearst openly flaunting his relationship with a young Hollywood actress named Marion Davies. By 1926, Millicent had

William Randolph Hearst's mistress, Marion Davies. The couple entertained Wilkins at 'Hearst Castle' near the end of the round-the-world flight of the *Graf Zeppelin*.

continued ↝

moved into her own residence in New York and the charade was
over.

Hearst and his mistress divided their time between various
mansions in California, the best known of which he had
architecturally designed on his 95,000-hectare ranch at San
Simeon, some 400 kilometres north of Los Angeles. Christened 'La
Cuesta Encantada' (the Enchanted Hill), the palatial spread is now
referred to as Hearst Castle and is one of California's top tourist
attractions. Guides there today tell of how Hubert Wilkins would
regularly fly over the mansion and dip a wing in deference to his
benefactor.

Hearst furnished the grand building with expensive antiques,
paintings by European masters, and vases and statues from ancient
Mediterranean civilisations. He even shipped in entire rooms from
some of the great châteaux and palaces of Europe. Nothing was
too good for his beloved Marion. Indeed, he'd already set up a
movie company, Cosmopolitan Pictures, dedicated to furthering her
career on screen.

The couple were renowned for the parties they threw at San
Simeon. During its 1920s and '30s heyday, there was hardly a
celebrity on earth that didn't make it to the ranch at some time or
another. Former US presidents and other political heavyweights,
Hollywood greats such as Lombard, Gable, Chaplin, Grant, Hope
and Pickford, celebrated gossip columnists, Olympic and sports
champions, aviation heroes and explorer-adventurers — all these
and more. Life truly was 'enchanted' at La Cuesta Encantada for
those inside Hearst and Davies' social circle. It was the stuff of
movies, and sure enough a movie-maker came calling.

Hearst's career and lifestyle, especially his relationship with
Davies, became the basis for Orson Welles' acclaimed 1941 film
*Citizen Kane*, an epic fable about the corrupting influence of
power. While the inspiration for its brooding, megalomaniacal
central character owed much to the legendary Howard Hughes

and others (and even to Welles himself, apparently), Charles Foster Kane was generally considered to be a caricature of William Randolph Hearst. The latter was incensed by the obvious parallels, and particularly by the portrayal of Davies as a singer with no talent.

As lead actor and director, and a larger-than-life presence in his own right, Welles was the one to feel Hearst's personal wrath most keenly. In truth, though, the direct Kane–Hearst parallels were the creation of Orson's co-writer, Herman J. Mankiewicz, who'd once been a favourite up at San Simeon. A notorious drunk, though a dazzlingly talented screenwriter all the same, 'Mank' had taken his subsequent fall from grace rather badly.

Just as *Citizen Kane* was being lauded with glowing reviews and tipped to clean up at the Oscars, Hearst unleashed a relentless campaign to sabotage its release. He is said to have offered RKO Pictures the then-whopping sum of $800,000 to destroy all prints of the film and burn the negative. RKO declined, so he banned all his newspapers, magazines and radio stations from even mentioning the movie. He called in favours from A-list friends, resorting to blatant blackmail if necessary, and pressured cinema owners in every city where he had a newspaper to refuse to show it. Welles himself was targeted one night at his hotel, with the familiar tabloid 'sting' operation (naked woman ready to leap into his arms, photographer on hand to catch the moment), but he received a tip-off beforehand and stayed elsewhere.

Thanks largely to Hearst's influence, *Citizen Kane* proved not to be the box-office success that industry insiders had predicted and was all but ignored on Oscar night. It would be almost a quarter of a century before Welles' masterpiece began receiving the unequivocal acclaim it deserved, frequently topping polls for the best film of all time. By then, Hearst was long dead. He passed away in Beverly Hills, California, in August 1951, at the age of eighty-eight.

# Chapter 15

# The Hired Hand

LINCOLN ELLSWORTH WAS determined to make a name for himself in polar exploration, just like Hubert Wilkins and Richard Byrd had done. And the seeds were sown when Wilkins stayed at Schloss Lenzburg on his honeymoon. As well as their long discussions about the proposed submarine expedition, there was a lot of talk about Ellsworth's plans for fame: he wanted to be the first man to fly across the continent of Antarctica. Wilkins had already beaten him to the honour of being the first to fly in the Antarctic, and Byrd had been the first to fly over the South Pole, in November 1929. No other plane had flown there since and so the honour of making the first trans-Antarctic flight was still up for grabs. Perhaps Wilkins was dismayed at his high-society friend's thirst for personal glory, but there could be no doubting Ellsworth's passion and commitment.

Wilkins spent most of 1932 extricating himself from the quagmire of debt that had resulted from the previous year's foray to the Arctic in the *Nautilus*. Financially broke after paying every bill from his own pocket, and owing a debt of gratitude to Ellsworth for his assistance, Wilkins agreed to lend his considerable expertise to the venture. And for the next four years he was a vital cog in Ellsworth's three expeditions that culminated in the successful flight across the Antarctic.

The link with Ellsworth heralded a change of pace and direction for Wilkins, and he would never again lead his own expedition. Maybe the failure of the *Nautilus* mission had raised some doubts in his mind about his capacity for leadership. Or perhaps this modest man was tired of continually having to front fundraising campaigns. No matter how generous were his major sponsors, extra financial support was always needed to ensure his expeditions were given every chance of success. And it was no easy task finding that money in the early 1930s, with the world reeling under the effects of the Great Depression.

One could only wonder whether he felt guilty at spending so much time away from Suzanne, who was often not in the best of health, plagued by chronic rheumatic fever. In their letters, however, neither of the pair broached the possibility.

EARLY ON IN 1933, at the age of fifty-three, Lincoln Ellsworth got married, after which he and his bride, Mary Louise, headed off on an extended honeymoon in the Pacific. Meanwhile, Wilkins went about organising the expedition. He hired Bernt Balchen as the senior pilot. The 33-year-old Balchen was a former airman in the Royal Norwegian Naval Air Service and chief test pilot for Anthony Fokker and had been Byrd's senior pilot in the 1929 flight over the South Pole — so he was familiar with the frozen continent. Next, Wilkins set about purchasing the best aircraft available. He found it in California: the *Polar Star*, an all-metal, low-winged, Gamma 2B monoplane, made by the Northrop Corporation. With a full load of fuel it had a range of almost 10,000 kilometres.

Wilkins then headed for Norway to find a suitable ship and soon settled on a 400-tonne, 41-metre former fishing vessel named the *Fanefjord*. She had been built in 1919 from the finest Norwegian pine and oak and was powered by both sail and a diesel engine; fully laden

American billionaire Lincoln Ellsworth persuaded Wilkins to help him in his flights over Antarctica and settled many of the Australian's debts from the *Nautilus* project.

with fuel, she had a range of 10,000 nautical miles. Wilkins had her renovated, with the crew's quarters made more comfortable and the addition of metal sheathing in the hull to withstand the might of the Antarctic ice. The ship was then renamed the *Wyatt Earp*, after Ellsworth's wild west hero.

The Australian also hand-picked the men who would sail on the *Wyatt Earp* — Captain Baard Holth and eight officers and crewmen, all of whom were Antarctic veterans, with years of experience on Norwegian whaling expeditions. Continuing to shop locally, Wilkins chose a nineteen-year-old navy pilot, Magnus Olsen, to be Balchen's understudy.

With Ellsworth having finally joined the team, the *Earp* left Bergen on Saturday, 29 July 1933, bound for the New Zealand city of Dunedin, via the Canary Islands and Cape Town. Having collected the last provisions, she headed off for Little America, Byrd's old base at the Bay of Whales in Antarctica, on 5 December, arriving thirty-three days later. The *Polar Star* had been brought to the camp by freighter and assembled ready for the attempt on the historic flight.

Balchen and Ellsworth carried out three test flights around the bay before disaster struck, on 13 January, announced by a fearsome rumbling like the erupting of a volcano. The *Wyatt Earp* shook like a leaf in the wind, while over on the ice, the runway on which the *Polar Star* was standing suddenly began to crack. Only the Northrop's wings, acting like a bridge between two of the broken pieces of ice, stopped the aircraft from disappearing into a watery grave. Crew-members jumped into a dinghy and risked their lives to secure the *Polar Star* to the ship with lines. It took them six hours to haul the plane back on board the ship, only for them to then have to confront the damage: its skis were smashed beyond repair and the wings grotesquely bent. There would be no cross-continent flight that summer.

The crew-members were shattered — many burst into tears. But Wilkins remained calm. He urged the team not to shed tears over the broken plane and soon had them all drinking champagne instead, toasting to success in the future. The Australian might not have been leading the expedition, but he certainly knew how to inspire the men.

The next day, when the disappointment had largely dissipated, Wilkins called the team together again. 'We've got plenty of fuel and supplies on board,' he said. 'Any of you who can spare the time can join me as we take them onto the plateau. That way, when we come back next spring, there will be a reserve of stores awaiting us.' Four of the Norwegians, including Olsen, volunteered. It was an exacting task as the supplies had to be dragged on sledges a distance of more than 80 kilometres, into a biting wind and in temperatures that hovered around minus 30 degrees Celsius. The five men slaved for ten hours each day doing the backbreaking work. It was the expedition's single achievement of that first summer of 1933–34.

That done, it was time to head back to Dunedin. From there an oil tanker, the *Texaco South Africa*, took the smashed aircraft to California for major repairs at the Northrop factory.

With money not an issue, there was never any doubt that Ellsworth would be trying again in November. This time he bowed to the experience of Wilkins, who suggested the American try the flight in the opposite direction, beginning at Wilkins' old stomping ground of Deception Island. But again, luck was not with them. First, it was angry storms that kept them grounded; then the *Polar Star* broke a connecting rod in its engine. By radio, Wilkins arranged for a couple of spare rods to be flown to Magallanes, the southernmost port in Chile, and the *Earp* set off on a 2000-nautical-mile round trip to collect them.

On 30 December, with the new part fitted and the skies clear at last, Ellsworth decided to make an attempt for his elusive prize. After two and a half hours, however, the *Polar Star* hit some treacherous weather and Balchen, valuing his own life, turned the plane around and flew back to Deception Island. Ellsworth was furious; it was the last time the pair worked together.

On 21 January 1935, the team sailed from Deception Island for Montevideo, where the *Earp* was laid up until the following spring. A second year had gone by with nothing to show for their efforts.

By this point, Wilkins wanted to call off the whole annual pilgrimage to Antarctica. Frustrated at the expedition's lack of scientific credibility, he was eager to make another submarine attempt on the North Pole. But when Ellsworth asked him to organise the third attempt, he reluctantly agreed; he had given the billionaire his word that he would help him finish the job, and he was not about to renege on a promise.

At Ellsworth's request, Wilkins sought out a replacement for Balchen and found it in Herbert Hollick-Kenyon. The latter had been born in London but emigrated to Canada with his family at the age of twelve and was an accomplished commercial pilot. Also signed up was an American flyer from Oregon, J.H. Lymburger.

For their 1935–36 assault, the team established a base at Dundee Island, on the northern tip of the Antarctic Peninsula. Twice Hollick-Kenyon and Ellsworth set out for Little America, but twice bad weather forced them to return to Dundee Island. Finally, on 23 November 1935, they were aloft without their flight being aborted. Part of Wilkins felt disappointed, but he kept his feelings to himself: he had done most of the organising and it was largely his expertise that had got them this far — but he wasn't going to receive any of the kudos.

Ellsworth wrote in his log: 'Heading for the unknown. Bold and rugged mountain peaks across our route lay ahead, some of which seemed to rise almost sheer to 12,000ft as far as the eye could see. I named this range "Eternity Range".' The radio operator on the *Wyatt Earp* knew nothing of this, however. The transmitter on the aircraft had ceased to work soon after take-off, and as a result there were soon fears that the duo had crashed.

It was estimated that the flight would take around fourteen hours; instead, it took twenty-two days to cover the 5600 kilometres. Three times bad weather forced them to land. On one occasion, the blizzard raged for three days and almost buried the *Polar Star* under snow. It took Ellsworth and Hollick-Kenyon another three days to dig the aircraft out and prepare a runway. Then, on 5 December, they ran out of fuel and were forced down again. Although they didn't know it, they were just 26 kilometres short of their destination. Setting off on foot, they twice trekked in the wrong direction and had to return to the plane for more supplies. On the third attempt they were successful, reaching Little America on 15 December, almost eleven days after being forced down.

Although there had been fears for the lives of the two men, Wilkins had been optimistic. Convinced that if the plane had come down it would have been nearer to its destination than to Dundee Island, he ordered the *Earp* to head for the Bay of Whales. After sailing halfway around the continent, the ship made it there on 20 January 1936, five days after an Australian ship, the HMAS *Discovery*, had arrived and taken the two airmen on board.

Several of the Ellsworth team managed to get one of Byrd's abandoned tractors running and headed with Hollick-Kenyon for the *Polar Star*, carrying a supply of gasoline. The aircraft was then flown to the Bay of Whales and loaded onto the *Earp*. The trans-Antarctic flight had been completed at last.

Ellsworth, Wilkins and the rest of the team arrived back in New York on 19 April. Having achieved his much-sought-after fame, Ellsworth had no further use for the *Polar Star* — so he gave it away. Today it is an exhibit at the National Air and Space Museum in Washington, DC.

And it was as easy as that for someone as rich as William Linn Ellsworth. It was like discarding a toy. One can only imagine how Wilkins must have felt about the privileged Ellsworth being able to 'buy' fame. Then there was Admiral Richard E. Byrd, who could call on the US Navy to provide all he needed for his similar brush with glory. Wilkins had to fight to raise every single dollar for his ventures, and unlike those others, he wasn't aiming to achieve celebrity status. Every one of his expeditions had one clear aim: to further scientific knowledge.

WILKINS HAD HARDLY arrived home at the New York apartment he shared with Suzanne before the two of them were heading back to the harbour, to join their old friend Dr Hugo Eckener at Friedrichshafen. The German's latest airship, the *Hindenburg*, was about to begin a regular service across the Atlantic. At 245 metres in length (the equivalent of three modern Boeing 747s placed end to end) and equipped with cabins for up to seventy-two passengers, it was bigger than the old *Graf Zeppelin*, on which Wilkins had travelled around the world seven years earlier. Unlike the former flagship, the passenger quarters were inside the body of the airship rather than in the rear gondola. There was a crew of sixty-one.

The *Hindenburg*, numbered LZ129, was originally intended to be filled with helium, but a US military embargo on the export of the gas meant that the Germans had to use flammable hydrogen instead. With the Wilkinses on board, the giant airship was to make its first voyage from Friedrichshafen to Lakeside, New Jersey, on 6 May 1936 — just over a month after its maiden voyage from Germany to Rio de Janeiro.

This time Eckener would be a passenger instead of at the controls, though. Some years back he had fallen foul of the Nazis, after considering running for the office of president against their candidate. More recently, he had refused the request of propaganda minister Joseph Goebbels to name the new airship the *Adolf Hitler*, instead opting to honour the late Prussian general and people's president Paul von Hindenburg, who had remained staunchly opposed to Hitler until his death in August 1934. It was during the *Hindenburg*'s maiden flight to Rio that Goebbels declared Eckener to be a 'non-person', which meant that neither Eckener's name nor photograph could appear in any German newspaper and that he could no longer run the airship company.

But Goebbels could not stem Eckener's influence, and the airship pioneer wanted his old friends on board for the blue-riband flight. Fellow passengers included Karl von Wiegand and Lady Drummond-Hay, both of whom, as in 1929, were covering the event for the

Hearst newspapers. It was like old home week as Wilkins, Eckener and the two reporters exchanged stories of what had happened in their lives since the previous historic flight.

Unlike the circumnavigation and the Wilkinses' honeymoon trip the following year, the flight was uneventful — although there was one truly memorable moment. The *Hindenburg* left Germany on 6 May and sixty hours later it was circling above New York, at which point Suzanne was asked to sing a song. She chose 'I'm in the Mood for Love', written by renowned composer Jimmy McHugh the previous year. It had become an instant hit, with versions released by the likes of Vera Lynn, Louis Armstrong, Frances Langford and the Bob Crosby and Jimmy Dorsey orchestras. Suzanne's rendition on the *Hindenburg* was transmitted down to a local radio station and broadcast to its listeners. It was the first time such a stunt had been attempted anywhere in the world. And it was obvious to all the passengers how much love she had for her husband.

Just a year later, the *Hindenburg* would seal a place for itself in history, in one of the greatest engineering disasters of all time. On 6 May 1937, as the airship came in to land at Lakehurst, it caught fire and exploded. Thirty-six people died and many more suffered agonising burns. The catastrophe spelled an end to the German Zeppelin industry.

The tragedy affected Wilkins profoundly. When he heard the news, he thought about the carefree hours he had spent on board with Suzanne and his good mate Hugo Eckener (who, fortunately, was not on board this time). And he couldn't help thinking about the missed telegram that had kept him from being aboard the *R-38* when it had crashed sixteen years earlier.

HAVING SPENT MUCH of the past twelve months finetuning his plans to return to the Arctic with a new submarine, Wilkins was relaxing at home with Suzanne when he received a telephone call from Constantin Oumansky on 15 August 1937. The chargé d'affaires at the Soviet Embassy asked him to come to Washington urgently. He would explain the reason once the Australian arrived.

Wilkins was intrigued. A former journalist with the official Soviet newsagency Tass, Oumansky was a shadowy figure whom FBI chief J. Edgar Hoover believed was a member of the Soviet secret service, the MGB (forerunner to the KGB). As a confidant of Soviet dictator Joseph Stalin, Oumansky was destined for greater prominence in years to come.

Once Wilkins had arrived in the capital, Oumansky told him of the disappearance of famed Russian aviator Sigismund Levanevsky and five others in a plane en route from Moscow to San Francisco. The Russians were looking for help from Arctic experts to conduct a search in Alaska, while they themselves would search from Europe. Stefansson had suggested that Wilkins would be the perfect choice to lead the North American mission and it was a sound recommendation: nobody could match the Australian for his combination of flight experience over the polar regions and navigational skill.

Wilkins was well aware of Levanevsky's reputation, the man that fellow aviators had dubbed 'Russia's Lindbergh'. He had first made international headlines in 1933 after rescuing Jimmie Mattern, an American flyer who had crashed in Siberia. In April the following year, Levanevsky was one of the pilots who helped rescue the crew of a research ship, the *Chelyuskin*, which was crushed by ice and sank in the Bering Strait. For that he was awarded 'Hero of the Soviet Union' status by Stalin. But there was more at stake now than simply saving the life of a gifted pilot once favoured by the notoriously fickle Russian leader.

In early 1937, the Soviet Union had shocked the world by announcing it planned to run passenger flights from Moscow over the North Pole to San Francisco. Although Stalin had stated that

Levanevsky would be at the controls for the first test flight, there was no sign of the celebrated flyer during either of the two trial flights, the second of which, on 12–14 July, saw a crew led by Mikhail Gromov make the longest nonstop flight in the history of aviation, having covered a geographical distance of just over 10,000 kilometres. In fact, rumours had begun reaching the West that Levanevsky had been arrested in one of Stalin's purges and was in jail awaiting execution. But there was a third test run still to come. For, although the two flights were the first across the Arctic since Wilkins and Eielson's epic journey nine years earlier — and had therefore brought the Soviet Union significant praise in the media — the aircraft used were slow, single-motor planes with huge fuel tanks, and were quite unsuitable for freight or passenger transport. A new Bolkhovitinov long-range bomber was to be trialled during the third journey. It was a 25.4-metre, four-engine monoplane, capable of carrying 5000 kilograms of bombs at speeds of up to 316 kilometres per hour, and with a range of 4500 kilometres. And Sigismund Levanevsky had either been forgiven by Stalin or the Western news reports about his arrest were wrong, for he was at the helm.

Levanevsky took off from an aerodrome near Moscow on 12 August 1937, with five other crew-members on board. Having less range than the Vega used by the two pioneers of the Arctic route, the big aircraft with its distinctive blue fuselage and red wings would have to stop to refuel in Fairbanks, Alaska. The plane passed over the North Pole at 5.53 pm on 13 August. It was 500 kilometres on the Alaskan side of the pole when Levanevsky sent a radio message explaining that he was having difficulties: 'Motor 343 [the code for engine trouble]. Flying heavily against 100km/hr wind. Losing altitude from 6000m to 4300m.' Moments later he sent a second, incomplete message, '48-3400 …', meaning: 'We are going to land in …'

Was he going to land in a few minutes? In the snow? It mattered little. The flight organisers in Moscow knew that Levanevsky and his crew had come down somewhere between the North Pole and Alaska. The important question was whether they'd survived or whether their plane had crashed through the ice and sunk in the icy ocean.

A search was swiftly organised. First to take to the air was 28-year-old Canadian Bob Randall, a pilot with the Mackenzie River Air Service. Randall flew along the Alaskan coast, landing and questioning every group of Eskimos he saw. Only one group, on Barter Island, just off the coast, reported hearing anything unusual: the sound of what they thought was an outboard motor. But they could see no sign of a boat.

Meanwhile, Wilkins was hunting for a suitable aircraft to use. He soon found one in New York — a Consolidated PBY Flying Boat. It was owned by a friend of Wilkins and Stefansson, aviator and explorer Richard Archbold, who was quick to lend the aircraft. To make up his team of pilots, the Australian turned to his old colleague Al Cheesman and the British-Canadian pilot who had flown across Antarctica with Ellsworth, Herbert Hollick-Kenyon. They were joined by Australian engineer Gerald Brown and a former US Navy radio operator, Ray Booth. The team flew north from New York on 17 August and five days later were at Coppermine trading post, well above the Arctic Circle, fully provisioned with food and gasoline and ready to begin their search.

On their initial sortie, Wilkins faced his first emergency. Getting up from his navigator's table to stretch his legs, he walked back along the fuselage to find the floor covered in gasoline, some 5 centimetres deep and slurping around with every jolt of the aircraft. Wilkins spent the next two hours on his hands and knees mopping up the fuel with old rags, which he then hung from the ventilators at the plane's aft to evaporate. 'It was a miracle that the fumes had not caused an explosion before I discovered the danger,' he'd report. It transpired that when the Eskimos at Coppermine were filling the ten extra drums of fuel that were to be carried in the cockpit, they'd filled them right to the top, so that when the plane rose, the gasoline expanded in the reduced air pressure and seeped out of the drums.

Because of changing weather, there was a need for accurate meteorological forecasts. Wilkins asked for help from all the countries in the region, and for the first time in history the United States, Canada, Soviet Union, Norway, Sweden and Denmark responded by sharing their knowledge. Such international co-operation was a boon, and something he had long advocated. But there was no way around the navigational problems caused by their proximity to the North Magnetic Pole and the resulting interference with his four compasses.

For a month the Flying Boat zigzagged across the icy wastelands, searching and sending radio messages to the frequency used by Levanevsky, but with no result. With the northern winter closing in, Wilkins was forced to abandon the search and return to New York.

The Soviet authorities were keen for Wilkins to continue during the winter, however, and through their embassy in Washington they purchased the Lockheed Electra that flamboyant aviator Henry 'Dick' Merrill had recently used to collect movie film and photographs of the coronation of King George VI for the American media. Wilkins gladly accepted the job, pointing out that, with the air free of dust, the reflection of the Arctic moonlight on the snow was bright enough to enable a person to read a newspaper. Plus, during the period immediately before and after each full moon, they could expect six full days of uninterrupted moonlight at that time of year.

Wilkins, Cheesman and the rest of the team reached Point Barrow in late November. For the next four months, the aircraft made wide sweeps across different areas of the Arctic, but again with no success.

248

In late March 1938, the Soviet Union called off the search; there was no way that, had Levanevsky and his crew survived the emergency landing on 13 August, they could still be alive now.

Wilkins arrived back in New York on 25 March. In his two aircraft he had spent some 285 hours in the air and had flown around 71,000 kilometres, searching an area of 440,000 square kilometres. It was a heroic effort, one that did much to re-establish his reputation in America while winning him admiration and new friends in Russia. With war looming, such a spirit of international co-operation was in short supply during the late 1930s.

In June 1938, Wilkins was invited to Moscow. It was the first time he'd been in Russia since the Quaker trip fifteen years earlier with Lucita Squier. In a ceremony at the Kremlin, Foreign Commissar Maxim Livinov offered the official thanks of the Soviet Union for the Australian's efforts during the search for Levanevsky and presented him with several awards for foreign heroes. Wilkins also addressed the Soviet Academy of Sciences and was then given carte blanche to tour Moscow and Leningrad, with all meals and the finest accommodation paid for by the Kremlin.

Back in London, MI6's C must have had a quiet chuckle at the way his man was being feted.

Chapter 16

# Exploring the Paranormal

WILKINS' ANCESTOR BISHOP John Wilkins had been an unabashed proponent of space travel, although, in his time, the whole concept seemed little more than a figment of a novelist's fertile imagination. But some 250-odd years later, once a generation of pioneer aviators had shown that man could fly, the idea of space travel was not that far-fetched. Similarly, although suspicion remains strong in some quarters, in the twenty-first century the area of psychic phenomena and the paranormal has become altogether more acceptable to the masses, whereas, back in the 1930s, it was only the more forward-thinking who even entertained the possibility of there being a world beyond our own.

Hubert Wilkins had always been a forward thinker, and it's safe to assume that during the '30s he had more time than before to turn his mind to other-worldly pursuits. Always active as he was with his plans for a second submarine venture and regular contributions to scientific journals, his exploration activities since 1932 had been confined to serving as expedition manager and consultant, albeit a tirelessly hardworking one. The months once lost each year to budget meetings, public fundraising and corporate public relations were therefore a thing of the past for the Australian — Ellsworth's open chequebook had seen to that.

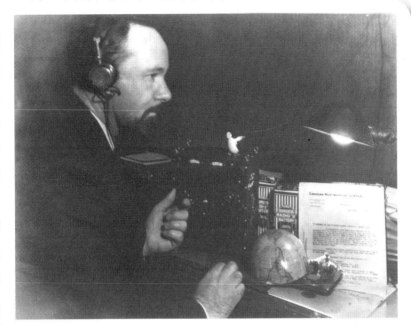

Wilkins believed radio was not the only way to communicate over long distances. Try mental telepathy!

Wilkins had befriended a well-known writer and clairvoyant named Harold Sherman. Many people regarded Sherman as a crank, but not Wilkins, who had been interested in mental telepathy and other psychic phenomena for quite some time. Born in 1898, Sherman turned to writing in his twenties. By the time he died in 1987, aged eighty-nine, he had churned out over eighty books, from sporting novels for young boys and self-help manuals to explanations of the paranormal. He also wrote thousands of magazine stories and pamphlets.

In August 1937, while Wilkins was making his hurried preparations before leaving to join the search for Sigismund Levanevsky, Sherman went to see him. 'While you're away, why don't we try a few experiments in mental telepathy?' the American suggested before elaborating: they could pick a time every few days, and for half an hour Wilkins would concentrate on a particular subject while Sherman attempted to read his thoughts from New York. Both men would write down what entered their minds during the half-hour and send their notes to a respected third party for comparison.

Wilkins loved the idea, seeing it as a great opportunity to throw some light on the incredible power of the human mind and perhaps silence a few sceptics along the way.

So arrangements were made. Every third day between 11.30 pm and midnight, New York time, Wilkins would sit quietly and visualise what had been happening to him that day. Thousands of miles away, Sherman would turn out the lights in his New York apartment and try to read Wilkins' mind. Sherman would send copies of his accounts to a psychologist at Columbia University, Dr Gardner Murphy, and to Samuel Emery, a resident of the City Club of New York, both of whom would later compare them with Wilkins' diary entries.

Wilkins later explained: 'It soon became apparent that Sherman, in some manner not understood by either of us, was picking up quite a number of thought forms — strong thoughts emitted by me.' It was like a replay of Wilkins reading the radio messages on the *Quest* in 1922.

More than 60 per cent of the entries matched — too many coincidences to give the sceptics any cause for derision. The pair later published the results in a book called *Thoughts Through Space: A Remarkable Adventure in the Realm of the Mind*. The degree of mirroring in the two men's accounts was quite eerie at times.

On 11 November 1937, Wilkins went to a formal ball in Saskatchewan wearing an ill-fitting, borrowed dinner suit. Among those at the ball were officers from the Canadian armed forces and the Royal Mounted Police, and government dignitaries and their wives. Sherman's entry for that day noted: 'You are in company with men in military attire — some women — evening dress — social occasion — important people present — much conversation — you appear to be in evening dress yourself.'

Almost four weeks later, on 7 December, Wilkins was in Point Barrow when one of the buildings caught fire. He watched the blaze from the window. Sherman's version read: 'I seem to see a crackling fire shining out of the darkness — get a definite fire impression as though a house is burning — you can see it from your location on the ice.'

Sherman was delighted with the number of accurate correlations. But he reckoned the experiments had proved that humans were 'in the kindergarten of their own mental processes'. As for Wilkins, he was unsure whether he and Sherman had proved beyond doubt that there had been mental telepathy between them. The facts seemed to suggest otherwise, however.

JOHN WILKINS WOULD surely have approved of his progeny's experiment, but what of the bishop's main point of paranormal interest, the existence of a civilisation living on the Moon? Or, taken further, could there be alien life forms on planets in another universe — aliens so advanced that they might one day come to Earth and teach humans about the past and perhaps the future?

Members of the Urantia Movement were convinced that such aliens were already in their midst. And Wilkins was to find himself a leading figure in the movement, keen that others should eventually share his excitement about the ideas passed on by the visitors. Because of the organisation's early demands for complete secrecy about its teachings and its membership, it's not known exactly when the famous explorer was drawn into this small group of thinkers, but one can well imagine that his interest in the paranormal peaked following the intriguing experiment with Sherman.

The Urantia Movement began to take shape in the mid 1920s. University of Chicago psychiatrist Dr William Sadler, a scientist well known for his often unusual approach to mental health, had decided to gather some friends and former patients together for an informal chat group. His wife, Dr Lena Sadler, was a key figure in the get-togethers, held on Sunday afternoons at their home in the windy city. Those involved grandly called themselves 'the Forum'.

Born in 1875, Sadler was also a leading figure in the Seventh Day Adventist Church and a teacher of pastoral counselling at the church's McCormick Theological Seminary. He had got his break in the scientific field while working for Dr John Harvey Kellogg, an Adventist surgeon, author of books on health and diet, and brother of Cornflakes magnate William Keith Kellogg. The ties with the clan didn't end there, for Lena Sadler was a distant relative of the famous breakfast-cereal manufacturer, and Lena's sister Anna had married her half-first cousin, Wilfred Custer Kellogg.

William Sadler had spent over a decade debunking and refuting spiritualism. To him, every psychic was a fraud — either that or a mentally disturbed person who honestly thought they were receiving messages from 'the other side'. But one Sunday during the early part of 1925, he told the Forum that he'd found an exception to this rule.

Sadler explained that since 1911 he and members of his family had been 'visited' by extraterrestrials from a place deep in another galaxy who were imparting knowledge unknown to other humans. These visitors called themselves Revelators or Midwayers, and referred to Sadler and his household — Lena, their son William Jr, and Anna and Wilfred Kellogg (both of whom lived with the Sadlers for a time) — as the Contact Commission. The Midwayers gave their revelations through a sleeping channeller, believed by many historians to have been Wilfred Kellogg. Whether it was his brother-in-law or not, the

Forum host wasn't saying, but this channeller was the one such psychic or medium who had proved to be the real thing in Sadler's opinion. From that moment on, the Forum became a discussion group for the aliens' theories of Urantia, the extraterrestrials' name for Planet Earth.

Details of the Forum and the resulting Urantia Movement are sketchy at best, and even Sadler's published account of the chronology of events that followed is difficult to piece together. It seems that after 1911 there was close to twenty years of preliminary contacts while the channeller and other Contact Commissioners were being tested or trained by the Midwayers; much of the information that the humans had gathered concerned Urantia's relationship to other planets in the galaxy of Satania and beyond. A dramatic change to this procedure occurred one night when a Midwayer replied: 'If you only knew what you are in contact with, you would not ask such trivial questions. You would rather ask such questions as might elicit answers of supreme value to the human race.' Suitably shocked by the response, and inspired, the small group began to seek outsiders to help compile the suitable questions and gain a greater understanding of the replies.

At the aliens' request, the Forum became a formalised club in around September 1925, debating the results of the contact sessions. Each member signed a pledge of secrecy — a useful tool, seeing as these educated men and women might well have been held up to public ridicule had their involvement become common knowledge. Sadler's house guests then began compiling the important, and increasingly more complex, theological questions the Midwayers had suggested, after which the Contact Commission would present them at the next sitting. The replies became known as the Urantia Papers. Much of the dense (to some, unfathomable) text concerned religion, with detailed references to the work of Jesus Christ —

who, it turned out, was the reincarnation of a prophet named Michael of Urantia.

According to Sadler, the replies would miraculously appear through the channeller as he filled the sheets of empty paper in front of him. Members of the Forum showed samples of these answers to handwriting experts, who were said to have agreed that they were not the writings of a human.

Another happening that defied logic concerned the safeguarding of the Urantia Papers. Copies of the replies were typed up and filed away while the originals were locked in a safe, together with the questions. But the next time the safe was opened, the documents had disappeared. With every new set of questions and answers that were subsequently collected, Sadler began placing $10 banknotes between the sheets of paper, only to find that the originals would disappear while the banknotes remained in the locked safe.

Sadler himself admitted that there were many anomalies in the Urantia Papers — or 'missing links', as he put it. He was never able to explain why the extraterrestrials made their revelations in English, for instance, and not in some other language. 'There is much connected with the appearance of the Urantia Papers which no human fully understands,' he conceded.

No date is available for the final contact session with the Midwayers, but by 3 April 1939 a study group called 'the Seventy' had been set up to help prepare the vast collection of typed papers for publication. Hubert Wilkins, fresh from a final expedition under Lincoln Ellsworth, was known to have been a member of the group. The last meeting of the Forum was held on 31 May 1942, three years after the death of Lena Sadler, but the Seventy would continue to meet until well into the next decade. During the seventeen years of the Forum's existence, it had attracted a membership of 486.

The extraterrestrials had given the humans permission to publish the work, and some 10,000 copies of the 2100-page *Urantia Book* were eventually printed in 1955, at a cost of $75,000. When Lena died in August 1939, she'd left $25,000 in the hope that one day the papers would be published; the first person to come forward with a donation of $1000 to help offset the remaining amount was Wilkins.

The book quietly appeared on the shelves of a few specialist bookshops. With their professional reputations on the line, perhaps the devotees wanted to avoid controversy. Sadler provided a different reason for the lack of publicity, however: 'We were told to study the methods employed by Jesus in introducing his work on Earth. Note how quietly he worked at first. So often after even a miracle, he would admonish the recipient of his ministry, saying "Tell no man what has happened to you".'

As a result, years after the deaths of both Sadler and Wilkins, those that are aware of the Urantia Papers are in a significant minority. For Hubert Wilkins, they became a book he would treasure for the rest of his life.

A YOUNG L. Ron Hubbard — soon to become world famous as a science-fiction writer, founder of the Church of Scientology and proponent of Dianetics — entered Wilkins' orbit around the time that the Seventy study group had got under way. Surprisingly perhaps, their meeting came about through an altogether more secular, Earth-based organisation than the Urantia Movement.

For every genuine adventurer who has gone about their exploration of the world methodically and with no thought for the acclaim that their exploits deserve, there have always been scores of others who have boasted of successes that in reality are no more than elaborate hoaxes. The Explorers Club, currently located in New York's fashionable East 70th Street, has had to separate the worthy from the frauds ever since it was formed in 1904 by a group of enthusiasts determined to encourage expeditions to every last corner of the world.

The prestige of the club can be gauged by the names of some of its best-known members. Robert Peary, the head of the team said to have been the first to reach the North Pole in 1909; Roald Amundsen, who two years later beat Robert Falcon Scott in the race to be first to the South Pole; Charles Lindbergh, the aviator who in 1927 piloted the *Spirit of St Louis* in the first nonstop solo flight across the Atlantic Ocean; Thor Heyerdahl, who sailed the balsawood raft *Kon-Tiki* from Peru to French Polynesia in 1947 in an attempt to prove that the Polynesians actually came from South America; Edmund Hilary and Tenzing Norgay, the first team to climb Mount Everest and return safely, in 1953; and Neil Armstrong, who in 1969 was the first man to set foot on the Moon.

In the eyes of many historians, Wilkins' efforts matched those of each of these twentieth-century heroes and his credentials to join the Explorers Club were watertight. He spent many an afternoon and evening mixing with like-minded men, discussing the boundaries of the world still to be reached and the future of the people who populated each and every nation on Earth. They would relax in the comfortable surroundings of the old club headquarters on 72nd Street, not far from the Tudor building that currently houses the club. Wilkins' regular companions there included his old mentor Stefansson and Richard Archbold, the heir to the Standard Oil Company fortune and the man who had willingly offered the Australian his Flying Boat for the Levanevsky search.

Wilkins and Archbold had a lot in common. The latter was a pioneer aviator and was particularly interested in the tribes, plants and animals of the uncharted highlands of West Papua (now the Indonesian province of Irian Jaya) and had led three separate expeditions to the area. It was shades of Wilkins' time with the Murri and the Yolngu in Australia.

In the late 1930s a Nebraska-born, self-proclaimed adventurer managed to join the trio in their regular soirées. Lafayette Ronald Hubbard was not a member of the Explorers Club, but his gift of the gab ensured he was allowed in whenever he turned up. He would tell club-members about his so-called Caribbean Motion Picture Expedition of 1932, on board the four-masted schooner *Doris Hamlin* — specifically, how he was the director and had filmed underwater movie footage for the US Hydrographic Office and the University of Michigan. As it turned out, neither group had any record of having ever received footage from the expedition. Hubbard also boasted of selling photos to the *New York Times* and film to Pathé News. Again, neither organisation actually received anything from him. Another of his regular discussion topics were the three expeditions he claimed to have led to Central America between 1933 and 1937, to study primitive native tribes in the region. US immigration authorities had no record of him even leaving the country during that period, however.

It mattered not, apparently. He was a great raconteur and Wilkins and the others enjoyed his company. Indeed, Hubbard wrote in his diary for 13 December 1939 that he'd been with Wilkins, Stefansson and Archbold that day and the three older men had 'made me much at home'.

Hubbard proved to be a good listener too, especially when the Australian was discussing the philosophy of Urantia. Published years after his meetings with Wilkins, a number of the plots in Hubbard's science-fiction stories bear more than a passing resemblance to Urantia ideas; and Scientology, of course, is based on the theory of aliens determining our lives on Earth. Rightly or wrongly, L. Ron Hubbard was elected as a full member of the Explorers Club in 1940.

Another controversial member of the club was Frederick Cook, a New York medical practitioner and pioneer Arctic explorer. Cook and the leader of the first expedition on which he visited the Arctic, Admiral Robert Peary, were to be involved in a bitter feud that stretched over decades.

In 1906, Cook was elected president of the Explorers Club before heading off on one of his expeditions. On his return, he claimed to be the first to have climbed Alaska's Mount McKinley (at 6194 metres, the highest mountain in North America), reaching the summit, he said, in September 1906. But a year later there were doubts cast about his claim and it was suggested that the photo allegedly taken at the summit was in fact from a ridge at 4700 metres. Then, within eighteen months, Cook and Peary were swapping allegations about who had reached the North Pole first: Cook claimed to have been there on 21 April 1908; Peary, whose counter-claim was for 6 April the following year, denounced Cook as a fraud. The general public, however, was unfazed, and 100,000 New Yorkers turned out to honour Cook in a ticker-tape parade through the city. Eventually, his claims were rejected by the scientific community. There were also grave doubts about Peary's assertion, and it was only the efforts of friends in the US Congress, who passed a bill recognising his claim, that saved him from being denounced, too.

Worse for Cook, he got further shamed while involved in the search for oil in the United States. In 1923, he and ninety-one other oil company executives were convicted on charges of using the US Mail to defraud the public in oil-stock sales. He was jailed for almost fifteen years (with parole, he served just over seven) and fined $12,000. While serving his sentence at Leavenworth Federal Penitentiary in Kansas, Cook worked in the rehabilitation of drug addicts in the prison population, was the resident doctor in the penitentiary's hospital and was superintendent of the school.

Wilkins had never lost his admiration for Frederick Cook, however, despite the accusations levelled against the medical practitioner. In late 1939, while the eyes of the world were on the war that had recently broken out in Europe, the pair met in New York. Wilkins was able to explain that, despite some remaining hostility from his peers, Cook's photo was once again hanging in the Explorers Club along with those of all the other presidents, including Peary. But there was still bitterness beating in Cook's heart. 'Whatever anyone thinks,' the old man replied, 'I *did* climb Mount McKinley and I *did* reach the North Pole. I will eventually stand before my maker with a clear conscience.'

Cook went to meet his maker only months later, on 5 August 1940.


IT WAS WITH some reluctance that Wilkins had agreed to take part in one last expedition with Lincoln Ellsworth. As it turned out, their 1938–39 Antarctic foray would be the final privately funded expedition in the history of polar exploration. In future, all missions would be funded by nations with a toehold on the frozen continent.

His reservations were twofold. Firstly, his preference for finishing what he had started with the *Nautilus* remained as strong as ever, and secondly, relations between the two old friends had cooled somewhat. Ellsworth was resentful of the publicity that Wilkins was able to engender, especially after his efforts in the Levanevsky search and the feting he'd subsequently received in Moscow by the Kremlin hierarchy. But with no financial backing for a second submarine mission forthcoming, Wilkins again found himself signing on with the American.

Although the stated aim of the expedition was to make a flight across the diameter of the Antarctic Circle — a rather pointless endeavour, given Ellsworth's 1935 flight from Dundee Island to Little

America — there was a hidden agenda on this trip. Ellsworth had been approached by the US State Department to lay claim to any unexplored areas of Antarctica, even if other countries had already staked their claim. The race to carve up the continent was now well under way. Ellsworth was to keep his instructions secret, especially from Wilkins. After all, Australia had a major stake in Antarctica thanks to the efforts of Sir Douglas Mawson, who had claimed vast areas adjacent to the Davis Sea for Australia without actually having set foot on the mainland. It was in this same area that Ellsworth planned to begin the expedition.

The *Wyatt Earp*, the American's 400-tonne, 41-metre converted fishing vessel, was dragged back into service after a refit in Norway. There would be two aircraft: a Northrop-built Delta, an all-metal monoplane with a 750-horsepower Wright cyclone engine; and a small two-seater plane, the Aeronca Scout, whose name described its

The perils of the Antarctic ... but the *Wyatt Earp* did manage to escape after being trapped in the ice.

purpose. As with previous expeditions, both planes were equipped with wheels, pontoons and skis. J.H. Lymburner, who had been with Ellsworth and Wilkins on the previous expedition, was the chief pilot, and a Canadian flyer named Burton Trerice would serve as stand-by pilot. Again as before, all the officers and crew of the *Earp* were Norwegian.

The ship departed from the New York seaplane base of Floyd Bennett Field on 16 August 1938. Having taken on supplies at Recife in Brazil four weeks later, they then sailed for Cape Town, where Ellsworth finally joined the team, fresh from a hunting trip in Kenya. On 29 October, two days before Wilkins' fiftieth birthday, the *Wyatt Earp* headed off again, sailing 3000 nautical miles south-east to Desolation (or Kerguelen) Island. There they hove to while the engine was cleaned before setting off on 17 November for the final leg of the journey to the Antarctic mainland.

After a hellish forty-five days spent battling mammoth seas and storms in the Southern Ocean, the *Earp* eventually reached the mainland on New Year's Day 1939. Then the search began for a suitable landing field for the Delta, during which Ellsworth could keep his secret no longer: he told Wilkins he intended to claim the land that Mawson had seen for the United States. Showing all the cool detachment of a great poker player, Wilkins did not react; instead of turning on his friend, he decided to stake a few land claims himself.

He had always carried an Australian flag with him on his expeditions, and without fail also had a miniature one in the cockpit of any aircraft in which he flew. Now, worried about America trying to grab vast areas of Antarctica, he went ashore at each island visited during the Ellsworth expedition and raised his country's flag, claiming the island for Australia. At Vestfold Hills, which had been named two years earlier by Norwegian Lars Christensen after the area that was headquarters for the Arctic whaling industry, Wilkins also left a copy of *Walkabout* magazine — what could be more Australian than that? Had the Australian Government acted on his efforts as Wilkins had asked, the legitimacy of his claims may have internationally tested.

On 11 January, Lymburner and Ellsworth took off in the Delta from where the *Earp* was moored, north-east of Vestfold Hills. The weather was such that they could manage only a short flight. But it was long enough for Ellsworth to open the cockpit window and drop a brass cylinder. Inside was the following message:

*To whom it may concern — Having flown on a direct course from latitude 68:30 S, longitude 79:00 E, to latitude 72° S, longitude 79° E, I drop this record, together with the flag of the United States of America, and claim for my country, so far as this act allows, the area south of latitude 70° to a distance of 150 miles south of latitude 72° S, longitude 79° E which I claim to have explored.*

Once he and Lymburner had returned to the ship, Ellsworth quickly radioed a story back to the United States. Readers of the 13 January 1939 edition of the New York Times were duly informed that there was new land in Antarctica over which the USA claimed sovereignty.

With his State Department obligations thus fulfilled and the weather preventing him from realising his plans to fly over so many more square kilometres of the barren land, Ellsworth called an end to the expedition. He ordered the *Wyatt Earp* to head for Australia. If Hubert Wilkins felt any emotion in returning to the country of his birth for the first time in almost fourteen years, it was surely overshadowed by the grave concern he had regarding Ellsworth's land grabbing.

The ship docked at the Tasmanian capital of Hobart on 4 February, where Ellsworth's claims were immediately rejected by the Australian Government. The race to carve up Antarctica was in full flight. Only the gathering clouds of war would halt the chase.

# A watery grave for the *Earp*

At the end of Ellsworth's final expedition, at Wilkins' behest, the Australian Government purchased the *Wyatt Earp* and the two aircraft, to use in the establishment of a permanent Antarctic base. It was a huge, long-overdue vote of confidence in Australia's forgotten son, George Hubert Wilkins, but the plans were soon shelved due to the more pressing events taking place in Europe.

Instead the *Earp* was commissioned as HMAS *Wongala* and spent the war years patrolling St Vincent's Gulf in South Australia. She then served as a Sea Scout training ship at Port Adelaide until December 1947, when, again as the *Wyatt Earp*, she was scheduled to be the mother ship for Australia's first postwar Antarctic expedition, with an RAAF Vought-Sikorsky Kingfisher seaplane on board. The ship proved to be too small and slow, however, and was sold to commercial interests. Later, as the *Natone*, she plied the east coast of Australia carrying potatoes. In January 1959, the *Natone* struck a rock off Double Island Point, near Fraser Island in Queensland, and sank. The wreck remains there today, at the bottom of the ocean.

The Northrop Delta aircraft stayed in storage at Sydney's Mascot Aerodrome (now Kingsford Smith Airport) until 1940. For the rest of the war, it was used first by the Department of Civil Aviation and later by the US Army Air Corps and the RAAF. The fate of the second plane, the Aeronca Scout, is not known.

Paltry treasures these items of expedition hardware might have been, but they remain the only ones that Australia has ever held in terms of a record of Wilkins' activities as a world-renowned explorer.

# Chapter 17

# A New Walhalla

THE SEVEN YEARS spent as Lincoln Ellsworth's expedition adviser and manager may have brought Wilkins little in the way of personal or professional satisfaction, but as a hired hand and the beneficiary of the billionaire's largesse, he was now well free of the spectre of financial ruin that had loomed over him for years, long before the *Nautilus* fiasco even. If an Englishman's home is his castle, perhaps all this South Australian farm boy needed was a property close to some water, with a view.

Suzanne had made a trip home to Melbourne during Ellsworth's last expedition, to catch up with family and friends. She returned to the United States early in the summer of 1939 to find that her husband had stopped off in South Africa on his way back from Australia. Searching for something to occupy her time, she decided to visit an abandoned farm in Pennsylvania state that an acquaintance had spoken about in glowing terms. One look was all that was needed. Suzanne was entranced and bought it on the spot.

When Wilkins finally returned to New York, later that summer, she was almost jumping out of her skin. 'I've got a surprise for you,' she said and handed him the deeds of the property. 'You will just *love* it!'

Suzanne then began listing the various attributes of the property: it matched his descriptions of the farm he'd grown up on; it was miles away from everything and anything; the farmhouse was set up on a hill, with lots of water around; it would be an ideal place to store all his treasures, books, and odds and ends of exploring equipment … On the downside, she added, it was rundown; field mice and other critters were running around inside; there was no glass in the windows, and sunlight shone through the roof. 'But we can fix it up and make it special,' she beamed.

When Wilkins went with her to see his new 'estate', a broad smile swept over his face. He nodded his approval and immediately bought a station wagon to ferry them to their new home. He decided to call it 'Walhalla', after Suzanne's home town. On their next visit, Wilkins made a closer inspection, still sporting a wide grin as he wandered around the property. Eventually he turned to Suzanne: 'You know, it will cost about a thousand to fix it up. But it will be worth every cent.'

Over the coming years, the new home would play host to some of the most famous names in the world, offering these visitors quiet comfort and Aussie hospitality. But for now Wilkins wouldn't have much time to enjoy the idyllic location. Within weeks of him beginning to turn the derelict farmhouse into a home in which they could live, a cloud descended on the world, with Hitler's invasion of Poland. As of 3 September, Wilkins' homeland and the nation that gave him his knighthood were at war with Germany.

Wilkins tried to enlist, but both countries turned him down. He was approaching fifty-one years of age — too old for the recruitment officers. So what if he had a Military Cross and Bar to his name and in the polar wilds could always keep ahead of his younger colleagues? Wilkins even offered his experience and expertise outside of his war record, but these services were also politely refused by the authorities in Britain and Australia. With his friends and contacts in the German aviation industry, such as Hugo Eckener, it's a wonder they didn't take him up on his offer.

Wilkins had influence in his adopted home, however. And he used it to talk to American aircraft and automobile manufacturers to enlist their help in the war effort. The United States may have been nominally neutral, but public sentiment was certainly pro-British. Then, as the conflict abroad was nearing the end of its first year, Wilkins' behind-the-scenes role took him away from American shores. Ostensibly, he would go to Europe to see how the US companies could help the war effort. But, as a former spy, he may well have had an altogether different brief.

In June 1940, he flew across the Atlantic on a Pan American Airlines Clipper to Lisbon, via the Azores. From the Portuguese capital, he travelled north into France. Much of the country was already under German occupation; the remainder was in chaos. Then, on 14 June, four days after he'd landed in France, Paris fell to the Nazis. There was no choice for Wilkins but to abandon the mission. He managed to hitch a lift to England on a French transport plane, but soon after they were airborne, a German Messerschmitt fighter shot it down.

Wilkins never revealed exactly what happened between the time the transport crash-landed and his arrival in England on one of the last RAF planes to escape France, two days later. The passengers on the French transport had managed to escape, obviously, but the rest of the story he dismissed with typical understatement: 'I just walked and cycled my way through German lines until I reached Nantes [a port in north-western France] and eventually reached England.' That mysterious hand had once more guided him to safety.

Cabins on trans-Atlantic ships were hard to find, but with a bit of influence from British Government contacts in Whitehall, Wilkins managed to obtain a berth on a ship carrying refugees back to the United States. Just like after the Stefansson expedition in 1916, he was on a ship that had to run the gauntlet of German U-boats, and did so successfully.

Back in north-eastern Pennsylvania, a half-renovated farmhouse was awaiting his final touches.

BY DEFINITION, SPIES lead a dark and shadowy life. That's why so little is known about Wilkins' missions for US intelligence organisations. Indeed, the very nature of these outfits help cloak the secrets, especially because until World War II the United States had no co-ordinated approach to espionage. The State Department had its own operatives, as did the Office of Naval Intelligence and the War Department's Military Intelligence Division (better known as the G-2). And they rarely shared their material, except with the president. The fledgling Federal Bureau of Investigation, and its ambitious boss J. Edgar Hoover, was also a law unto itself.

So it's not certain to which organisation Wilkins owed his allegiance and who received his secret reports. He certainly didn't confide in his wife, Suzanne. After his death, she was to reveal a conversation they had in 1941 after he'd returned home from a mysterious trip to Asia. She asked him what his job with the US Government entailed. Wilkins looked her straight in the eye and asked: 'Can you keep a secret?' When she replied in the affirmative, he smiled and said, 'So can I!' She never broached the subject again.

Rather than a mystery, however, that Asian trip is an episode that has merited a place in history, if only for its leading to one of the huge lost opportunities of modern times. And first stop on Wilkins' itinerary was one of the great hotels of the world.

The Imperial Hotel in central Tokyo was (and still is) the most famous in Japan. Since the hotel first opened in 1890, the establishment had played host to scores of the world's royalty, foreign heads of state, diplomats, captains of industry and stars of the day. The Imperial's owners had always prided themselves on the discreet service offered to their guests: the staff could be relied upon not to repeat any conversations they happened to overhear and to turn a blind eye to any unusual assignations. Wilkins would have been quite aware of this when he took a room there in July 1940. He had stayed at the hotel before, briefly, while on the around-the-world flight in the *Graf Zeppelin*. But this time it was a very low-key visit.

He wanted to meld into the background. Officially, he was gathering information for an economic survey of the Far East on behalf of the US Government. His swing through Asia would also include China, Manchuria, Burma, Singapore and the Dutch East Indies (now Indonesia), and then Australia. Most of the people he met must have had their suspicions about Wilkins' true motives, but his cover was sound enough.

With China and Manchuria already the targets of Japanese military aggression, everyone knew a war in the Pacific was inevitable (not that it had stopped the Americans from exporting strategic goods such as oil to Japan until very recently). It was simply a case of when the conflict would break out. The Imperial Hotel was teeming with German guests, who could be seen in deep and serious conversation with uniformed members of the Japanese Imperial Forces. Wilkins could hardly have failed to feel the mood in the hotel while he renewed the acquaintanceships he'd made during his first visit to Tokyo. Back in 1929, the Japanese bureaucrats had gone out of their way to provide him with facts and figures relating to local aircraft production. He could never hope for such candour now, but any details he was able to garner would be welcomed by his intelligence chiefs.

What he couldn't learn directly from his contacts about Japan's readiness for war, his keen eye picked up while observing life in the towns and cities he visited during the trip. In the Manchurian city of Chunking, the capital of the Nationalist Chinese under Chiang Kai-Shek, Wilkins witnessed Japanese bombing raids in all their ferocity. But it was over drinks with an old friend in another famous hotel, Raffles in Singapore, that he was handed a startling piece of intelligence, one that could have dramatically changed the course of future events in the Pacific had it been taken seriously at the time.

The friend, a senior Japanese diplomat, told him how the Imperial Navy planned to bomb Pearl Harbor, near Honolulu, and initiate war with the United States. It was a shocking scenario, but quite viable, Wilkins realised. Years later, Suzanne Wilkins would explain that the drunken Japanese friend had laughed when revealing the plans to her husband.

'It's so absurd that no one in Washington will believe you if you tell them,' he told Wilkins. 'But, believe you me, it will happen within the next few months. When we take out the American ships, we will have a free passage down here to Singapore and across to Australia. Without the Americans' help, your fellow countrymen in Australia will be unable to stop us. Anyway, why would the Americans believe a fellow silly enough to try to take a submarine under the Arctic icecap?'

The final quip upset Wilkins, but he contained his anger. And the Japanese diplomat was right: no one back in the US intelligence 'community' believed him.

The prediction was to come back to haunt them on Sunday, 7 December 1941, when some 353 aircraft from six Japanese carriers anchored off Hawaii bombed the US naval base at Pearl Harbor. In two hours of mayhem, five battleships and nine other vessels were sunk and 188 aircraft destroyed. Three other battleships were severely damaged, and a total of 2335 servicemen and sixty-eight civilians were killed. The Americans were suddenly drawn into World War II. They called it a 'sneak attack', but Wilkins had already given them a warning.

WHEN THE UNITED States belatedly entered the war after the Pearl Harbor attack, it was soon realised that its equipment was absurdly out of date. A joke doing the rounds at the time suggested that the American soldiers were using gear left over from World War I. In fact the situation was possibly worse.

Because most Americans had vowed that their country would never again enter a foreign war after the Great War, the military planners had based all their efforts on the assumption that any future conflict would take place on American soil, with the armed forces protecting US sovereignty. So clothing was designed for a Florida summer or a Montana winter. It took a series of disasters during the first half of 1942 to force a quick rethink. Tents shipped to the New Hebrides in the Pacific disintegrated within weeks because their fire-resistant fibres lacked a fungicide to prevent mildew. Food cans rusted after being drenched by salt water on the sea journeys across the Atlantic and Pacific. And when American troops fought in the Aleutian Islands, west of Alaska, their uninsulated boots were of little or no use.

The rethink came with the US Government appointing Wilkins as a consultant to the Military Planning Division, with a brief to redesign equipment and soldiers' uniforms to ensure they were suitable for the extreme conditions in which the battles were being fought — from the deserts of North Africa and the tropical jungles of the Pacific to the alpine areas of Europe. His expertise on survival in Arctic conditions, as well as the lessons learned from living in the heat of northern Queensland, was to be invaluable. He would then fly to wherever it was necessary in order to personally 'test-drive' the new equipment and uniforms. It was a hectic life, with Wilkins often going for two or three days with little if any sleep.

But he did manage to get time off occasionally, to spend precious moments with Suzanne in the quiet serenity of Walhalla. There, no doubt, he would have pondered his own life and the sad fact that the people of the world had failed to learn from lessons of the past. The last of six volumes written by his old commanding officer, Charles Bean, for the *Official History of Australia in the War of 1914–1918* had finally appeared in 1942, featuring so many of Wilkins' photographs. Any pride he felt regarding his contribution must surely have been overwhelmed by dismay that another world conflict had arrived just a generation later.

And perhaps he wondered about the changes between the two wars. The major battles of World War I were won through a constant and frightening barrage of artillery fire. This new conflict was primarily an aircraft war — Pearl Harbor, the Battle of Britain, sorties waged from aircraft carriers in the Pacific, and eventually, the two atomic bombs dropped on Japan. Hubert Wilkins had been one of the pioneers of aviation, and the scientific advancements that he and others helped bring about had led to the vital role of aircraft in the waging of war. It was a bittersweet legacy indeed.

# Chapter 18

# Ashes to Ashes, Pole to Pole ...

WORLD WAR II finally ended on 15 August 1945 with the surrender of Japan. But then a war of a different kind began between the former allies: on one side, the Soviet Union and the satellite nations it helped set up in Eastern Europe, and on the other, the United States and Britain. It was soon known as 'the Cold War', after a term used by novelist George Orwell in an English newspaper article in October of the same year. It described a conflict of ideologies, economic conflict, nuclear proliferation and the build-up of military troops and weapons, or, as Orwell put it, 'a peace that is no peace'.

The Americans, worried about what might happen as relations with Moscow deteriorated, continued to take advantage of Wilkins' experience, at a research laboratory in Natick, Massachusetts, at what is now known as the US Army Soldier Systems Center. The experiments there produced everything from food for astronauts that could be squeezed from a toothpaste tube, to the ubiquitous chicken nuggets. Wilkins turned sixty in October 1948, but he still continued to consult at Natick, and would do so for the rest of his life.

Today, visitors to the research establishment are told of an incident that took place not long before the Australian's death. A local policeman had been walking his beat one night in January

1958 and found a fellow asleep in the snow. He jabbed his nightstick into the man, hoping to arouse him and save him from freezing to death. But he needn't have bothered. The man in the snow was Hubert Wilkins, and he was road-testing a new survival outfit stuffed with chicken feathers. Wilkins had no intention of freezing to death. At the other end of the scale, in 1952 he made a gruelling swing through Pakistan, the Middle East and North Africa in temperatures that rose to above 50 degrees Celsius, and coped better than colleagues almost half his age.

In his writings, he gave little indication of life away from his work. In fact, there's no mention at all of this postwar period in his 'autobiography', ghosted by Lowell Thomas, not even in the book's epilogue, written by Suzanne. It was as if Wilkins regarded anything not associated with exploration as insignificant.

He was to make one last trip to Antarctica in his lifetime. It was in 1957, when Admiral Richard E. Byrd, titular head of the US Operation Deep Freeze, invited him to be part of the celebrations for the International Geophysical Year. From 1 July 1957 to 31 December 1958, a dozen countries — namely Argentina, Australia, Belgium, Chile, France, Japan, New Zealand, Norway, South Africa, the Soviet Union, the United Kingdom and the United States — established more than forty bases on the Antarctic continent and another twenty on the Antarctic islands. Despite suspicions fed by the Cold War, there was a true spirit of international co-operation, and four years later the twelve nations signed the Antarctic Treaty, which has controlled affairs in the area ever since. On this final visit to Antarctica, Wilkins stressed his Aussie heritage by being photographed with a miniature Australian flag and a long-neck bottle of beer. The trip south had begun with a plane flight from US shores — a relative luxury and a far cry from the many treacherous sea voyages the veteran explorer had had to endure between the two world wars.

The efforts during the International Geophysical Year were what Wilkins had been calling for over so many decades. For too long, his words had fallen on deaf ears, but he was back in his beloved Antarctic, witnessing his dreams becoming a reality. Perhaps it had taken another horrendous international conflict and the attendant human sacrifice to make the world appreciate the planet's natural wonders.

As he surveyed the icy continent one last time, he must have thought of the nickname coined by young Norwegian pilot Magnus Olsen, back on the first Ellsworth expedition in 1933. Olsen had dubbed Wilkins 'the King of the Antarctic', and that he was.

HUBERT WILKINS MAY have been the butt of many a joke over his 1931 *Nautilus* venture, but for the next quarter of a century he'd remained convinced that his theory of travelling under the polar icecap was correct — even if he couldn't find an enthusiastic billionaire to finance another challenge in the Arctic. It would take someone else to prove him right, and the quantum leap in submarine technology, again resulting from recent international hostilities, to make a new mission possible.

On 24 January 1954, Mamie Eisenhower, wife of President Dwight Eisenhower, launched the world's first nuclear-powered submarine. Fittingly, the craft was named USS *Nautilus*. She was commissioned ten months later. The first commander of the *Nautilus* was Eugene 'Dennis' Wilkinson, but he was soon kicked upstairs and replaced by Commander William Anderson, who was at the helm when the *Nautilus* made her first foray under the northern icecap. The submarine left Seattle on 9 June 1958 and headed north. The voyage wasn't planned in a spirit of exploration; the United States was keen to find a way to position submarines close to the Soviet Union as a nuclear deterrent during the Cold War.

The first effort of the *Nautilus* was aborted after a fuse blew on her twin gyroscopic compasses. Without their aid, the submarine was moving blind under the ice and courting disaster. Anderson managed to work his way back south to safety in open water and returned to the United States, awaiting better conditions and a thorough compass repair job.

For his next attempt, Anderson would have the weight of the whole of the United States on his shoulders, since the Russians had by now launched their first two satellites, Sputnik I and II, and the White House needed a propaganda boost for America. But the voyage was to be conducted in secrecy, in case it had to be aborted once again. In a wonderful irony, the navy dubbed the venture 'Operation Sunshine'.

On 22 July that same year, the *Nautilus* headed off on a voyage that Anderson hoped would take her from the Pacific, under the North Pole, and across to the Atlantic. Again, it was not to be, this time because Anderson had been unable to find a way under the deep ice on either of the two routes he'd taken. As he waited at Pearl Harbor for his third attempt, the US Navy was taking no chances and prepared a second nuclear submarine to serve in a follow-up effort, should it become necessary — the USS *Skate*, skippered by Commander James Calvert.

The *Nautilus* finally succeeded on her fourth attempt. The nuclear-powered submarine travelled along a deep valley under the Arctic Ocean east of Point Barrow and, on 3 August 1958, reached the North Pole. Wilkins had been vindicated. Anderson continued on and two days later broke the surface in open water in the Atlantic.

To complete the propaganda blitz, a naval helicopter lifted the commander from the deck of the *Nautilus* and took him to a US Air Force base in Iceland, from where he was flown to Washington. As the *Nautilus* sailed to Britain, Anderson was facing the media at the White House. He was then flown across the Atlantic, after which another helicopter deposited him back on the submarine to enable him to be at the helm as she sailed triumphantly into Portsmouth Harbour, in the south of England.

Less than twenty-four hours after the *Nautilus* reached Portsmouth, the *Skate* followed her to the North Pole and headed for Bergen, the last resting place of Wilkins' *Nautilus*. A great admirer of the Australian, Calvert sent a cable to Wilkins: 'The men of *Skate* send a sincere salute to a man who has many times shown the way.' Vindication and due acknowledgement, all in a matter of weeks.

On 23 October, the *Skate* was back at the US Navy's command base at Groton, Connecticut. That day, Commander Calvert played host to the pioneer of Arctic submarine exploration, Hubert Wilkins. Still as spritely as ever at the age of sixty-nine, with only his hearing beginning to fail him — a legacy of his time on the battlefields of Europe, not to mention the decades of exposure to the racket of primitive aircraft engines — the Australian spent most of the afternoon on board, marvelling at the changes that had taken place since his days as a fledgling submariner. It was to be his last official public appearance.

ON THE NIGHT of Wednesday, 30 November 1958, Wilkins had been staying at the Grand Central Hotel in Framington, Massachusetts, a rundown establishment that was his home away from home when working at nearby Natick. The next morning a cleaning maid entered his room and found Wilkins dressed in his suit and tie, lying dead on the floor beside the bed. The seventy-year-old had suffered a massive heart attack.

The night before, he'd spoken by telephone to Suzanne in Walhalla. The *Herald Tribune* that day had featured a special supplement on Australia, and the couple had discussed their respective reactions to the positive stories about the land of their birth. Wilkins assured his wife he would be back at Walhalla in plenty of time for Christmas.

It wasn't to be, just like the promise he'd made to Suzanne before their wedding in August 1929, that they would be married for thirty years. 'It turned out to be twenty-nine,' his widow later wrote, 'but I won't quibble.'

In a more reverent tone, Suzanne would eulogise her husband, the man she constantly referred to as 'Wilkins' in correspondence with others, in the following terms: 'There are those who will argue that a man never dies before his time. Hubert, for his part, had lots of important work left to do. But he had a full life, three score and ten, packed with action and great achievement. He died seventy years young, with a slight smile on his lips.'

A funeral service was held in Framington on 4 December. As well as Suzanne, he was survived by his two elder siblings Thomas and Annie, seventeen and five years his senior, respectively.

Other comments on his life would vary from praising his achievements to the heavens, to deriding him for being pro-Russian, particularly in America. In Britain, generous accolades poured forth for one of the nation's knights of the realm, while New York's Explorers Club would observe how, to many, Wilkins was a good thirty years ahead of his time. In Australia, the response was muted, predictably so. Sir Douglas Mawson, a national treasure down under, had continued to deride the man he dismissed as a gifted amateur until his own death the previous month, and it seemed his influence had caught on.

Lady (Suzanne) Wilkins had much to say about what she saw as Australia's antagonism towards both Wilkins and her. 'They even suggested that I was a mere nothing in Wilkins's life,' she told Captain John K. Davis, a famous Antarctic navigator and skipper under both Shackleton and Mawson. 'The reverse is understanding the truth. They are writing him up but with a patronising air, and if not damning him with faint praise, they're coming close to it. I was told at the funeral that there was a lot of jealousy towards him and I can see that. There seems to be outright hatred for me.'

'A lot of jealousy' … could she have been talking about Mawson, perhaps?

Away from the fickle court of public opinion, the fact remained that Wilkins was without peer in twentieth-century exploration. He had made almost forty different expeditions, from life-threatening ventures in the icy wastelands of the two polar caps to scientific sorties in the untamed Australian bush and climate experiments in the midsummer heat of North Africa. His exploration and research took him to every continent on the globe. He had been honoured by many of the world's leaders. Sadly, the only country in which Wilkins did not receive due recognition was that of his birth, Australia. Successive governments had ignored his offers to come home and lend his expertise to Australian scientific projects. And few members of the general public even knew his name. There would be no image of Hubert Wilkins on the nation's banknotes, as Mawson's received. Even Wilkins' own likeness was inexplicably 'airbrushed' out of the photograph used by the Royal Australian Mint in the design of a 20-cent coin issued in 2011 to commemorate the nation's war correspondents.

'Hubert *who?*' so many Australians ask. The answer is simple enough: Captain Sir (George) Hubert Wilkins, MC and Bar, pioneer aviator, war hero, photographer, explorer, meteorologist, spy, naturalist, author, Fellow of the Royal Geographical Society and the Royal Meteorological Society, and Honorary Doctor of Science at the University of Alaska.

A proud Australian also but, more importantly, a truly international man.

It was left to the United States to pay him the ultimate tribute.

Just before dawn on 17 March 1959, the USS *Skate* broke through the icecap at the North Pole. Three flags were hoisted — that of

Australia, the Union Jack of Great Britain, and the Stars and Stripes of the United States. Commander James Calvert and a colour party of twenty emerged from the submarine and filed onto the ice and snow. An officer, holding an urn containing the ashes of Hubert Wilkins, brought up the rear. The sailors stood to attention in the pre-dawn gloom.

The icy winds ripped at the notes from which Calvert read with the aid of flares held by a couple of his crew. He paid tribute to, in his words, one of the great men of the century. Calvert declared that the adventurous spirit and incredible courage of Wilkins had set a standard for which everyone who followed in his footsteps should aim.

As a rifle salute rang out, the officer holding the urn calmly scattered Wilkins' ashes to the wind. George Hubert Wilkins was finally at rest, in the environment in which he was so much at home during his life.

# POSTSCRIPT

While most Australians have never heard of Sir Hubert Wilkins, those in the area of South Australia in which he was born and raised are determined that, there at least, his name will live on forever. On 29 November 1966, eight years after his death, some 350 locals braved a heatwave and an all-enveloping storm of red dust to attend the unveiling of a memorial to the great explorer at the town of Hallett, on the Barrier Highway, just north of his birthplace at Mount Bryan East.

But a generation later, the local population wanted more. They enlisted the aid of modern-day adventurer and pilot Dick Smith and *Australian National Geographic* magazine to help raise $80,000 to restore the Wilkinses' family cottage at Mount Bryan East. On 29 April 2001, Smith officially opened the renovated icon, which is now a museum devoted to the intrepid explorer. A replica of Sir Charles Kingsford Smith's *Southern Cross* — the Fokker monoplane sold to him by Wilkins — circled overhead at the start of the festivities, before dipping its wings in farewell and heading back to Adelaide.

As Smith explained: 'He's my hero. He was Australia's greatest adventurer. He had a go at everything from submarines under the Arctic to balloons around the world, to being the first person to fly in Antarctica. He's forgotten because he was too successful. No one ever died.'

# ACKNOWLEDGEMENTS

Sir Hubert Wilkins was a modest man who dwelt on the achievements of others rather than his own. In his writings he would often dismiss one of his heroic acts in just a sentence or two, when it deserved many thousands of words. So the task of finding out just what made this man great has been a difficult one.

His good friend Lowell Thomas, the renowned American television newsman, gave us an insight when he ghosted Wilkins' autobiography, *Sir Hubert Wilkins: His World of Adventure*, half a century ago. Although too many incidents finished up as little more than throwaway lines, the picture of Wilkins' scientific approach to life was quite evident.

One of those select few Australians who did know about the exploits of Hubert Wilkins was of immense help. Fellow Aussie travel writer Roderick Eime has been researching Wilkins for the past twenty-odd years, tracking down photographs and memorabilia. Rod offered me his assistance with no strings attached; he just wanted the deeds of Wilkins recognised. There is virtually nothing Wilkins-related that Rod hasn't read and he has tried to alert fellow Australians and people overseas alike to the great man's achievements by penning a number of newspaper and magazine features. As Rod puts it himself:

*Ever since I was soundly berated for my ignorance by the late William Mills, keeper of collections at the Scott Polar Research Institute [in*

*Cambridge, England], I have made it my business to correct the gross oversight in Australian history that omits Sir Hubert Wilkins from much of our literature. His exploits are now re-emerging as some of the most significant feats of twentieth-century exploration. So fantastic are they, that if they were fiction they would be dismissed as 'unbelievable'. I tip my hat to you, Sir Hubert, none will ever match you.*

A huge thanks also to Rod for sharing so many photos from his private collection.

I must also express my thanks to Melbourne broadcaster Simon Nasht, whose book and television works, particularly his 2005 publication *The Last Explorer*, have helped clear up many an apparent contradiction between contemporary reports and Wilkins' self-effacing explanations of the same events. Nasht is a thorough historian and, I hope, will be rewarded for his painstaking research when Wilkins eventually gets the recognition he deserves.

This book would never have seen the light of day but for the foresight of the former boss of ABC Books Stuart Neal, who recognised the need for Wilkins to be given his due historical recognition, and the enthusiastic encouragement of his successor Brigitta Doyle, a true friend of authors whose belief in the project kept me inspired.

And, finally, a massive thanks to editor Jon Gibbs. Passionate about the English language and the need for every date and location to be spot on — right down to the day of the week in which some extraordinary piece of history took place — Gibbs made sure Hubert Wilkins received the kudos he deserves in the text, while also seeing to it that the unassuming Aussie hero never lost any of that *Boy's Own Annual* derring-do that endeared me to Wilkins more than a decade ago.

# BIBLIOGRAPHY

Stephanie Barczewski, *Antarctic Destiny: Scott, Shackleton and the Changing Face of Heroism*, Hambledon Continuum (London), 2007.

Robert Bartlett, 'Bartlett's Story of the *Karluk*', *New York Times*, 1 June 1914.

C.E.W. Bean, *Official History of Australia in the War of 1914–1918, Volume III — The Australian Imperial Force in France: 1916*, Angus & Robertson (Sydney), 1929.

C.E.W. Bean, *Official History of Australia in the War of 1914–1918, Volume IV — The Australian Imperial Force in France: 1917*, Angus & Robertson (Sydney), 1933.

C.E.W. Bean, *Official History of Australia in the War of 1914–1918, Volume V — The Australian Imperial Force in France: December 1917–May 1918*, Angus & Robertson (Sydney), 1937.

C.E.W. Bean, *Official History of Australia in the War of 1914–1918, Volume VI — The Australian Imperial Force in France: May 1918– the Armistice*, Angus & Robertson (Sydney), 1942.

Simon Callow, *Orson Welles: Hello Americans*, Jonathan Cape (London), 2006.

Commander James Calvert, '*Skate*'s Breakthrough at the Pole', *Life*, 4 May 1959.

Commander James Calvert, *Surface at the Pole: Extraordinary Voyages of the U.S.S. Skate*, Naval Institute Press (Anapolis, Maryland), 1996 [first published 1960].

Oliver Carlson & Ernest Sutherland Bates, *Hearst — Lord of San Simeon*, Kessinger (Whitefish, Montana), 2010 [first published 1936].

Peter Cochrane, *The Western Front 1916–1918*, ABC Books (Sydney), 2004.

Commander John L. Cope, various newspaper articles, *New York Times*, 1920–21.

Richard J. Diubaldo, *Stefansson and the Canadian Arctic*, McGill-Queen's University Press (Montreal), 1998.

Lady [Grace] Drummond-Hay, various newspaper articles, 1928–36, including *Daily Express* (London), *Sydney Morning Herald*, *The Argus* (Melbourne), *Canberra Times*, *Brisbane Courier*, *Courier-Mail* (Brisbane).

Roderick Eime, various newspaper, magazine and online feature articles, 2005–11, including *Sydney Morning Herald*, *Heritage Australia*, *Cruise Passenger*, *Outer Edge*, traveloscopy.com, travography.com, totaltravel.yahoo.com

Nelson Eustis, *Australia's Greatest Air Race*, New Holland (Sydney), 2008 [first published 1977].

Philip Gibbs & Bernard Grant, *Adventures of War with Cross and Crescent*, Methuen (London), 1912.

Ian Hodges, *Wartime* magazine, Australian War Memorial, September 2003.

Roland Huntford, *Shackleton*, Hodder & Stoughton (London), 1985.

Stuart Edward Jenness, *The Making of an Explorer: George Hubert Wilkins and the Canadian Arctic Expedition, 1913–1916*, McGill-Queen's University Press (Montreal), 2004.

William Joy, *The Aviators — True Adventures of Australian Airmen*, Shakespeare Head (Sydney), 1965.

Alfred Lansing, *Endurance: Shackleton's Incredible Voyage*, Weidenfeld & Nicolson (London), 2011.

James Marr, *Into the Frozen South*, Cassell (London), 1923.

William J. Mills, *Exploring Polar Frontiers — A Historical Encyclopedia*, ABC.CLIO/Greenwood online, 2003.

Simon Nasht, *The Last Explorer: Hubert Wilkins — Australia's Unknown Hero*, Hodder Australia (Sydney), 2005.

Vilhjalmur Stefansson, *The Friendly Arctic*, Kessinger (Whitefish, Montana), 2010 [first published 1921].

Lowell Thomas, *Sir Hubert Wilkins: His World of Adventure*, McGraw-Hill (New York), 1961.

*The Urantia Book*, Urantia Foundation (Chicago), 2000 [first published 1955].

Captain Sir George Hubert Wilkins, *Flying the Arctic*, G.P. Putnam's Sons (New York), 1928.

Captain Sir George Hubert Wilkins, *Under the North Pole: The Wilkins–Ellsworth Submarine Expedition*, Brewer, Warren & Putnam (New York), 1931.

Captain Sir George Hubert Wilkins, *Undiscovered Australia: Being an Account of an Expedition to Tropical Australia to Collect Specimens of the Rarer Native Fauna for the British Museum, 1923–1925*, Putnam (London), 1929.

Sir Hubert Wilkins & Harold M. Sherman, *Thoughts Through Space: A Remarkable Adventure in the Realm of the Mind*, rev. edn, Fawcett (New York), 1971 [first published 1942].

Commander F.A. Worsley, *Shackleton's Boat Journey*, Folio Society (London), 1974.